THE ECONOMIC MODERNISATION
OF FRANCE

The Economic Modernisation of France

ROGER PRICE

CROOM HELM LONDON

First published 1975
© 1975 by Roger Price

Croom Helm Ltd
2-10 St John's Road London SW11

ISBN 0-85664-227-4

Printed and bound in Great Britain
by Redwood Burn Ltd Trowbridge and Esher

CONTENTS

ACKNOWLEDGEMENTS

I would like to record my appreciation of the help and advice I have received from my colleagues in the School of European Studies at the University of East Anglia, and especially to Michael Balfour, Morley Cooper and Stephen Wilson. The University librarian Wilhelm Guttsman and his staff, in particular Barry Taylor and Ann Wood, have provided invaluable assistance. Christopher Johnson of Wayne State University, Detroit, and Charles Tilly of the Centre for Research on Social Organisation of the University of Michigan read the first draft of the manuscript and it benefited greatly from the comments they made. It goes without saying that I bear full responsibility for any errors of judgement or fact which might have been made.

Marianne Bhavsar, Sally Redgrave and Hilary Roberts typed the manuscript from my original hand-written draft. I am extremely grateful to them for persevering with my horrible writing. I am also grateful to David Croom and Malcolm Ward for their help and encouragement.

I owe a great debt of gratitude to Robert and Jane Frugère for their many kindnesses. Above all I want to thank Heather, Richard and Siân.

ABBREVIATIONS

A.B.	Annales de Bretagne
A.D.H.	Annales de démographie historique
A.E.S.C.	Annales (Economies, Sociétés, Civilisations)
A.F.	Année Ferroviaire
A.G.	Annales de Géographie
A.H.R.	American Historical Review
A.H.R.F.	Annales historiques de la Révolution française
A.M.	Annales du Midi
A.N.	Annales de Normandie
B.H.E.S.R.F.	Bulletin d'histoire économique et sociale de la révolution française
B.S.H.M.	Bulletin de la société d'histoire moderne
C.H.	Cahiers d'histoire
C.I.S.	Cahiers internationaux de sociologie
C.A.	Le Contrat Social
E.A.	Economie appliquée
E.C.	Etudes et Conjoncture
E.E.R.	European Economic Review
E.H.R.	Economic History Review
E.S.	Economies et sociétés
E.R.	Etudes rurales
I.H.	Information historique
J.E.B.H.	Journal of Economic and Business History
J.E.H.	Journal of Economic History
J.I.H.	Journal of interdisciplinary History
J.P.N.P.	Journal de Psychologie normale et pathologique
M.S.	Le mouvement social
P.	Population
R.D.M.	Revue des deux mondes
R.E.	Revue économique
R.F.S.P.	Revue française de science politique
R.G.A.	Revue de géographie Alpine
R.G.C.	Revue générale des chemins de fer et tramways
R.G.L.	Revue de géographie de Lyon
R.G.P.S-O	Revue géographique des Pyrenées et du sud-ouest
R.H.	Revue historique
R.H.E.S.	Revue d'histoire économique et Sociale
R.H.L.	Revue d'histoire de Lyon

R.H.M.C.	Revue d'histoire moderne et contemporaine
R.H.S.	Revue d'histoire de la sidérurgie
R.N.	Revue du Nord
S.L.G.	Société Languedocienne de Géographie
T.A.S.	Techniques, arts, sciences

INTRODUCTION

The periods into which history has traditionally been divided by historians, solely for their own convenience, have generally been determined by political criteria. Thus 1789 and the Revolution are usually regarded as a major turning point in French history, a place for one book to end and another to begin.

In political and ideological terms the Revolution was no doubt of crucial importance, but humanity was not transformed thereby. Most of the population continued to be subjected to the age-old constraints of their environment. At the end of all the political upheavals of the Revolution and Empire little had changed in the daily life of most Frenchmen.

Continuity deserves a place in history equal with the prominence given to change. The two are inseparable — the one conditioning the other.

This volume is intended to be a study of economic developments in France between c.1730 and c.1880. The period is conceived as one of growth in production within pre-industrial economic structures, succeeded from 1840—50 by rapid structural transformation and the creation of an industrial economy.

The Ancien Régime économique et sociale was characterised by the predominance of agriculture and of artisanal forms of industrial production, and by technically backward, slow and expensive modes of transport inducing the compartmentalisation of market structures and of human societies. The hallmarks of this kind of society were isolation and localism. The exchange of goods, people and ideas was restricted. The economy was far from stagnant but the volume of trade and, in consequence, the volume and technological development of production, was restrained by the costs of transport. Regardless of the needs of the population the difficulties of distributing the goods produced restricted the potential for development. These basic structures restrained the potential for dynamic action. Changes within them were slow to occur and slow to have extensive effects. It is worth remembering however that if France was underdeveloped in 1850 this was only in relation to Britain, the most economically advanced country in the world, or in relation to her own future development.

If a remarkable event such as the Revolution is placed within such a social context, its human significance can be more accurately assessed. Man does not live by bread alone, and yet until his bread ration is assured, its gaining can dominate his existence. In a pre-industrial society sustained interest in politics is the privilege of a small minority. For the vast majority the real revolution must be the one that transforms their material conditions.

Paradoxically this change imprinted itself less forcefully on the human consciousness. Its progress was more gradual and less dramatic, even in the case of major technological innovations like the railway. Yet the social consequences of such changes affected the lives of far more people more profoundly than political revolution in the nineteenth century.

The Revolutions of 1789, 1830, and 1848 occurred within different evolving social situations, characterised by pre-industrial structures. These Revolutions had significant consequences for economic development but contributed far less to its evolution than did the transformation of the structure of the market.

Structural transformation of the market, on a scale sufficient to radically alter the characteristics of demand and the conditions of production occurred with the development of the railway, which was undoubtedly faciliated by prior industrialisation. It however contributed enormously to the acceleration of economic growth, to the establishment of a national market, and of a more national society. This development and its broad consequences was the major revolution in French society in the nineteenth century.

By c.1880 the effects of the transport revolution were manifest. Although demographic stagnation, the immobility of rural labour, low productivity in many sectors and the relative slowness of urbanisation restricted changes in the scale and character of the market so that substantial areas of technological archaism survived, society had nevertheless been transformed. If a terminal point has to be assigned to the *Ancien Régime*, perhaps this could be the period 1850–80 rather than 1789.

Before this time economic structures, material conditions, and even social and political relationships had changed only slowly and to a limited extent. The position adopted here is not that of a transport determinist but rather the view that the transport system was the most important single component in the economic mechanism. By examining the development of communications and its economic consequences it is hoped to validate this assumption.

1 COMMUNICATIONS AND THE DEVELOPMENT OF COMMERCE

Economic development is dependent upon means of transport as this alone permits the exchange of goods. The transport technology of any one time imposes limits — defined by its carrying capacity, speed and the consequent cost of transport — upon the amount of trade and determines its character. For example, when transport depended on animal power and the wind trade in expensive luxuries was more likely to flourish over long distances than trade in basic but bulky human necessities like foodstuffs.

In France there were basically two types of region. First, and most numerous, were those which might be characterised as continental interiors, overwhelmingly agricultural, autarchical and inward looking, although never totally; second, areas, either coastal or placed on navigable rivers (i.e. on commercial axes), where communications, exchange and production for sale might be more highly developed. All the major towns developed due to such a situation.

If in spite of poor communications the cloths of Amiens and Reims were sold in the markets of Lyon, Marseille and Toulouse and the wines of Bourgogne were brought down the Seine to Paris and Rouen, it remained true that circulation was difficult whether by road or water. Commerce was active but primarily carried out on a local or regional basis. In contrast with future development it was diffuse. Markets were fragmented and isolated and to a great extent, had to be self-sufficient.

This weakness of the transport infra-structure was the main reason, in the French situation, for a state of relative underdevelopment and for the survival of the *Ancien Régime économique* into the 1840s. The economy was characterised by the predominance of a low yield agriculture devoted to meeting local needs and by the preponderance in the industrial sector of the production of consumer goods, primarily by means of artisanal techniques.

Within this economy change was inevitably slow until the existing equilibrium was decisively upset when rail construction brought about a revolutionary transformation of conditions.

Roads

Roads form a network which slowly evolves with the evolution of the economy, although the relationship between cause and effect is a complex one. In the early eighteenth century the roads of France were

1

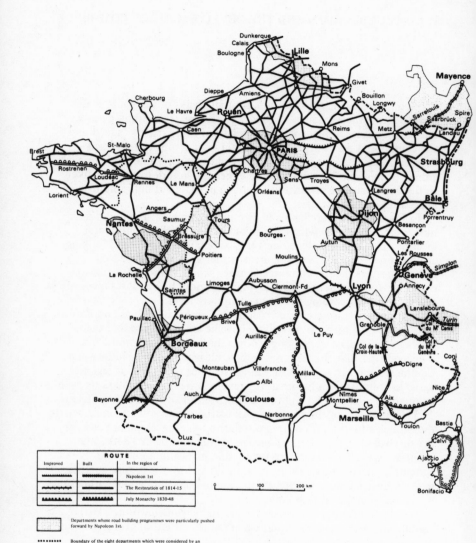

Map 1. The Development of the Road Network 1780–1850.

Source: J.-A. Lesourd in *Atlas Historique de la France Contemporaine 1800-1965*, Colin, 1966

generally mediocre. A network of royal roads ran from Paris to the frontiers and major towns, but even they were only very irregularly maintained. The structure of the national traffic was very much influenced by the role of Paris as a political capital and also as a commercial centre and consumer market. Traffic concentrated in the north and north-east because of the greater industrial and commercial activity in those regions and the facility of movement along plains and sills. There was a marked contrast with the west and the south-west in particular, where dispersed habitat and the greater predominance of agriculture minimised exchange.

The position of the roads was closely dependent on geography. They tended to follow high land above the valley bottoms to avoid marshland, floods and the need for bridging, and also from the desire to take the shortest route almost irrespective of relief. Between any two points there often developed a multiplicity of routes as economy of effort encouraged users to open a new path rather than repair an old. Roads were usually narrow and constantly threatened with incorporation in the neighbouring fields of land-hungry peasants. Their physical condition was determined by the structure of local soils. The lack of foundations meant that pot-holes and flooding were constant dangers to their users. Upland areas were likely to be dependent on narrow paths impassable for carts and used solely by pack-animals and beasts on the hoof.

There were four basic types of cart in use: in the north where relief was easy and traffic dense, large four-wheeled carts, very stable and with large capacity, drawn by five to seven horses were common, but were rare elsewhere. More common were the small four-wheeled carts drawn by one horse — used almost everywhere save in the Midi — large two-wheeled carts pulled by several horses in line, and smaller two-wheeled carts drawn by one horse. In the sourthern plains ox-carts, often pulled by cows, were more common than horse-drawn vehicles. Most of the carters were peasants who turned to this activity during the agricultural dead season; horse-owners tended more often to be specialised merchants. The drawing-power of animals generally tended to be limited by undernourishment and poor roads. Slopes of more than 15° were impossible and much easier gradients caused serious difficulty. The consequence was the frequent dependence on pack-animals — a mule could manage about 120 kilograms although roughly half of this weight was taken up by the pack.

Merchandise was largely transported by peasants, and passengers by a host of small companies. If there were some signs of concentration, particularly at Paris, Lyon and Lille, the process was slow. The *messageries royales* was not to be established until 1775.

River and especially road traffic gave employment to large numbers of peasants who hired out their animals or transported goods themselves. A rural zone close to major roads profited from the sale of food and fodder and from the supplies of manure, whilst the animation of roadside villages with their postmaster, innkeeper, carter and blacksmiths has often been portrayed. In spite of high transport costs there were always substantial movements of some heavy goods — e.g. salt, a necessity produced only in some regions, and a variety of foodstuffs and fuels.

Improvement of transport conditions depended upon the evolution of road building techniques, on the development of a widespread awareness of the economic and social utility of roads, and in the last resort upon the political decision to establish a permanent administrative organisation to plan, construct and maintain.

Colbert had envisaged a national system of communications in order to strengthen control over the provinces by the central authority. This political motive, combined with the growth of towns and trade in the early eighteenth century, created interest in road improvement and increased State intervention. Under Orry and the Trudaines, father and son, the administrative framework of such a system was established in the 1740s, including the foundation of Ecole des Ponts et chaussées (1747) to provide a continuous supply of trained engineers. In 1737 a general plan established priorities: the first goal was to link Paris and all provincial capitals, strengthening political control; the second to improve roads from the administrative centre of each generality to those of neighbouring generalities; and finally, to improve roads of strategic and economic importance. From the 1750s techniques of road construction were systematically improved and codes of practice drawn up, resulting particularly in improved surfaces and drainage. The process was aided in some provinces by subsidies voted by the provincial estates. In Languedoc, Bourgogne and Franche-Comté funds were specifically designated to secondary roads of essentially local economic interest, which were often ignored by the royal engineers.

The major problems faced by engineers were those of finance and labour. An attempt was made to solve both of these by the extension of corvée — of labour service for thirty days per year for all men aged 16–60, save those living in the towns — to the whole country in 1738. This permitted the mobilisation of large numbers of men at relatively low cost. Most of the major works of the eighteenth century were achieved with corvée labour, but labour dues were performed reluctantly and to be effective required careful surveillance by engineers.

Critics of the system, and notably Turgot in his Edict of February 1776, saw its taking of peasants from the fields as arbitrary, unjust, and inefficient. He determined that the work should be paid and financed by taxation, annexed to the *vingtième* so as to minimise exemptions. This change was opposed by the Parlement of Paris and the edict was revoked in August 1776, although in recognition of the strong feeling against the corvée communities were allowed to introduce a tax if they wished. Generally, to avoid increasing the tax burden on the poor the labour corvée was retained until the Edict of 27 June 1787 which made definitive the introduction of a tax. This met little opposition from the privileged as tax exemptions were retained.

Growing interest on the part of central and provincial authorities in the improvement of communications is revealed by the growth of expenditure at both central and provincial levels. Thus the state, which spent an average of 771,200 livres per annum in the period 1683–1700, was spending 3 million during 1715–36, over 4 million in 1770, 6,900,00 in 1780 and 9,445,000 in 1786. In the diocese of Toulouse an average of 1,200 livres per year was spent on road repairs in the first half of the century. The sum reached 40,000 in 1765, 127,000 in 1782 and 190,000 in 1789.

Significant improvements were being made. Between 1740 and 1780, an estimated 25,000 km. of road had been constructed or improved. The essential technical and administrative infra-structure had been created. Moreover the pace of improvement was clearly accelerating towards the end of the century.

In some areas, notably Bourgogne, road works had been carried out on a scale sufficient to change profoundly the conditions of commerce. A new commercial spirit was developing — thus in the Auvergne, villages, particularly in vine growing areas, pressed for better roads and even offered contributions. In the Dauphiné in the 1780s, efforts were being made to improve the links of the small industrial centres of the pre-Alpine region with the plain. The great bulk of the improvements made, however, had been to existing major roads — roads with undoubted economic rôles, but defined essentially by their political functions — the roads of the royal couriers, of the military and Maréchaussée, and the roads which bore waggons carrying taxes.

Transport conditions had been considerably improved in many areas, but not fundamentally changed. Irregular maintenance ensured this. In entire provinces — in Picardy, Limousin, Brittany and Provence — the network even of major roads was obviously inadequate. Bridges were rare, particularly it seems in the Franche-Comté. Above all the transversals leading from these major routes were insufficient, and vast zones remained isolated, most obviously in the west and Massif Central. Mountain areas suffered most from the deficiency in roads. In the future Ariège during the eighteenth century roads had only been constructed on the plateaux and in the valleys, with none above 700 metres. Mountain villages depended on mules and humans to carry goods. In the Dauphiné around 1800 the iron of Allevard and the coal of La Mure could only be moved by pack-animal. The creation of a network of secondary roads, feeding the major routes, had hardly begun. The privileged axes linked the major provincial capitals and market centres. Villages close to them flourished, but most other rural communities were only able to enter into contact with external markets by means of a network of rural pathways, often impassable to carts, which turned into mire after rain. Planks of wood across streams frequently took the place of bridges. These rural roads depended for maintenance on the owners of the land alongside them, and since neither individual landowners nor communities had the energy, money or appreciation of the value of good roads which might have stimulated action, they were neglected. The condition of the rural roads reflected, above all else, the particularism of eighteenth-century France, and was a powerful factor in preserving this.

Along the main roads commerce and individual physical and intellectual liberty increased with reductions in travelling times. Between 1765 and 1780 the length of journeys between some major cities was reduced by 30—50 per cent. Paris to Marseille in eight instead of twelve days; Paris to Toulouse in eight instead of fifteen; and Paris to Nantes in five instead of eight.

But the cost of travelling at such speed was high. It was a facility available only to a small minority of wealthy people. The coach accelerated, but the cart still crawled along at three to four kilometres per hour. Merchandise could reach Lyon from Paris in thirteen to sixteen days in 1787, compared with twenty in 1715, but movement was constantly subject to delays, which were expected and accepted with resignation, and off major roads nothing had changed.

It has been claimed that in some regions — in Bourgogne most notably — a transport revolution did occur. There, between 1745 and 1760, improved roads led to a reduction in transport costs to about one-fifth to one-sixth of the price of the merchandise, compared with a tripling or a quadrupling at the end of the seventeenth century. One should perhaps be sceptical about this. Generally where economies were achieved they were nowhere near this scale. On the Paris-Lyon route between 1715 to 1769 rates fell by around 13 per cent and on the Lyon-Rouen route between 1778 to 1787 by around 31 per cent. Even this was not general. It is infact very difficult to generalise about transport costs, which varied greatly between regions and over time.

For short distance transport peasant carts were primarily used, and in the agricultural quiet season, when otherwise draught animals might have been idle, competition was sufficiently intense to keep costs low. In the northern plains where land transport was easier but faced competition from waterways, it tended to be relatively cheap and well organised.

Due to improved road standards, transport costs rose less rapidly than the general increase in prices, and nominally unchanged rates thus in fact represented a real reduction. Security on the roads increased, and the burden of internal customs and tolls was reduced to a relatively small part of the cost of transport due to State action. But costs inevitably remained high when carts moved slowly, particuarly in winter when roads were at their worst and the days short. The major element in costs was the expense of food for men and horses, which obviously increased in proportion to the travelling time.

Even on the relatively few well-maintained roads high costs limited traffic and ensured that even at the end of the eighteenth century the internal market remained compartmentalised, and evolved only slowly.

The succeeding period of the Revolution and Empire saw a reversal of the tendency towards improvement. Roads, save those of strategic interest, were increasingly neglected. There was at best no increase in the speed of movement on major roads, but often this was accompanied by substantial increases in costs. It cost 13.50 fr. to transport 100 kilograms from Paris to Marseille in 1770–1, 20 fr. in 1785–9, 23 fr. during the Empire. The return journey cost respectively 19.50 fr., 25 fr. and 33 fr. The English blockade of sea routes increased the burden on the roads, accelerating their degradation, and the rise in costs.

Perhaps the only positive achievement of the period was the growth of administrative intervention. The Decrees of 16 September 1811 and 7 January 1813 classified roads into those of national and those of departmental importance. This was to be of some importance in the future.

With the restoration of the Bourbons in 1815, the work of road improvement recommenced. The annual budget rose immediately from fr. 14 to 20 million, and generally 3–4 per cent of the government budget continued each year to be spent on roads. Of the network of around 40,000 km. of *routes royales* existing on the eve of the Revolution, 15,000 km. with 82 bridges needed to be reconstructed after years of neglect. The urgency of the problem was revealed by such events as the poor harvests of 1816. To meet food shortages grain was imported into Marseille, but in the autumn of 1816 and spring of 1817 the flooding of the Rhône, the usual means of transport, threw the whole traffic onto the roads. It soon cost 200 francs, compared with the more usual 80 francs, to hire one cart to move cereals to Lyon, with obvious consequences for food prices, and disruptive effects on the transport of all other goods.

Once reconstruction had occurred, then improvement could follow — roads were widened, gradients were reduced, bridges were built to replace ferries; in mountain areas protection against flooding was assured by building dykes, raising road levels, and cutting galleries. The period has been described as one of importance in the development of road building techniques, particularly in the adaptation of the road to its environment.

By 1827 it took twenty-five days by ordinary haulage to transport foods from Paris to Marseille, at a cost of 14.50 fr., and 18 fr. for the return journey. In 1815 it had taken thirty days, and cost 23 fr. and 33 fr. respectively. By accelerated transport the journey took as little as thirteen days at a cost of 32 fr. and 36 fr. The main complaints now were not about slowness but irregularity.

However, for passengers in 1830 it still cost 40 fr. to travel from Paris to Bordeaux in an ordinary coach, i.e. not on a mail-coach. The total charge was doubled when the cost of food, lodging and tips were added. This represented perhaps one month's wages for a worker, so few people travelled.

As before, work was concentrated on major roads. Awareness of the need to improve local roads existed, but financial resources remained inadequate. The departmental councils voted funds for those roads classified as of departmental importance but rarely provided much. A law of 28 July 1824 authorised, but did not oblige, communes to create special funds to finance local road works. Relatively little was achieved and progress in agriculture, as a result, was severely limited.

From 1830, during the July Monarchy, activity again accelerated — an estimated 15,500 km. of road and 283 bridges were added to the network of routes royales. Government expenditure on roads increased to an average of 30 million francs per annum, in addition to which extraordinary grants, most notably one of 84 million in 1837, were voted.

This appears to have been a period of substantial increase in road traffic, and in general economic activity. As the following table indicates the rhythm of construction of major roads was unsurpassed.

Rhythm of construction of national and departmental roads

	brought into use	av. per year
pre-19th century	43,035	—
1800–14	2,943	196
1814–30	6,781	399
1831–47	22,550	1326
1848–60	7,618	585
1861–70	2,400	240
Total:	85,327	

1835 road traffic has been estimated at 2,760 million km. tons (number of tons x distance moved), and this is calculated to represent *c.* two-thirds of the total movement of merchandise by land and water. The exact quantities must remain unknown because of the paucity of accurate information but this is probably the best estimate we have. In Paris in 1841 there were 4,650 transport companies, often very small, with 29,725 carts. On the routes between Lyon and the Midi in the early 1840s some 34,940 carts and 86,050 horses and mules are estimated to have been active.[1] In spite of the relative cheapness of transport on the Rhône, for less bulky commodities like silk road transport was preferred because it was quicker, even at a charge of 70—80 fr. per ton from Lyon to Marseille.

The continued improvement of transport conditions is revealed by falling tariffs. On the Le Havre to Paris road, even before steamboat competition, it took only two days by fast cart, and tariffs had fallen from 135 fr. to 55 fr. per ton between 1828 and 1837. The road was used, however, only for the movement of goods of high value in relation to bulk, like coffee, raw cotton and spices. Wine, salt, soap and bulkier goods took the Seine.

In spite of continuous improvement areas of neglect remained. Work was still concentrated on major roads, and in the plains, so that discontent was registered in such places as the Alpine region at what was felt to be government neglect. As a result some mule tracks were replaced by roads in the Dauphiné and major roads constructed to establish links with Geneva and open the area to international trade.

In most areas the roads of departmental importance were significantly improved and the process of administrative control and supervision of works intensified, but in spite of this the majority of rural communes remained unaffected until the law of May 1836, which made the maintenance of local roads by the local authorities, for the first time, compulsory. This led eventually to the creation of a vast network of local roads. It remained the case, however, in spite of improvements, that the cost of transporting most heavy goods was prohibitive thus keeping the volume of traffic low, which did not encourage large expenditures on roads.

In the last decade before the construction of a rail network, the roads of France, although much improved in the previous 150 years, were still a fundamental restraining factor on economic activity and personal movement. There was, of course, a great deal of variation in the level of road use between departments, which reflects their differing levels of economic activity — intense in the departments of the north, in Normandy, the Paris region, in the Loire and Rhône areas, and around Marseille; feeble in the east, Brittany, the Alps, Pyrenees and Massif Central.

The positive achievement of this century and a half can be seen by examining the increase of the average speed of the passenger coaches operated by major companies — this (including stops) is calculated to have been 2.2 km. per hour in the seventeenth century, 3.4 by the end of the eighteenth century, 4.3 in 1814, 6.5 in 1830 and 9.5 in 1848.[2] Illustrating the same point — the normal tariff for transporting goods fell from around 0.33 centimes per ton per kilometre in 1808 to 0.20 centimes in 1851 due to the multiple effects of price depression, technical progress and increased competition. But it must be emphasised that these improvements did not affect a fundamental change in the conditions of transporting merchandise. Off the major, national and departmental roads, movement remained difficult, even in summer, and often impossible in winter, and since these minor roads were the essential feeders of the major ones much of the country was cut off from the stimulating effects of commerce and wider horizons. Also the high transport costs on the major roads were multiplied once off them.

The more important towns with previously developed commercial functions controlled the more developed networks of communications for people and goods. Less important towns — a multitude of administrative and judicial centres — had more limited networks linked to these functions and so were increasingly incapable of satisfying growing commercial needs. The case of Bourges has been examined.[3] It possessed road links with other communities within a radius of 150 km., the roads leading to Paris and Clermont-Ferrand being exceptions to this. The most busy roads led to canal and river ports, to Moulins and Orléans, but even in those cases traffic remained small — at the Pont-de-Nevers in 1835 daily traffic rarely exceed 50 tons with a seasonal low of 14.41 tons on 17 February.

The Le-Havre-Mulhouse road was used to transport raw cotton from port to mill. By using big four-wheeled carts each drawn by eight horses, which were changed in relays the journey could be made in six days in perfect conditions, but it might take as long as one month. At the other extreme was the Vivarais, where mule traffic remained more significant to the economy than ox-carts. Between these two extremes there was considerable variation but at best transport was expensive, whilst most rural communes still lived in a state of isolation, orientated towards self-subsistence rather than exchange.

Government expenditure on roads averaged around 34–35 million francs in the 1850s, rising to around 43–44 million francs in the 1860s. The network of *routes imperiales* grew from 35,500 km. to 38,300 km. from 1850 to 1870, mainly due to the process of reclassification of departmental roads. Considerable improvements had already been made to major roads, and with the development of a competitive rail network, their importance declined. Thus from the Second Empire a far larger

10

proportion of resources was devoted to the hitherto neglected local roads.

The law of 21 May 1836 on local roads (*chemins vicinaux*) had been essentially a declaration of intent. It was only from the 1850s that substantial progress was made in reducing the isolation of most rural communes. Priorities were established according to estimates of the importance of local roads. Subsidies were increasingly accorded to local authorities too poor to finance improvements — a policy culminating in the law of 11 July 1868. This was both a vote catching measure designed to counter complaints that the embellishment of Paris contrasted with the neglect of the countryside and a response to genuine economic and social needs.

In many respects this legislation too would only bear fruit in the future. Nevertheless by 1870 a network of around 370,000 km. of maintained local roads existed, contrasting with the 13,825 km. in 1840, feeding 47,026 km. of departmental roads and 38,300 national roads. By 1914 the local road network would be increased to 534,000 km.

Even this programme did not entirely recognise the importance for agriculture of farm to farm, and farm to road movement, especially difficult in regions of dispersed habitat like the *bocage* of the west. Particularly where land-holdings were dispersed the farmer spent considerable time and energy moving from farm to fields.

Far from reducing road traffic, railways stimulated activity. The patterns of road use did however change. Traffic on roads parallel to the railway declined, as did long-distance traffic generally, but activity on transversals, on roads serving as feeders to the railways, increased with general levels of economic activity.

Existing road networks were indispensable to the development of rail transport, but rapidly became inadequate. The existence of the railway stimulated the development of roads leading to its stations. Where formerly road services had radiated out from important regional centres, increasingly they led from places without a railway to the nearest railway station. In this age of animal traction the small station was as attractive as the large.

There are no accurate statistics for the period prior to 1851, but road traffic in that year has been estimated at 2,400 million km. tons. In that year the railways carried far less, and their significance for the national economy was still far from evident. Road traffic, however, rose to 3,200 million km. tons in 1856, then declined to 2,860 million in 1876 under the dual effect of changed economic conditions and the loss of Alsace-Lorraine. Tariff competition clearly evinces the problem faced by road transporters, forcing them on to non-competing routes. In 1840 ordinary carting had cost 18—20 francs per ton, per kilometre, accelerated transport 30—35 francs, and coach transport 1 franc. By contrast the average price per ton, per kilometre, by rail was 12 francs in 1840, 0.77 francs in 1851 and 0.059 francs in 1800, whilst the existence of large fixed costs encouraged railway transporters to concede special tariffs to large-scale users.

Road transport was not entirely uncompetitive. On the Clermont-Reims road in 1860, five years after the opening of the railway line between these two places, around 122,500 travellers are estimated to have used the coach which offered lower prices and greater convenience due to the siting of the railway stations outside the two towns. For short distance transport of merchandise in particular, road transport had the advantage of greater flexibility; the cost of loadings and unloadings necessary on arrival and departure at the rail-head and the often complained about inadequacies and slowness of handling at railway goods depots served to increase the real cost of rail transport.

In the decades during which the railway network was being established, the overall transport network was subject to constant structural change. Movement by road was progressively transformed; when a railway line reached a particular town, that town became, for some time, a place of transhipment. At the same time the functions of the road in the area already crossed by the railway, were modified. The consequences of the arrival of the railway at Bourges have been analysed in detail.

Road services parallel to the lines Bourges to Paris, and Bourges to Vierzon quickly disappeared, but services to Fourchambault and Nevers increased, providing a connection for these towns with the railway to Paris. Once the line had passed beyond Bourges, further modifications occurred, so that by 1861 only strictly local services survived, transporting, however, a growing volume of commodities.

By means of the railway and the accelerated development of local roads leading to it — even in the least favoured areas of the Massif Central or the uplands of the Dauphiné — the transport revolution and a consequent transformation in the conditions of rural life were achieved. The era of isolation and semi-closed social and economic systems was over.

Waterways

The waterways provided a much used alternative to land transport. By canal construction and canalisation the natural potential of rivers was increased. Naturally the areas in which water transport was favoured were limited to sea and river ports and a surrounding, narrow economic region.

Coastal shipping was estimated to have carried around a million tons a year between 1786 and 1789 — being especially important for the

Breton peninsula, otherwise largely isolated due to the difficulties of moving goods by land. The most significant element of the internal transport system was the Loire, the essential link between the Mediterranean, the south-west and the east and north. Goods brought by sea to Nantes were transhipped at Orléans, which performed an important entrepôt function, and reached Paris by the Canal de Briare or by road across the Beauce.

Traffic on the Loire in the eighteenth century might have been as much as double that on the Seine, and 20 per cent above that of the Rhône, the next most important waterway.[4] Numerous other rivers were also used for transport — if only of wood by floatage — even where natural conditions were not particularly favourable. The smallest navigable streams were used, at least during their periods of high water. The character and capacity of boats varied greatly between rivers. The *chalands* used on the Loire, with a capacity of up to 150 tons, and the *bateau* on the Seine between Paris and Rouen, carrying usually 25 to 70 tons, were exceptionally large.

The economic role of the Loire reveals above all the inadequacy of the pre-rail transport infra-structure. Its sandbanks and irregular flow imposed serious difficulties and delays on navigation. Because of these it could take as long as six to eight months for goods to reach Paris from Nantes. That this route was nonetheless preferred to road transport is indicative of the high costs of the latter.

Navigation on the Seine was slow and expensive because its meanders made the use of a sail almost impossible — expensive human or animal power was necessary. The Rhône was of unequal draught and subject to torrential floods which made up-river movement extremely difficult.

Besides seasonal fluctuations in the water-level, rapids and sand-banks, there were numerous artificial obstacles — notably bridges with insufficient headroom, and weirs designed to increase the water-level for mills.

The economic importance of the waterways should not be under-estimated. The major iron producing regions were dependent on them — the Foix area used the rivers Ariège and Garonne to move iron products to Toulouse which served as an entrepôt, as did Nevers, La Charité, Cosne, Orléans, Saumur, Nantes and St Nazaire along the Loire. The Seine and Marne permitted the movement to Paris, Rouen and Le Havre of iron from Champagne and Bourgogne. The Aisne and Oise transported the products of the Soissonnais and Thiérache, while the Loing and Yonne those of Nivernais. Most important for the transport of iron was probably the Saône which was used by the products of Franche-Comté, Champagne and Bourgogne.

The whole economy of the Auvergne was orientated towards the

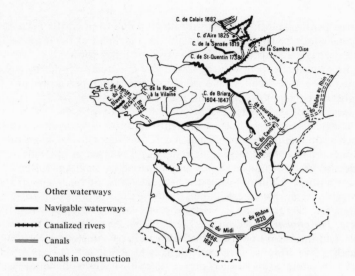

Other waterways
Navigable waterways
Canalized rivers
Canals
Canals in construction

Source: J.-A. Lesourd after E. Dutens, *Histoire de la navigation intérieure de la France*, Sautelet, 1829

Map 2. Waterways in 1830

north by use of the Allier. On the eve of the Revolution the Bec
d'Allier carried an average of some 2,000 boats in a year, each with
20—25 tons, i.e. 40—50,000 tons. The Dauphine was similarly
dependent on the Isére.

The cost of transport on these rivers varied seasonally with water-
levels and the carrying capacity of boats. On the Loire between Digoin
and Briare for a 50-ton boat it would cost around 160 livres down-river
and 200 livres up-river in ordinary times, but rising to 420 in
unfavourable conditions. Slowness, delays and frequent accidents often
rendered the apparent cheapness of water only illusory. It was not a
dependable means for moving either manufactured products or
foodstuffs.

Canal construction was one way of improving the conditions of
water transport. The Canal du Midi, opened in 1661—2 had provided a
link between Agde and Bordeaux — connecting also upper Languedoc,
an area which normally had a surplus of cereals to sell, with lower
Languedoc, an area of normal deficit.

By the beginning of the eighteenth century there were some 670 km.
of canal, and around 300 km. more were added during the century, to
the already existing 8,000 km. of navigable water. Apart from this
achievement, the century also saw the planning of canals which were to
be constructed mainly in the following century.

During the Revolutionary and Imperial periods little of note was achieved, although some works commenced earlier were completed — such as the Canal du Centre in 1793. Formerly communications between the Rhône corridor and Paris had been difficult due to the heights of Bourgogne and Morvan. Goods had been transported by the circuitous route Rhône—Tarare—Loire. Now Paris was made accessible by means of the Saône and Canal du Centre, and by 1810 about 4—5,000 boats of some 60 tons capacity annually took this route, carrying especially wine. During this period oceanic and coastal shipping was disrupted by the war at sea.

The post-war stagnation of the Atlantic ports — of Bordeaux, La Rochelle and Nantes — compared with the increasing prosperity of those on the Mediterranean or in the north, was indicative of the permanent effects of the war years on currents of trade. Through Le Havre would come an increasing proportion of the raw cotton needed by the developing textiles industry of Normandy, the north and Alsace. It played a vital rôle in the trade of these regions and of Paris. Marseille was the leading centre for imports of cereals — 71 per cent of the total in 1840 — coming mainly from the Black Sea area and Egypt. The poor domestic harvests of 1846—7 clearly revealed its significance in this sphere and also that of the Rhône by which foodstuffs were moved into the heart of France.

The renewed prosperity of coastal trade in the years following the wars of the Empire reveals something of the development of internal commerce. It has been estimated that in 1786—9 1 million tons per annum were carried, but by 1837—46 this had risen to 2,009,000 tons, and by 1847—56 to 2,556,000.[5] In 1846 some 10,000 ships were involved, using a multitude of mainly small ports.

Under sail, in the summer months, the Bordeaux—Le Harve voyage might take 20 days costing around 42 fr. per ton in the 1840s. In the winter, however, the same trip might take 42 days. Bordeaux-Nantes-Paris, by way of the Loire gave additional security and shortened the journey but at additional cost.

Coastal shipping, under sail, did not provide a reliable form of transport. Steam increased its appeal temporarily. In 1849 the *Morlaisien* permitted travellers to get from Morlaix to the railway line at Le Havre and thence to Paris in 32 hours — by far the quickest means of making the journey. But direct rail competition would soon make this uncompetitive.

The period of the Bourbon Restoration was one of importance in the improvement of waterways. Canal links from the coal-fields of the north to Paris, from the Loire basin to the Seine and the Rhône-Rhine link were completed. Barrages to maintain water-levels during periods of low water and better tow-paths were provided, and the first steamers appeared on the major rivers, rapidly replacing horse-drawn boats for passenger traffic. The first railway transporting coal from St Etienne to Andrezieux, served only as a feeder for the Loire traffic.

The developing demand for coal was of major importance in stimulating these improvements. In 1825, of 1,725 barges using the Canal de St Quentin — the link between the north and Paris — 1,540 were engaged in transporting coal. In 1824, 4,000 boats brought coal to Paris from the Loire basin. This latter was an entirely more primitive operation than the former, for once boats from the Loire reached Paris, it was difficult and uneconomic, because of the lack of cargoes, to take them back upstream. They were consequently broken up and sold as firewood, an operation resulting in a large waste of capital. This contrast was symbolic of the dethronement of the Loire from its pre-eminence in the communications network, and its replacement by the waterways of the north and by those linked to the Rhône as the main arteries of France. By the 1840s traffic on the Loire was only about one-sixth of that on the canals of the north and half that on the Rhône.

The Rhône in spite of the fact that it was unusable for some three months in the year due to water-levels which were either too high or too low, was, prior to railway development, the key to the prosperity of Lyon, which received by way of the upper Rhône the transit traffic from Switzerland and Savoy; by the Saône the products of the west and the Loire basin which had taken the Canal de Berry and those of the Centre; by the Canal de Bourgogne the products of the Seine basin; and by the Rhine-Rhône Canal those of the east. Of the 700,000 tons of merchandise estimated to have been marketed in Lyon in each of the years between 1841 and 1845, about 500,000 had been transported by water.[6]

Illustrative of the problems of navigation on the Rhône is the fact that there a force of one horse-power was necessary to pull one ton, while on the Rhine the same force pulled seven tons; up-river movement was especially difficult. In the 1830s 2,500 boats with a total capacity of 150,000 tons moved down-river from Lyon to Arles but only 1,300 with 71,000 tons up-river, pulled by groups of horses or oxen and supplemented by a sail when possible.

The first half of the nineteenth century was the major period of canal construction: from 1800 to 1825 about 15 km. a year were added to the network. From 1825 to 1840 this rose to 154 km. after which the pace slackened as railway development commenced, but it remained at 33 km. a year from 1841 to 1868. By 1847 there were 4,170 km. of canals.

The consequences of this development were limited both by faults in the design of the canals themselves and more significantly by the failure to adequately canalise the rivers the canals were meant to link.

Thus traffic from Lyon to the north-east — to Mulhouse or Strasbourg — required two transhipments to smaller boats, one at the entry to the Upper Saône, another at Verdun. On the route to Paris, by way of the Canal de Bourgogne, the problem was the inadequate depth of the river Yonne. The Canal de Berry, part of the Loire-Rhône link, completed in 1841 after eighteen years' work, had sufficient water, even for small coal barges with a capacity of 32—36 tons, for only four to six months each year. A more successful enterprise, the Canal du Centre carried 149,000 tons in 1828, 346,000 in 1844, 527,000 in 1846 and 573,000 tons in 1851, although traffic from the Rhône corridor often preferred the Canal de Bourgogne with its 195 locks which doubled the time taken to Paris, but was state-owned and charged far lower tariffs.

Most successful of all were the waterways of the north, and their links with Paris. The convergence of navigable waterways around Paris encouraged their use as a means of supplying the city's needs. This was the most important French port, the quays of the 12th arrondissement, and the ports of Bercy and Ivry in 1839 received 19,664 boats carrying 1,920,000 tons of merchandise — including most of the city's needs of wood, iron, grain and wine. Paris was linked to the centre of the country by the canals of Bourgogne and the Centre, with the east by the Marne-Rhine canal, to the sea by the lower Seine, and with Belgium and the north by the Canal de St Quentin and the Oise. The latter was the most effective link and in 1849 carried a traffic of 1 million tons — more in fact than the lower Seine and Rhône together.

This substantially reduced coal prices in Paris and stimulated the development of mining in the north. In contrast the slowness with which links with the Loire coal basin were improved, hindered its development. By 1842 it cost 17 fr. to transport one ton of coal from Mons to Paris, but 30 fr. from St Etienne.

The development of steam navigation on rivers and canals seemed to herald a new period of prosperity. By 1826 there were 26 steamers in use on the lower Seine, 2 on the upper Seine above Paris, 7 on the Loire, 10 on the Garonne. On the Rhône 6 steamers were employed in 1837, and 29 in 1843. In that year French inland waterways were furrowed by 242 steamships, concentrated mainly on the lower stretches of rivers.

The effects were diverse. The Rhône enjoyed its greatest period of prosperity in the 1840s. The journey up-river from Arles to Lyon took only 35 hours in 1843, compared with one month by barge. Most steamers were capable of carrying 120—130 passengers and 25—30 tons of merchandise. Growing competition both on the river and with navigation on the Rhine for transit traffic, stimulated rapid technical improvement.

The consequences were most notable for passenger traffic and up-river movements where the greater power of steamers was of great advantage. In 1841 steamers transported 49,015 tons of merchandise up-river, the other boats 58,090. Down-river steamers moved only 27,115 tons, compared with 204,553 tons carried by the traditional boats.[8] The speed advantage of steamers was less significant down-river whilst their tariffs remained higher. The major victim of the development of steam transport in the Rhône valley seems rather to have been road traffic. But the restrictions on river movement imposed by varying water-levels continued to prevent the establishment of regular and reliable services. Haulage contractors in the Rhône valley having been driven out of business by steamer competition, there was often nothing to complement the river during stoppages, so in this vital respect the transport situation worsened.

On the Seine in the 1840s, steamers carrying around 300 tons and tugs towing a string of barges were replacing horse-drawn traffic, the tugs completing the Rouen-Paris run in a maximum of 60 hours compared with a previous fast run of 4 to 5 days. The use of steamers on the Seine rapidly undermined the role of the Loire. Steamers drew too much water to be used extensively on this shallow river, and the advantage it had formerly offered to sailing vessels, due to its orientation and relative lack of meanders, was now lost. By 1842 traffic on the lower Seine had reached 435,000 tons as compared with some 310,000 tons on the Loire between Nantes and Orléans.

Although relatively few communities enjoyed access to them, the programme of canal construction made possible economic development, particularly in coal-mining and metallurgy, which could not otherwise have occurred. However, the structural weaknesses of these waterways limited the reduction in transport costs that could be achieved. Adverse water conditions often forced manufacturers to stop production due to shortages of raw material or through an inability to move their finished products. The waterways did not provide a reliable means of preventing food shortages after a localised harvest failure, since the numbers of boats which could pass through the system of locks on the canals in a single day was limited. On the Canal de Berry, for example, the locks could handle only 40 at most, carrying some 2,400 tons.

In short, the waterways were a palliative, incapable of changing basic transport conditions. Improved roads and railways would substantially reduce the dependence of the economy on them.

Furthermore waterways, unlike roads, could not develop as feeders of railways. The two were in direct competition. In this situation total waterway traffic increased slowly from 1,831 million km. tons in 1847 to 2,007 million in 1880, as the economy expanded. Their share in the carrying trade declined, however, and their competitiveness was increasingly restricted to the carriage of heavy goods of little value, and that primarily on the waterways of the north, lower Seine and east. By 1881, the year for which the first statistics are available, coal constituted 23.7 per cent of the total tonnage carried, building materials 40.9 per cent, and non-perishable foodstuffs 11.9 per cent. Concentration on particular routes was evident — with marked decline in the west, south-west and south-east.

The completion of the railway lines in the upper Loire and Rhône valleys led to a rapid decline in river traffic. The port of Blois registered 120,000 tons of merchandise in 1855. By 1859 this had already fallen to 64,000 tons, and by around 1880, even downstream traffic had almost disappeared. Offering lower tariffs than the railway companies was of no avail as regularity could not be guaranteed.

On the Rhône in 1856 536,000 tons were transported, but only three years later it had dropped to 273,000 tons. This situation was repeated on most of the waterways of France, and along the coastal shipping routes. Resistance to change, the siting of factories on waterways, the temporary increase in traffic in areas not already reached by rail, e.g. railway locomotives were until the early 1850s sent from Le Creusot along the Saône — these things delayed their decline, but on most waterways this delay was not prolonged. Few modern canals existed, and these almost entirely in the north. Elsewhere locks were too narrow and water-levels inadequate.

Distances, too, were quite often shortened by the railways, which were designed to follow a straight line between two points — Paris-Le Havre was half the distance. Lens was 370 km. from Paris by water, but only 220 km. by rail. In 1855 the average goods train covered these distances at a speed of 35 km. an hour whilst the average barge could only manage 30—40 km. per day. Competition became increasingly difficult as rail efficiency increased and its tariffs fell.

Transporters were helped by the more efficient waterways cutting their profit margins to the minimum and by the state repurchasing canals and operating them as a public service, but it could not halt the decline. State expenditure on waterways was increasingly concentrated on those of greatest economic importance, particularly those carrying coal in the north. A policy of improvement rather than construction was pursued. Large-scale port-works after 1859—60, especially at Marseille, Le Havre and Bordeaux indicated a concern to improve maritime communications. Now, undoubtedly, the railway was king.

It has been estimated that around 1835, 173 million tons of merchandise was either produced in or imported into France. Of this some 127 million tons were consumed at the place of production, indicating the predominance of semi-closed economic systems, and the remaining 46 million were consumed at an average distance of 60 km. from the place of production or import. Furthermore something like 15 million tons of the goods transported were moved by water, 10 million tons by professional hauliers, and 21 million tons by agricultural carts.[9] Such calculations cannot be statisticaly accurate, but probably this is as good a judgment of proportions as we can hope for.

In the 1840s communication remained very difficult, and the volume of traffic restrained. Large regions remained impermeable. The economy was characterised by the survival of the compartmentalisation and juxtaposition rather than interpenetration of regional economies.

Railways

Industrial tramways had long existed — for example at Le Creusot and Montcenis from the end of the eighteenth century. More akin to the modern railway was the line from Saint-Etienne to Andrezieux on the Loire (18 km.) opened in 1827, with traction provided by horses and stationary engines. This and subsequent lines, like those from Andrezieux to Roanne (1829) and Epinac to Pont-d'Ouche (1830) were simply tributaries of the river, designed by mining engineers to solve the problem of access from pit-head to waterway, and supply the growing demands of industry.

In contrast with these the line from St Etienne to Lyon used locomotives from the first. Opened in 1832 essentially to carry coal, it also carried 171,000 passengers in 1834.

More significant in the long run was the Paris-Saint-Germain-en-Laye line inaugurated in August 1837 which gave most influential people their first experience of travel by rail. This was a convincing success, and was followed by the opening of the Paris-Versaille line (right bank) in August 1839, and the Paris-Versaille line (left bank) in September 1840. In the provinces 1839 saw the opening of lines between Mulhouse and Thann, Montpellier and Cette, and Nîmes and Beaucaire; in 1841 the Strasbourg to Basle. Progress was slowed by economic depression from 1837 to 1841, but willingness to invest in railways subsequently increased, encouraged above all by the opening of the first major lines — the Paris to Rouen and Paris to Orléans in 1843.

The utility of the short, coal carrying lines had soon been proved — their construction effectively reduced the cost of coal at Marseille, for example, from 45 to 25 francs per ton in the 1830s. There was initially great scepticism about the possibilities of long-distance transport by rail, but in spite of sustained bitter opposition from carting and river interests, by the early 1840s it was generally accepted that railways would be of crucial importance for industrial development. Their significance for agriculture was rarely envisaged.

Compared with other countries the construction of a railway network in France was a slow process. Between 1838 and 1842 the issue was debated many times in the Chamber of Deputies, between those who favoured construction and control by private companies, and those who favoured a state network. The key law of 1842 laid down the basic plan for a network radiating from Paris, whose infra-structure was to be financed by the State, who would then concede the lines to private companies which provided the capital for the superstructure. The concept was as much determined by political as economic considerations. It seemed to government engineers and ministers to be a means of satisfying the old dream of assuring effective control from the political centre over the provinces.

Never had there been a need for so much capital to be amassed, so many workers, clerks, and engineers to be gathered, so much money to be distributed in wages, so much metal and building materials to be produced, and so many buildings to be constructed, as in these years. In spite of the appeal to English expertise, capital and labour, inexperience and the very scale of the organisational problem led to major difficulties of administrative and financial control.

But progress was made — by March 1846 Orléans had been joined to Tours. in 1846 the Paris-Lille-Brussels route was opened, and by the end of 1847 the railway had reached Compiègne, Abbeville, Le Havre, Tours, Vierzon, Bourges and Chateauraux. 1,830 km. of track were being exploited and a further 2,872 were under construction.

Even in 1844, when rail tariffs were significantly higher than they would be in later years, substantial transport economies were possible on the few lines under exploitation. The following comparisons have been made between road and rail tariffs for the movement of one ton over the 80 km. between Vierzon and Orléans:[10]

	Cost			Time Saved		
	Road	Rail	Economy	Road	Rail	Economy
Ordinary haulage	20 fr.	12.8 fr.	7.2 fr. (36%)	60 hrs	4 hrs	56 (93%)
Accelerated haulage	30 fr.	15 fr.	15 fr. (50%)	24 hrs	4 hrs	20 (83%)
Coach or express	80 fr.	32 fr.	48 fr. (60%)	8 hrs	2 hrs	6 (60%)

The economic crisis of 1847 however brought refusals to pay the amount outstanding on partly paid up shares, and the withdrawal of English capital. Companies with inadequate financial backing found themselves in difficulties at a time when traffic and receipts were declining. The Revolution of February 1848 intensified the crisis of confidence. The shares of the Paris-Rouen company fell rapidly from 858 to 280 francs. Nationalisation of the companies was for some time discussed but the idea was dropped in the period of political reaction following the June Insurrection in Paris. The basic result of this period of unrest was a slowing of construction. In 1851 there existed 3,600 km. of track, exploited by eighteen relatively small companies — a network without coherence, but whose significance in respect of transport costs was already being clearly felt in at least some regions.

The *coup d'état* of December 1851 ended social disorder by repression, and in new conditions of security, and, fortuitously, of international economic prosperity, a pent-up wave of speculation was released, encouraged by an administration aware of the crucial importance of improved communications in economic development and political control. In place of long parliamentary discussions, decisions were taken rapidly by meetings of ministers, engineers and financiers. By 1852, the difficulties of the crisis years had resulted in the formation of syndicates with far greater financial resources than the groups of capitalists in the 1840s who financed strictly localised lines. The new authoritarian régime had more confidence in its ability to control these powerful financiers than had the July Monarch. Feeling itself unable to finance public works on the scale required because of the orthodox pressure for balanced budgets as essential to financial confidence, the government sought to create a climate favourable to massive private investment. Instead of competition, it encouraged mergers. Its success can be seen in the growth of investment in railways. In 1847 this had been 252 million francs; in 1852 — a year of concession rather than construction — 131 millions; in 1853 269 millions; in 1854 339 million; and in 1854 496 millions.

Concessions were now generally made for ninety-nine years — creating a long-term schema which encouraged long-term investment in shares, and the companies to improve their techniques and profitability. In January 1852, for example, the Paris-Lyon line was conceded for this period to a consortium including the bankers Rothschild, Pillet-Will, Hottinguer, and Mallet, and the English engineers Locke and Brassey. The conventions agreed to between the Government and such groups included also certain guarantees of interest, designed to provide security for investors. This policy was to be extended in the later conventions.

Related to this was the policy of encouraging mergers between companies which was designed to create strong entities able to construct secondary lines with less potential for profit than the lines of the first network. By the end of 1853, 15 companies had been reduced to 4, each operating on a regional basis. In March 1852, for example, the Paris-Orléans, Centre, Orléans-Bordeaux, Tours-Nantes companies amalgamated as the P-O Company, and in return were given further concessions. National as well as regional coherence of operation was improved by the establishment of an influential railway section in the Ministry of Public Works from November 1853, which was followed in

1854 by the institution of regular meetings between company representatives.

By 1857 the main lines of the network provided for by the 1842 law were completed, extending for some 6,520 km. In that year, for the first time, the tonnage transported by rail exceeded that by water. In 1851, 1,718 million tons were moved by water, compared to 462 million by rail, but in 1857 the relation was 1,693 million to 2,142 million. By 1866 it was 2,225 millions compared with 5,825.

What was true of the northern company in these years seems to have been true of most of the others: until the 1860s extension of the network produced a sufficient increase in traffic to maintain profitability, so that until 1867 receipts rose more rapidly than expenditure. The return on the heavy fixed costs involved in the initial establishment of the network increased as traffic grew more dense, permitting tariff reductions which further encouraged this growth. Although the inadequacy of original station facilities increased handling costs for merchandise, this was slowly reduced by reconstruction, the growing carrying capacity of waggons, and increased pulling power of locomotives. The administrative control of traffic flow and operating costs was for long a particularly difficult problem, but as these techniques were improved costs were reduced. This problem illustrates the difficulties where technological innovation, in this case the steam locomotive, was injected into an established situation. A broad spectrum technical advance was necessary before its potential advantages could be maximised. Deficiencies in signalling, brakes and control systems were restrictive, whilst the human beings, who were used to working with human and animal power, were for some time unable to fully appreciate the problems and potential of steam.[11]

Outside the basic network of major lines, large areas still remained untouched and likely to remain economically stagnant. To the financiers it did not appear that regions like the Massif Central or Brittany would generate sufficient traffic to make railway operations profitable. The Grand Central, established to open the Massif Central, was primarily intended as a speculative venture, it being presumed that other companies would be interested in making take-over bids to reduce competition — as indeed occurred.

In return for potentially profitable concessions, and for permission given to amalgamations, the Government was able to exert some pressure on companies to induce them to accept responsibility in 1857 for a second network of 8,600 km. However the economic depression beginning in that year reduced receipts and the burden of financing the Crimean War created a shortage of investment capital. The Government responded by making new conventions with the companies. A law of 8 February 1859 extended state guarantees of

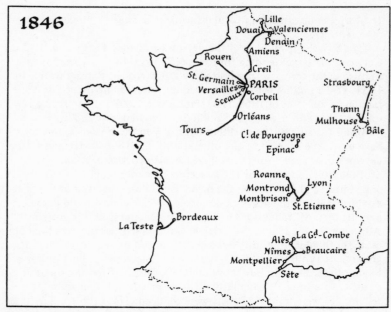

Map 3. Railways in France 1846.

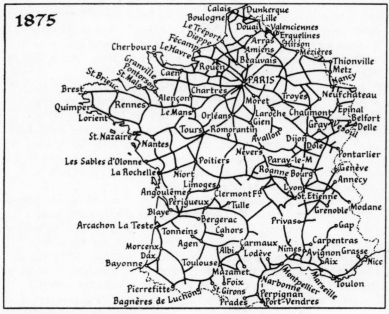

Map 4. Railways in France 1875.

profits to this second network and this ended public reluctance to invest. Further agreements in 1863 and 1868 induced the companies to accept increased responsibilities, in return for increased financial aid from the state. A law of 12 July 1865 established the legal conditions for the creation of a third network, of lines of strictly local interest to be constructed with local capital, but these were slow to develop.

By 1870 22,530 km. of railway line had been conceded and 17,466 of these were in use. During the Second Empire 13,900 km. had been conceded and 13,600 km. brought into use. Moreover, this network had been given coherence: instead of discontinuous sections divided between a large number of companies, a small number of large units had been established. But in according priority to the development of lines in areas where traffic was most dense, i.e. in promoting the economic development of the regions which were already most advanced, the needs of the more geographically isolated and economically backward regions, particularly of the Massif Central, Alps and west, had inevitably been neglected. Few lines had yet penetrated them. Moreover as the initial stimulus to modernisation waned, the rate of development of regional economies slowed towards the end of the Empire, and the economic incentive to invest further capital in transport facilities declined. This was particularly marked by 1876.

Even though large numbers of concessions had by then been made to local companies in an effort to satisfy the needs of localities not served by the lines of the major companies, large areas remained isolated and dependent on road transport. Because previous construction had followed existing currents of trade regional divergencies in economic development had been accentuated, making the formation of local companies with the necessary finance unlikely.

Consequently the Freycinet Plan was formulated to overcome the lack of support and was approved in 1878, but its implementation was postponed by the economic depression of 1882 and the unwillingness of the major companies to extend their networks. The Plan gave concessions to these major companies and discontinued the policy of encouraging local companies in an attempt to give greater coherence and financial stability to the extended network. The conventions of 1883 providing guarantees of dividends again overcame company reluctance; in consequence the rail network grew from some 22,000 km. in 1880 to 39,500 km. in 1914, supplemented from the 1890s by narrow gauge and tramway lines.

Even in 1914, in areas like the Massif Central, large areas would still remain isolated from the railway, but for all its imperfections this enlarged network permitted social and commercial intercourse on a scale which would have otherwise been impossible.

Unlike the pre-1883 network, subsequent additions did not provoke substantial modifications of the economic structure, or even a very considerable increase in the volume of goods transported: the new areas served were not economically dynamic. But in strictly local terms the consequences were often revolutionary. In Brittany, for example, the clearance of wasteland was stimulated by the new possibilities of transporting lime and developing dairy farming.

Political factors and the pressures of local interests often had a secondary influence on the routes taken, and the significance of this programme has perhaps been partly obscured by the accusation that lines were constructed in order to win over votes. But basically this third network responded to the real needs of what was still in large part a rural economy and society. Prior to the advent of the motor car, if vast areas of the countryside were to advance economically and socially there was no alternative means to bring it about other than the railway. This was the basis of the Government's decision. Nowhere was the economic and social transformation achieved by the railway as marked as in these backward areas, although their relative backwardness was not altered.

Telegraph

Complementary to the railway in reducing isolation and accelerating communication was the electric telegraph. The first line was constructed in 1844 between Paris and Rouen; by 1849 there were 500 km.; and in 1851 2,133 km. Subsequently progress accelerated. In 1852 a further 1,325 km. were added to the network, and by January 1855 all the prefectures were linked to Paris. The lengthening of the line was accompanied by reductions in charges and growing use. Unlike the previous semaphore telegraph this network could be used by the public. From a charge of 2 fr. per 20 words in 1861, the tariff fell to 0.50 francs in 1868. From 9,014 telegrams in 1851, the number sent rose to 3,503,182 in 1869. In combination with the railway the telegraph enormously facilitated the development of centralised political and economic controls, and transformed day-to-day administrative and commercial practices.

Conclusions Concerning Communications

The development of investment in railways as a proportion of total industrial investment has been estimated as follows:[12]

1835–44	0.56%	1865–74	3.85%	1895–1904	4.41%
1845–54	2.71%	1875–84	5.27%	1905–1913	4.58%
1855–64	5.50%	1885–94	4.39%		

This creation both modified the use made of other means of transport and caused an unprecedented increase in the volume of traffic which cannot simply be explained in terms of a transfer from other forms of transport. New traffic was created. Thus in the period of economic expansion – effectively one of structural change in the economy – from 1851 to 1876 traffic, measured in ton kilometres, increased by 1,590 per cent on the railways (11.2 per cent per year), whilst waterway traffic increased by only 18 per cent and road by 19 per cent (c. 0.5 per cent per year). The railways, which in 1851 moved some 11 per cent of the total volume transported, by 1876 transported 63 per cent, compared with the 15 per cent and 22 per cent, respectively of the waterway and roads.[13]

In spite of the improvement in road conditions from the eighteenth century, a real transport revolution was not possible before the development of railways and steamships. No other method of transport on a large scale, with regularity and at low cost existed. The following table indicating the evolution of the transport costs of merchandise clearly reveals this.[14]

Price in centimes per kilometre	Ordinary carting	Accelerated carting	Railway av. tariffs Ordinary Speed
c. 1750	40–60		
c. 1775	25–35		
1799	42		
1800	10–20	35–40	
1810	36		
1812	30		
1820	30		
c. 1840	20–25	30–45	
1841			12.0
1834–46	23–28	43–45	
1851	20		7.7
1860			6.9
1870			6.1
1880			6.0

Commerce

In the countryside in a pre-industrial society the search for independence of the market was one of the basic characteristics of daily life. Self-sufficiency provided security against price fluctuations and those who speculated on the necessities of life. When transport was slow and expensive most people could rarely afford to buy those goods which had not been produced locally. In the case of foodstuffs, only local supplies could be depended on, and so a polyculture, restricting the need for exchange was essential.

In practice this self-sufficiency was intruded upon by the need to obtain those things the family unit either did not produce or not in sufficient quantity, such as cereals, salt and iron, and by the demands of royal taxation. These were paid for by the sale or barter of whatever surplus the family might produce — wheat, cheese, wine, olive oil, animals, etc. — by the sale of labour, or in the last resort by begging. Normally a system of exchanges developed with a primarily local basis. In Provence some communes produced a surplus of wine; others olive oil; and yet others sheep and vegetables. In another the inhabitants might be engaged traditionally in pottery, producing household vessels and storage jars for a small region. Between such communes trade would develop, becoming especially important where two 'complementary and contrasting' zones met, for example where the Alpine foothills met the plain.

The volume of trade and the direction it takes is clearly dependent upon the facilities for transport. These fundamentally determine the structure of the market. Much of this local trade was conducted on a direct basis between producer and consumer, but also involved were pedlars and merchants who served sometimes as economic links with a wider world. Even in the middle of the nineteenth century, in most villages the only commerce was that of the innkeeper, and even in the larger market towns were too few potential clients for there to be many shops.

Only the richer families broke away from such patterns of self-subsistence. They might develop more refined tastes, which they had the money to indulge. This provided a continuing link with inter-regional trade circuits.

The growing intensity of trade in the eighteenth century is revealed by the number of fairs and markets. The latter were generally held weekly and to them the rural population took what they had to sell, and bought in return, above all, cereals. The scale of transactions tended to be very small. More important economically were the fairs. At least in the plains, these had already tended to decline in number as communications improved. A further process of selection occurred, resulting in fewer but larger fairs which remained until the middle of the nineteenth century the most important opportunity for commerce, when the peasant made his big and infrequent purchases of manufactured goods, and merchants bought and sold.

In areas of growing volume of trade the lack of easy communications demanded the existence of a dense network of small towns with commercial functions in relation to small surrounding areas. They served as centres at which the rare but indispensible exchanges could occur, and at which artisans could reside. The larger towns attracted more trade and merchants from further afield and distributed products involved in inter-regional trade. The whole system in developing areas was highly developed by the end of the eighteenth century. The extent of proletarianisation in agriculture and the development of rural industry are indicative of this. But due to the slowness and irregularity of communications it remains characterised in comparison with development later in the century as relatively feeble in exchange both in terms of distance and volume.

Cities like Paris, Lyon, Orléans, and Toulouse attracted trade by virtue of the demands of their populations and their location on the lines of communication. They performed entrepôt functions, their merchants collecting goods from far afield and then organising their transport and redistribution. Orléans provides one example of a major commercial centre whose importance was due to location and transport conditions. Situated on the Loire, it linked north, south and centre. Irregularity in river communications made it impossible for merchants in the areas it linked to know with any degree of certainty when supplies of a product ordered from far afield could be expected. Thus entrepôts were established at Orléans and merchants addressed themselves to these rather than directly to the producer.

The famous fair at Beaucaire on the Rhône performed similar functions, but it declined in importance as communications improved and more direct transactions became possible. In the 1820s new roads brought about the development of commercial activity at Marseille and hastened Beaucaire's decline. Her rôle in international trade was first reduced and then with the advent of rail construction she sank to the level of a regional market.

Money remained a necessity, even in the most self-sufficient rural communities; therefore the significance of the merchant in rural society should not be underestimated, or the participation of most peasant farmers in the market. Even though it was marginal, it was nonetheless of crucial importance. As communications improved and market structures adapted to this, intermediaries with a certain commercial expertise had an increasingly important part to play, and began to replace the face-to-face character of many transactions between farmer and merchant. The mass of small vine cultivators or workers in rural industry, with limited knowledge of market conditions themselves were especially dependent upon intermediaries.

The extent to which goods can be exchanged is obviously fundamentally dependent upon the condition of communications, from which proposition it follows that in a situation of underdevelopment the geographical limitation of the market limits the incentive to increase production. In short, rural societies, living essentially off themselves, provide only a very limited consumer market within which relationships between buyers and sellers are quasi-static, with little effort on either side to develop new business.

During the eighteenth century market structures slowly changed, commercial activity increased and provided a growing and vital stimulus to productive activity. The growing animation of the fairs reveals this. The turnover at that of Caen increased from 2½ million livres per year in 1715 to 9 million in 1767, and at Beaucaire from 14 million livres in 1750 to 41 million in 1788. This increase in value was due only in part to the general increase in prices. In the Auvergne the growth in the number of fairs held from the 1740s — from 344 in 1743 to 407 in 1777 — also reveals the development of a money economy. In the Bourgogne the improvement of roads from 1740 encouraged some men in most villages to set themselves up as merchants. Around Toulouse, the number of grain merchants grew. Along the roads the number of small speculators on the exchange of goods increased, stimulating economic activity.

The taxation requirements of the State can act as a powerful force, stimulating production for the open market to secure money with which to pay taxes. But this does not apply to everyone. The undertaxed large landowner does not have this stimulus. His security and status are secured by ownership of land; his revenue is guaranteed by increasing demand through population pressure to rent or share-crop his land, and on price fluctuations of foodstuffs. If the rest of the population in the area is living around subsistence level, they obviously have little surplus purchasing power which might generate demand. Until the possibility of producing for more extensive markets appears the restrictions outlined in this paragraph will continue to operate, and only the improvement of communications and the introduction of capitalistic conceptions into both agriculture and industry will provide that possibility.

The development of roads, of new markets, the increase in the number of merchants and the improvements in their methods, all this was a cumulative process, stimulating production. But if the volume of trade evidently did grow, this, and its consequences, should not be exaggerated. Before the railway, exchanges were still over very limited distances and, compared with subsequent development, small in volume, due to which, the basic marketing structure remained unchanged, still taking the form of a series of localised markets with only low levels of exchange between them.

Toutain has calculated the average distance travelled per metric ton of merchandise as a means of indicating the development of a national market. The bases of such a calculation are questionable. How, for instance, can short-distance movement of the type farm to nearest market centre be known? As a result it is probable that his estimate of average movement by road in 1830 is far too high. Use of the commercial records of the railway and canal companies by contrast promises a far more accurate estimate. The following statistics, whilst indicating the great significance of railways in the extension of the market, are probably an underestimate.

Average distance transported (kilometres per metric ton)[15]

	Road	Rail	Canal
1830	50–60	–	
1841–44		39	
1845–54		108	
1855–64		167	
1865–74		195	
1875–84		191	110
1885–94		190	136
1895–1904		191	147
1905–13		189	150

Whilst making this point, it would be unwise to underestimate the general stimulus given by the long-distance trade which did exist, particularly international trade. Although quantitatively far inferior to internal trade, it undoubtedly acted as a 'pilot sector', its demands stimulating the development of new techniques, the amassing of larger capitals, and improvements in quality. Involvement in international trade inevitably influenced productive and commercial methods generally. This can be clearly seen in the development of silk, glove, cloth and paper production in an area like the Dauphiné. Although most of this trade was with European countries (63.2 per cent in 1775), the loss of colonial trade during wars reduced the stimulus afforded, and can be said to have reinforced the determinism of internal geographic and demographic factors.

During the eighteenth century direct state intervention in the economy tended to decline, since in a prosperous and expanding economy regulation was less necessary than in a depressed one. Businessmen cried out less for help and protection than for freedom to make profits. The restrictions imposed by corporative regulations designed to limit production and competition made less sense when there appeared to be enough for everyone. Turgot's policy reflected this feeling. Its partial reversal represented the hesitation of the régime in the face of opposition from the privileged and its inability to engage in more than piecemeal reform.

The positive government action that there was seemed designed essentially to reduce the impediments to commerce. An *arrêt* of 16 May 1766 favoured uniformisation of weights and measures. Efforts were made to reduce the various taxes and tolls which, by increasing transport costs, reduced the movement of goods. Only on 5 November 1790 were internal customs barriers between provinces removed, but previously important exemptions had been introduced, for example in 1761 on the movement of coal, 1763 for grains, and in 1776 for wine. A variety of tolls were levied, in theory for services which were often no longer rendered — for the opening of mill dykes on waterways, for the upkeep and improvement of waterways, bridges and roads. Many of these charges were fixed so that their collection became uneconomic as prices rose, and they lapsed. Others were suppressed by local *parlements,* whilst a decree of 1774 exempted the grain trade from all tolls. A similar fate befell the taxes on merchandise entering fairs and markets, which were intended to provide for the upkeep of market halls, weights and measures, etc. These, in the Auvergne, varied between 5 per cent and 0.8 per cent of the value of a product but were gradually eliminated by towns anxious to increase trade.

Large towns often raised money by a tax on goods entering within their boundaries — the *octroi.* This and the similar tax on drinks were abolished by a decree of 19 February and 2–17 March 1791, but in the absence of adequate alternative sources of municipal revenue they were restored by laws of germinal year *V* and Frimaire year *VII,* in the case of the *octroi* and by a law of 1804 in that of drinks. The relatively high level of both of these taxes continued to be a serious cause of grievance for wine producers and merchants until their gradual elimination in the last third of the nineteenth century. At Paris, for example, a tax of 6.60 fr. per hectolitre of wine was paid in the year *VII,* which by 1880 had risen to 10.60 fr. Inferior wines paid a disproportionate amount in relation to their value.

The trade commodity which caused the most intense discussion was grain, and here economic arguments mixed inextricably with questions of morals and of public order. On the one hand it was argued that freedom of trade would ensure the movement of grain from areas of surplus to areas of deficit under the sole impulse of the profit motive, and on the other that it was immoral to profit from the hunger of the poor. J.-P. Lenoir, Lieutenant-General of Police in Paris, 1774–85 clearly believed in the concept of a just price and the responsibility of the Government towards the hungry.

In practice Government policy varied according to the supposed state of the harvest. In crises severe restrictions might be imposed on the movement of grain outside the kingdom, and even between provinces. Lack of information, and the failure to appreciate differing local situations often tended to make supply worse than it already was. Thus in September 1784 when there was a good harvest in the Toulouse area, restrictions on movement were introduced there because there had been a poor crop in the Paris basin, an area which the central government was obviously more aware of.

The series of general laws, particularly those of 1764 and 1770, designed to increase freedom and the flexible response of commerce and agriculture were thus neutralised by edicts made to meet particular shortages. On the other hand restrictive legislation often failed in its objectives, since a coalition of rural interests could make effective controls difficult to maintain. Movements by sea could most easily be observed by the Government, but even here local influence could secure exemptions. In most areas large landowners favoured free trade which permitted them to speculate on the massive fluctuations in cereal prices. In 1772 the Parlement of Toulouse repealed the restrictions imposed by the Controller-General Terray and had to be brought to heel by an *arrêt* of the Council of State which significantly condemned its collusion with the great grain producers.

There was thus often a contrast between government policy and actual practice. The principles of economic liberalism were clearly affirmed in 1789, but the Constituent Assembly was hesitant to allow complete liberty — free trade in cereals was permitted, but municipal controls over bread and meat prices, and over marketing practices, were retained. Faced with renewed problems of supply and price fluctuation the Convention turned to the most extreme restrictions yet seen and even attempted to establish the administrative apparatus necessary to implement them. The decree of 4 May 1793 regulated the trade in grains and introduced the principle of a maximum price fixed on a departmental basis. In July the direst penalties were proposed for food speculators.

This was an over-reaction against the principles of freedom, but nevertheless municipal price controls were retained until the 1860s. As long as the fear of famine survived, and as long as speculators were able to profit from large price fluctuations on a market characterised by compartmentalisation and inelastic supply, the supply/demand mechanism favoured by the liberal theorists could not work effectively. It required the transport revolution beginning in the late 1840s before the free play of market forces could become a reality.

Tariff restrictions on the import of cereals from other countries were removed only in 1861. This, combined with the steamship then made the French cereal market part of an international market, introducing new factors into supply conditions and the determination of price levels.

Currency

For trade to occur on a significant scale money must circulate. In an age when paper money still had limited acceptance — during the Restoration for example the Bank of France issued only 500 and 1,000 franc notes which circulated mainly in Paris — monetary supply was determined primarily by the bullion available, and by the use of commercial paper both as a means of payment and of securing credit. In January 1825, compared with some 150 millions in bank notes, the metallic currency in circulation was estimated at 2,713,000,000 francs. In 1815 the Bank of France discounted 206 millions francs worth of commercial paper — rising to 617 millions in 1830, a fact indicative of the growing intensity of trade.

During the eighteenth century it has been estimated that the monetary stock perhaps doubled and certainly that the use of commercial paper increased. Generally, and increasingly so, there was a division of function between the two. Money served for daily transactions, for purchases in rural markets, for the payment of workers, and short-term commercial transactions, whilst commercial paper served large-scale operations where payment was postponed. The growth of monetary supply increased people's ability to make purchases and led to an acceleration in economic activity. The more rapid circulation of money had the same effects as enlarged supply in stimulating activity.

To our eyes the rate of circulation of money appears very slow. Hoarding was an important aspect of the use of money: money was saved to provide a reserve with which to buy food in time of crisis; it was hoarded for the eventual purchase of land, or for the payment of dowries. Money remained a scarce commodity often available only at a premium. It was a commodity with which to speculate. Its limited supply, combined with the necessity of its possession helped maintain extremely high rates of interest. Small manufacturers and merchants, and indeed businessmen at all levels, lacking the security necessary to float commercial paper, were constantly plagued by problems of liquidity.

This was especially evident in periods of crisis. The political unrest of the Revolution and the introduction of paper *assignats* — serving to drive out good money — reduced supply through hoarding and interfered with the cirulation of money by the interruption of trade.

To a very large extent the circulation of money continued to depend on those in agriculture and the conditions they lived under. The acquisition of money required the sale of agricultural products susceptible to the natural hazards of harvest failure or disease amongst livestock. Besides rural industry, cash crops like silk, saffron or madder,

34

flax and hemp, and above all the vine, were important for procuring money.

Poor crops inevitably led to an outflow of money both locally and nationally to pay for imports of food. Crises of subsistence were due in large part to the sheer lack of the money necessary to buy food. In this situation that small minority of the wealthier inhabitants who possessed money wielded considerable social power, and through money lending were able to make enormous profits.

The other major drain on currency reserves was by taxation. This varied with the needs of the Government, becoming particularly high in time of war. Its burden was obviously greatest when food prices were high.

The circulation of goods depends upon a corresponding circulation of the means of payment, which were vastly improved by the railways and the telegraph. The railways and the economic and social changes accompanying them ended isolation and finally removed the fear of famine. Improved circulation of foodstuffs brought a decline in the amplitude of price fluctuation making the hoarding of money less necessary, and this together with the psychological release associated with the transition from closed to open societies created a new attitude towards money. It circulated more freely and more rapidly, thus stimulating commerce. Although gold retained much of its favour and continued to be hoarded, the value of bank notes in circulation grew from 500 million francs in 1850, to 1,350 million in 1869. Moreover small value bank notes were now issued and found widespread use.

The railway and telegraph networks made it possible for banks like the Crédit Lyonnais and Société Général to create in the last third of the century a network of branch banks far more extensive than that of the departmental banks and the Bank of France established in the 1830s and '40s. They permitted administrative control of the various branches by the centre, and the rapid movement of cash from areas of surplus to those where it was in demand. Credit resources were increased, the raising of capital facilitated and the means of payment simplified — notably by the use of bank cheques following the law of 1865. The increased amount of money, both bullion and paper, in circulation, and its growing mobility provided unparalleled means for the mobilisation of trade.

Conclusions

The growing importance of the railway network for commerce, not simply *vis-à-vis* other forms of transport, but due to its rôle in stimulating the growth of trade can be seen from the following table:[16]

Internal transport : merchandise (milliards ton kilometres)

	Road	Rail	Canal	Sea (coastal)	Total
1830	2.0	–	0.7	1.1	3.8
1841–44	(2.3)	0.06	1.1	1.2	(4.7)
1845–54	2.6	0.46	1.7	1.3	6.1
1855–64	2.7	3.0	2.0	0.9	8.6
1865–74	2.8	6.3	1.9	0.8	11.8

At a time when the volume of trade was expanding, when the elasticity of demand for transport was high, a pronounced reduction in transport costs led to an enormous increase in traffic. The tariff policies of the railway companies did much to determine the scale of this increase and its regional variations. The tariffs of the northern railway company on such bulky merchandise as coal were particularly low because of canal competition. Those of the Midi company remained relatively high because from 1858 it controlled the Canal du Midi and prevented the establishment of rail-canal competition.

Rail tariffs were not determined by operating costs but by a confusion of commercial principles and government pressure. The railway companies were never able to freely manage their tariff policies. The conventions they negotiated with the State guaranteed dividends but in return allowed for state interference. Given their quasi-monopoly position state intervention was probably inevitable.

The railways provided new opportunities for commerce and the quantities and diversity of goods produced and commercialised increased. The currents of traffic became more and more rapid and dense, which required inevitable changes in the structure of commerce and in the habits of merchants. These changes had begun before rail construction as part of a growth in trade, but now their evolution was accelerated. A growth in the importance of the tertiary, service sector of the economy, was a clear mark of this modernisation.

With rail and telegraph the commercial traveller became a far more common feature of business life. He produced his samples, took orders and the goods were speedily delivered. During the Second Empire the first large department stores were established in Paris displaying a large variety of goods at clearly marked prices, heralding a commercial revolution which, especially in the last quarter of the century, would extend to a mass of retailers represented in every town or village.

In this reorganisation of commerce, one layer of intermediaries was forced out. Many ports and markets and major entrepôts like Orléans declined. They had existed for centuries due to the slowness and irregularity of transport. The commission agents who had acted as relays between a series of regional transporters were no longer necessary once the railway served as a single transporter between sender and destination. The railway thus permitted the reduction of charges for the commercialisation of products, both directly through the reduction of tariffs, and indirectly by simplification of the network of intermediaries.

The railway, in ending geographical isolation from competition, made it impossible for producers and merchants to profit from monopoly situations, and thus contributed to the stabilisation of prices. Factors, wholesalers, and retailers continued however to require large profit margins. In 1861, for example, the cost of transporting a *piece* of wine from Dijon to Paris should have been only 7.50 fr. but the actual charge was 12.90 fr. Cheaper transport meant a reduction in prices for the consumer yet at the same time an increase in returns for the producer and for the merchant. This served to increase purchasing power and consumption.

Regions already more heavily engaged in commerce tended to be more alert to new possibilities, and this is a part explanation of the fact that if the rail network accelerated the development of poor regions, that of the richer was even more rapid, and regional disparities were maintained or even increased.

Special reduced tariffs, made available by the railway companies to bulk users were a major factor tending to confirm existing patterns of traffic. The concentration of traffic on Paris became more marked than ever.

The responsiveness of producers and consumers to the new situation should not be exaggerated. The business world needed to be assured of the potential for profit of a new market opened up by rail before they would enter it, and this took some time. It seems unlikely, because of this factor, that a genuine national market existed before the 1880s.

Notes

1. Lévy-Leboyer, M., *Les banques européennes et l'industrialisation internationale dans la première moitié du 19e siècle*, 1964.
2. Toutain, J.-C., 'Les transports en France de 1830 à 1965', *E.S.*, 1967, p. 15.
3. Wolkowitsch, M., *L'économie régionale des transports dans le centre et le centre-ovest de la France*, n.d.
4. Ibid., p. 33.
5. Toutain, op. cit., p. 19.
6. Rivet, F., *La navigation à vapeur sur la Saône et la Rhône*, 1962.
7. Lévy-Leboyer, op. cit., p. 278.
8. Rivet, op. cit., p. 162.
9. Lévy-Leboyer, op. cit., p. 290.
10. Wolkowitsch, op. cit., p. 51.
11. This section owes a great deal to E. Caron, *Histoire de l'exploitation d'un grand rèseau. La compagnie du chemin du fer du Nord, 1846–1937*, 1973, pp. 86–7.

12. Caron, F., 'Recherches sur le capital des voies de communication en France au 19ᵉ siècle' in *L'industrialisation en Europe au 19ᵉ siècle*, 1972, p. 240.
13. Renouard, D., *Le transports de Marchandises par fer, route et eau depuis 1850*, 1960, p. 39.
14. Bairoch, P., *Revolution industrielle et sous-developpment*, 1969, p. 329.
15. Toutain, op. cit., p. 258.

Further Reading

The following works were found to be particularly useful. The list is selective and not inclusive. Where not given place of publication is Paris for books in French and London for those in English.

Agulhon, M., *La vie sociale en Provence intérieure au lendemain de le révolution*, 1970.
Arbellot, G., 'La grande mutation des routes de France au milieu du 18ᵉ siècle', *A.E.S.C.*, 1973.
Armengaud, A., *Les populations de l'est-aquitain au début de Epoque contemporain*, 1961.

Babonaux, Y., 'L'evolution contemporaine d'une ville de la Loire: Blois', *I.H.*, 1955.
Baehrel, R., *Une croissance: La basse – Provence rurale*, 1961.
Bairoch, P., *Révolution industrielle et sous-developpement*, 1969.
Bergeron, L., *L'episode napoléonien*, 1972.
de Bertier de Sauvigny, G., *La Restauration*, 1955.
Blanchard, M., *Essais historiques sur les premiers chemins de fer du Midi languedocien et de la vallée de la Rhone*, Montpellier, 1935.
Blanchard, M., *Géographie des chemins de fer*, 1942.
Blanchard, M., 'The Railway Policy of the Second Empire' in Crouzet, F., *et al.*, *Essays in European Economic History*, 1969.
Bloch, R., 'Les chemins de fer francaïse et les transports de céréales', *R.G.C.*, 1901.
Bouvier, J., *Histoire économique et histoire sociale*, Geneva, 1968.
Bouvier, J., 'Le mouvement d'une civilisation nouvelle' in Duby, G. (ed.), *Histoire de la France*, II, 1972.
Bozon, P., *La vie rurale en Vivarais*, 1963.
Brunet, P., *Structure agraire et économie rurale des plateaux tertiares entre le Seine et l'Oise*, Caen, 1960.

Caralp-Landon, R., *Les chemins de fer dans le Massif central*, 1959.
Caron, F., *Histoire de l'exploitation d'un grand réseau. La compagnie du chemin du fer du Nord*, 1846–1937, 1973.
Caron, F., 'Recherches sur le capital des voies de communication en France au 19ᵉ siècle' in *L'industrialisation en Europe au 19ᵉ siècle*,

1972.

Chevalier, M., *La vie humaine dans les Pyrénées ariégoises,* 1956.

Chombart de Lauwe, J., *Bretagne et pays de la Garonne,* 1946.

Clark, C. and Haswell, M., *The Economics of Subsistence Agriculture,* 1964.

Clozier, R., *Géographie de la circulation,* 1963.

Cobb, R., *The Police and the People,* 1970.

Crouzet, F., 'Les origines du sous-développement économique du sudouest', *A.M.,* 1959.

Darnton, R., 'Le lieutenant de police J.-P. Lenoir, la guerre des farines et l'approvisionnement de Paris à la vieille de la Révolution', *R.H.M.C.,* 1969.

Dauzet, P., *Le siècle des chemins de fer en France,* Fontenay-au-Roses, 1948.

Desert, G., 'L'agriculture et les paysans sarthois au 19ᵉ siècle' in M. Lèvy-Leboyer, *et. al., Un siècle et demi d'économie sarthoise,* Rohan, 1969.

Desmarest, J., *Evolution de la France contemporaine. La France de 1870,* 1970.

Dion, R., 'Orléans et l'ancienne navigation de la Loire', *A.G.,* 1938.

Dunham, A.L., *The Anglo-French Treaty of Commerce of 1860 and the Progress of the Industrial Revolution in France,* Ann Arbor, 1930.

Dunham, A.L., *The Industrial Revolution in France,* New York, 1955.

Dupeux, G., *Aspects de l'histoire sociale et politique du Loir-et-Cher,* 1962.

Faucher, D., *L'homme et le Rhône,* 1968.

Fel, A., *Les hautes terres du Massif Central. Tradition paysanne et économie agricole,* 1962.

Festy, O., *L'agriculture pendant la révolution. Les conditions de production et de récolté des céreales,* 1947.

Fohlen, C., *The Industrial Revolution in France,* 1970.

Forster, R., *The Nobility of Toulouse in the Eighteenth Century,* Baltimore, 1960.

de Foville, A., *La transformation des moyens de transport et ses consequences économiques et sociales,* 1880.

Frêche, G., 'Etudes statistiques sur le commerce cérealier de la France méridionale au 18ᵉ siècle', *R.H.E.S.,* 1971.

Galtier, G., *Le vignoble du Languedoc méditerranéen et du Roussillon,* Montpellier, n.d.

Gautier, M., *Chemins et vehicules de nos campagnes,* St Brieuc, 1971.

Gille, B., *Les origines de la grande industrie métallurgique en France,* n.d.

Girard, L., *La politique des travaux publics du second Empire*, 1952.

Goubert, P., *L'ancien régimé*, II, 1973.

Guichard, P., 'D'une société repliée à une société ouverte, l'évolution socio-économique de la région d'Andance' in Leon, P., *Structures économiques et problèmes sociaux du monde rural dans la France du sud-est*, 1966.

Guiral, P., 'Le cas d'un grand port de Commerce, Marseille' in Labrousse, E. (ed.), *Aspects de la crise et de la dépression de l'économie française au milieu du 19e siècle*, 1956.

Imberdis, F., *Le réseau routier de l'auvergne au 18e siècle. Ses origines et son évolution*, 1967.

Jardin, A. and Tudesq, A.J., *La France des notables, 1815–1848*, 2 vols, 1972.

Jouffroy, L.M., *L'ère du rail*, 1953.

Jouffroy, L.M., 'Les relations du rail et de la route à l'origine des chemins de fer', *A.F.*, 1950.

Labasse, J., 'La circulation des capitaux en France au 19e siècle', *I.H.*, 1955.

Labasse, J., *Les capitaux et la région. Essai sur le commerce et la circulation des capitaux dans la region lyonnaise*, 1955.

Labrousse, E., *La crise de l'économie française à la fin de l'ancien régime et au début de la révolution*, 1944.

Labrousse, E., *Aspects de l'évolution économique et sociale de la France et du Royaume-Uni de 1815 a 1880*, 1949.

Labrousse, E., *et al.*, *Histoire économique et sociale de la France*, II, 1970.

Laurent, R., *Les vignerons de la Côte d'Or au 19e siècle*, 1958.

Laurent, R., *L'octroi de Dijon*, 1960.

Lebrun, F., *Les hommes et la mort en Angou au 17e et 18e siècles*, 1971.

Lefevre, A., *Sous le second Empire: chemins de fer et politique*, 1951.

LeFranc, G., 'The French Railroads 1823–1842', *J.E.B.H.*, 1929–30.

Lemarchand, G., 'Le 17e et le 18e siècles en France: bilan et perspectives de recherches', *A.H.R.F.*, 1969.

Leon, P., *Economies et sociétés pre-industrielles*, II, 1970.

Leon, P., *La naissance de la grande industrie en Dauphiné (fin du 17e siècle – 1869)*, 2 vols, 1954.

Letaconnoux, J., 'Note comparative sur la distance en temps entre l'intérieur de la Bretagne et la mer, aux 18e, 19e et 20e siècles', *A.B.*, 1907–8.

Letaconnoux, J., 'Les transports en France au 18e siècle', *R.H.M.C.*,

1908–9.

Lévy-Leboyer, M., *Les banques européennes et l'industrialisation internationale dans la première moitié du 19ᵉ siècle*, 1964.

Livet, G., 'La route royale et la civilisation Française de la Fin du 15ᵉ au milieu du 18ᵉ siècle' in Michaud, G. (ed.), *Les routes de France depuis les origines jusqu'à nos jours*, 1950.

Meyer, J., *La noblesse bretonne en 18ᵉ siècle*, 2 vols, 1966.

Picard, A., *Les Chemins de fer français*, 4 vols, 1884.

Pinchemel, P., *France: A Geographical Survey*, 1969.

Pitié, J., *Exode rural et migrations intérieures en France. L'example de la Vienne et du Poitou-Charentes*, Poitiers, 1971.

Poitrineau, A., *La vie rurale en basse-Auvergne au 18ᵉ siecle*, 1965.

Renouard, D., *Les transports de marchandises par fer, route et eau depuis 1850*, 1960.

Rivet, F., *La navigation à vapeur sur la Saône et la Rhône*, 1962.

Rochefort, M., *L'orgnisation urbaine de l'Alsace*, 1960.

Rousseau, P., *Histoire des transports*, 1961.

de Saint-Jacob, P., 'La corvée royale en France à la fin de L'Ancien Régime', *I.H.*, 1953.

de Saint-Jacob, P., *Les paysans de la Bourgogne du nord au dernier siècle de L'Ancien Régime*, 1960.

Seignour, P., *La vie économique du Vancluse de 1815–1848*, Aix-en-Provence, 1957.

Soboul, A., *La France à la vieille de la révolution*, I, 1966.

Sorlin, P., *La société française: 1840–1914*, 1969.

Thuillier, G., *Aspects de l'économie nivernaise au 19ᵉ siècle*, 1966.

Toutain, J.-C., 'Les transports en France de 1830 à 1965', *E.S.*, 1967.

Truchon, P., 'Les transports et voies de communication au service du Commerce Lyonnais sous la Restauration', *R.H.L.*, 1911.

Vidalenc, J., *La société francaise de 1815 à 1848, II, Le peuple des villes et des bourgs*, 1972.

Vigier, P., *La seconde république dans la région alpine*, I, 1963.

Wolkowitsch, M., *L'économie régionale des transports dans le centre et le centre-ouest de la France*, n.d.

2 AGRICULTURE

Part I: Ancien Régime Structures c.1730–1850

This chapter is concerned with human action within and upon given
natural environments which limit the effectiveness and scope of that
action, but which, by the changes wrought upon them, stress the
dynamic activity of men struggling to master natural conditions.

Geological structures change slowly, which means that they can be
taken as given throughout the period we shall consider. The effects of
human action are most evident in changes to increase fertility
introduced in the composition of soils, and so this is one of the
processes of change in agriculture which will be considered at some
length. The only other variable of decisive importance which needs to
be considered is the climate of France, since it is evident that
temperature controls the length of the growing season and consequently
determines which crops can be cultivated and with what degree of
security. Climate is a decisive determinant of land use. France can be
divided into two major climatic zones: the north and north-east, which
form part of the temperate region of the world, and the south, which is
part of the subtropical. The situation is complicated by the existence
of mountains — the Massif Central, Jura, Alps and Pyrenees cause
northern climatic traits to appear in the south, so that only the
Atlantic lowlands south of the Loire, the Aquitaine Basin, the
Mediterranean area south of the Massif Central and the southern Alps
have the dry summers and high temperatures characteristic of a
subtropical climate.

In both north and south the further inland one proceeds the more
continental climatic tendencies intrude on a predominantly oceanic
régime. Conditions become especially severe in mountain areas, where
due to low temperatures the growing season is restricted to some 3–6
months, and where variations of exposition induce major local
differences.

Optimum growing conditions for the production of cereals would
seem to be, in northern France, cold dry winters, warm dry springs,
and a dry summer, with a certain amount of rain to increase yields. The
main danger for this sort of crop is excessively wet conditions in both
winter and summer, whilst a cold spring delays the vegetative cycle. In
the Mediterranean area the main danger is excessive dryness.

The sort of food provided by agriculture is determined not solely by geological and climatic factors but by those which might loosely be labelled institutional, the first place belonging to the nature and effectiveness of the transport infra-structure and of the marketing conditions founded principally on it.

Before the creation of a railway network in the 1850s, transport, whether by road or water, and in spite of improvements, remained slow, expensive and insecure, so that the survival of a compartmentalised market structure in a period of growth in agriculture is what gives continuity to the period from *c*.1730 to *c*.1850. In the vast majority of localities foodstuffs were produced not for sale, but for immediate consumption. Only a surplus was sold, and poor communications anyway limited the size of the potential market. Demand was inelastic even if supply varied, with the result that prices fluctuated widely. When harvests were bad supplies could not increase, which encouraged speculation and panic; when harvests were good, the limits imposed on the size of the market by inadequate communications often made it difficult to sell even at very low prices. Eastern France, for example, most parts of which in normal years had a surplus of wheat always found this difficult to market, and in consequence usually had the cheapest wheat in France.

This is obviously not to deny that a substantial commerce existed, above all for the provisioning of large towns, and that this, together with local population growth encouraged innovation. In the eighteenth century no region was totally outside commercial circuits, although the south-west, Massif Central and the east certainly contributed less than other regions. But until the mid-nineteenth century the market structure remained characterised by fragmentation. It was composed of a series of semi-closed local and regional markets with only limited and irregular relations between them.

Due to the slowness, unreliability and cost of transport and the limited supply of money, most of the food consumed was produced near the place of consumption. To a large extent production and consumption were able to adapt to each other, and most consumers would not dream of demanding anything other than the foods grown locally. Therefore diet varied profoundly between regions according to natural resources and local traditions, although also affected by the products offered by neighbouring localities and by the more vigorous commercial currents. Cereals were, however, the basis of all diets. Since they were difficult and expensive to bring from elsewhere, most people tried to grow their own. Moreover as money remained in short supply it was necessary to use it as little as possible.

Almost everything was produced locally. Vines grew in all save three northern generalities at the end of the eighteenth century, flax in 40 departments, and hemp in 57 near the middle of the nineteenth.

Cereals grew in the mountains at heights and on slopes which required a massive human effort to produce low yields. Because of the dominant preoccupation with the supply of bread, other crops were neglected. The unwillingness to cultivate pasture because people needed to be fed restricted the abandonment of fallow, and restrained the growth in numbers of livestock which might have provided manure to fertilise the land.

Yet, even if French agriculture as late as the mid-nineteenth century remained overwhelmingly productive for local subsistence, certain major contrasts within it had already appeared. Limited specialisations, serving as bases for trade had always existed, and were being deliberately developed as communications improved. A slow process of integration into the market took place. Neighbouring, but physically contrasting zones — the obvious example being mountains and plain — often traded on a sort of complementary basis. But given the condition of the transport infra-structure the market for most products remained restricted to a narrowly circumscribed region, as seen in the example of Paris, the most significant urban market. The intensity of commercialisation of products varied with distances from it. Within a circumference of 25—30 km. daily transport by cart to the city's market places was possible and farms in this area were entirely preoccupied with its supply. Further away an increasingly small proportion of the product was marketed, less money could be earned and self-subsistence entered more into the cultivators' thoughts.

Natural conditions and transport infra-structure combined to limit access to markets. The result was a particular kind of agriculture: essentially, though with some exceptions, a subsistence polyculture, the product of the necessity for the peasant to produce all or almost all he needed. Regional nuances were determined by varying physical environments. These have been generally described in terms of two basic types. In the north and east, agriculture was based on a three-year rotation composed of an autumn sown cereal, such as winter wheat, a spring sown cereal such as oats, barley or rye, and fallow — the latter allowing the land to rest and providing grazing. This rotation was inevitably accompanied by collective restrictions on the use of land, essential where one of the three large fields into which the arable was divided would be opened to the village animals. In conditions of relative over-population in these regions, throughout the eighteenth century the maximum area of land was devoted to the production of cereals. Natural pasture was minimal, animals few. There thus existed a vicious circle — too few animals, insufficient manure, low yields and the apparent necessity to produce cereals on an extensive basis, but with fallow necessary to allow the land to rest because there was not enough manure to fertilise it, and the consequent inability to use one-third of the arable each year.

Most of France was outside this system of strict rotation. Geographers tend to affirm the existence of a southern polyculture, based on the rotation of wheat and fallow, where conditions were too hot and dry for the cultivation of spring cereals. Both northern and southern polycultures were based on the production of cereals, but beyond this the distinguishing features need to be stressed.

Generally in the south the area of cultivated land adjoined large areas of waste where flocks could move freely without danger to the crops. This situation permitted a greater flexibility. It was here that the three elements of the agricultural exploitation distinguished by Ernest Labrousse, namely garden, field and pasture existed. Compared with the north more land was available — the peasant could possess a garden close to his residence in which he could cultivate whatever he wished and particularly vegetables in an intensive manner producing high yields. The exploitation of the fields, where collective restraints would apply was less intensive. Manure was insufficient and badly used by being spread over too wide an area. Finally an area of waste provided pasture for sheep and goats and wild harvests such as bark for tanning, lavender and thyme.

In the south natural conditions permitted the development of a number of supplementary resources, adding variety and balance to diet, and some sort of a guarantee against the failure of the primary cereals crop. A marketable product was also often cultivated, the proceeds from which might be employed to purchase food: vines, and fruit-bearing trees providing fresh fruit in summer and dried in winter, chestnuts and olives. In this situation the fear of famine was less intense. In comparison with the amount of human labour applied the product might often look mediocre, but the lesser dependence on the single cereal harvest increased security.

Greater climatic instability and local variations in soil structure contributed to this element of variation in southern agriculture. Land was usually held dispersed in a number of separate parcels in an effort to gain some security against often extreme local variations in climate.

The greater freedom from collective restrictions encouraged innovation even by peasants. Significantly, major developments seem to have coincided with crises, when the normal relative inertia was shattered by the threat of starvation and new crops like maize, haricots and potatoes introduced. Maize, cultivated first in Aquitaine, had the particular virtue of benefiting from climatic rhythms adverse to wheat, and often doing well in years in which the wheat harvest was bad. It made possible the suppression of fallow and the reserving of the wheat crop for sale. In many situations, by empirical processes, peasants seem to have made innovations akin to those recommended by agronomists.

In the north, where there was less variety, and fewer opportunities for innovation the collective restrictions had as a counterpart a series of rights which afforded some protection to the poor — the right to graze their few animals on the fallow, and on the cultivated fields following the harvests, the right to glean, and a whole series of rights of usage in forests and on common land.

This generalised division between north and south should not be allowed to obscure the fact that no clear boundary existed. Two-year rotation was found in the north, in areas of poor soils such as the sandstone Vosges, Lorrain plateau and Morvan and also in fertile areas like the Pays de Caux, Burgundy and north-east Alsace, for a complex mixture of physical and social reasons. Three-year rotation could be found in parts of the south, especially in mountain areas, on fertile ground able to take cereals two years in succession, or where due to pastoral farming large quantities of manure was available.

Mountain areas stand out because of their particular natural and agricultural conditions — the problems of altitude, exposition and winter. In spite of often unfavourable conditions poor communications forced the cultivation of cereals. Wheat and rye are extremely susceptible to climatic variations so that yields tend to be poor in quantity and quality, though paradoxically often better in the higher areas of settlement than the lower because more manure was available and lower population density permitted concentration on the better soils.

Here, as elsewhere, if in spring the wheat and rye crops were obviously not maturing, barley and oats were often hurriedly sown as an emergency measure. Buckwheat, with a short vegetative cycle provided another standby in precarious conditions as did the potato from the end of the eighteenth century. Mountain areas never grew enough food and to obtain more, and in addition oil, wine, salt and iron, money was raised by pastoral farming, rural industry and seasonal migration. Nevertheless each community must aim at self-sufficiency because there was no guarantee that outside supplies would be available.

Descriptions of upland areas from as late as the middle of the nineteenth century are indicative of the precarious balance between population and resources. Terraces were constructed on hillsides, held in place by walls with their soils reconstituted after the eroding effect of rain by the simple process of carrying the soil in panniers on human backs, from the valley floor back up the hill. This more than any other feature reveals the survival of a subsistence agriculture in which strictly economic motives for production had little meaning.

Distinguishable from this broad picture of a subsistence polyculture were the relatively small areas of specialisation — areas benefiting from exceptional natural conditions and especially having access to large markets. The obvious example is market-gardening around towns; the vine is predominantly a commercial culture, and its existence in the Loire valley, for example, was due less to optimum natural conditions than proximity to a means of communication. There was clearly no absolute link between physical conditions and systems of culture.

The relative prosperity of Flanders, Alsace and the Garonne valley was due to similar reasons. Flanders in particular stands out as the most advanced area technically, where use of canal mud and urban waste had long permitted the suppression of fallow and its replacement by fodder crops. Coastal areas too were relatively privileged — fishing coexisted with farming, seaweed and sand permitted the increase of soil fertility, and winters were mild. With the exception of Flanders, however, a true monoculture, genuine specialised production for the market, was exceptional. Areas such as Picardy, the Île de France, and Languedoc, which eventually would specialise and which even in the eighteenth century exported substantial surplus to other areas, continued to produce all their basic needs.

Cereals

The dominant aim of this agriculture was to obtain bread. Jean Fourastie has stressed the simple determinism of a situation in which, given on the one hand the amount of land available, the need for fallow and the low yields, and on the other the size of population, then the cultures adopted must be those which permitted this population to subsist. To produce a given number of calories meat demands five or ten times the area of cereals and in most areas extensive pastoral farming could not be considered, even in the absence of other obstacles. The age-old fear of famine impelled men to plant the maximum possible area with cereals, whatever the cost in human labour, and in spite of the very poor yields obtained.

The statistics on productivity are not too precise and vary greatly in quality. It has, however, been estimated that in the eighteenth century the average yield per grain of wheat was 5 or 6, with a maximum in Flanders of some 15 for 1. On less rich or less well worked land yields as low as 3 or even 2½ for 1 were not exceptional. By the period 1821—5 the national average wheat yield remained as low as 1:5 or 6 having changed little in the eighteenth century. It should however be remembered that even a small increase in yields, say from 1.5 to 1.55 represents a 10 per cent increase in production.[1]

The major estimates of production prepared by Toutain have been subjected to justifiable criticism on the grounds that he used 1700—10 as his base period.[2] This was a period of cyclical crises, and comparisons of subsequent harvests with those of this period must exaggerate the growth in productivity. It has been suggested that if the comparisons were made with the period of cyclical maxima 1660—80 then Toutain's optimistic picture of the eighteenth century might have to be replaced with one of recuperation from crisis rather than genuine growth, certainly in Auvergne, lower Languedoc, the Midi and perhaps the Lyon regions, Normandy and Alsace. Real growth, above seventeenth century levels is likely to have occurred in the Cambresis and Hainault and possibly in the Paris region.[3]

The more reliable agricultural enquiry of 1840 revealed an agriculture described as 'stagnant, backward, even primitive'. In over half the departments of France production of 12 hectolitres of wheat per hectare could not be achieved. Yields varied between the 20 hectolitres commonly obtained in the department of the Nord to the 6.78 hectolitres of the Lot. All but seven of the departments with above average yields were found to the north of a line Les Sables-Belfort, and all those below, save six, south of the line.[4]

Other characteristics of a backward agriculture might be mentioned. The enquiry of 1840 revealed fallow to still represent 27 per cent of the arable land, with artificial cultivated pastures as only 6 per cent — statistics indicating the massive retention of the traditional two- and three-year rotations. In other words over 20 per cent of the land was being wasted each year.

Ideally, manure should have been concentrated on a smaller area to produce higher yields there, whilst pasture could have been cultivated on the land so freed from cereals to increase the number of animals, of manure and so further increase yields. Most cultivators still favoured extensive cultivation as a better guarantee against starvation — the manure available was consequently spread too thinly. For similar psychological reasons seeds were broadcast thickly but with little consideration of their quality. Usually they were badly cleaned, badly conserved, unselected and consequently often represented degenerate strains. The poor results of farming in Picardy were castigated by Arthur Young and have been blamed primarily on inadequate ploughing. This might have been adequate on large exploitations, but where four-fifths of the peasant were without horses and ploughs and had to borrow or rent them after their owners had used them, they were likely to plough too late and insufficiently.

Possession of a plough and the draught animals necessary to draw it was a mark of social distinction in the plains of northern France, but in most of the country this was not so. The light ploughs of the *araire* type in most general use were simple enought to be constructed by the peasant himself and required little animal-power — they could even be pulled by a man.

The soils of the north were deeper, and the typical three-year rotation

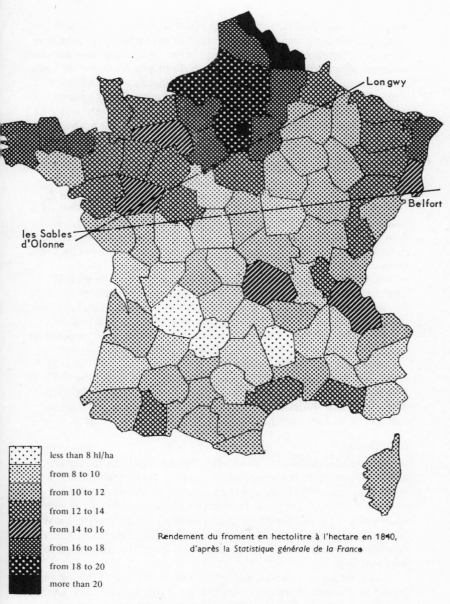

less than 8 hl/ha

from 8 to 10

from 10 to 12

from 12 to 14

from 14 to 16

from 16 to 18

from 18 to 20

more than 20

Rendement du froment en hectolitre à l'hectare en 1840,
d'après la *Statistique générale de la France*

Map 5 Wheat Yields in 1840 (hectolitre to the hectare)
Source: Statistique générale de la France

meant that each year two-thirds of the land was under cereals and required ploughing compared with only half where two-year rotations were more common. More animals and better equipment were therefore essential. The northern plough with its train of wheels, its mould board, its deeper plough, contained more metal, required specialist fabrication, and was expensive. It required more powerful animals and a team of a size that Mediterranean regions, lacking in pasture, were rarely able to sustain. There, to a certain degree, the ploughing tool was adapted to the energy for traction available — undernourished cows, small oxen, mules or men. Similarly carts often remained small because the available horses were small and ill-fed.

Moreover, the *araire* was better adapted to the soil, relief and climate of most southern areas. It was the tool of Mediterranean dry farming, adequate to clear weeds and aerate soils, but not capable of ploughing deeply, which was not desired on thin, light soils. It was light and manoeuvrable, factors vital on undulating terrain and in small, irregular fields. Archaic in appearance the *araire* was often well adapted to its environment.

Another determinant of agricultural techniques was the general abundance of labour. Methods of production were in part determined by the availability of cheap labour but also by the social necessity to give employment and subsistance to as much of the population as possible. This was most evident in mountain areas where in response to population pressure and with knowledge of vegetative cycles more attention was paid to exposition than the declivity of fields, so that often only hand tools could be used. The continued use of the sickle as a harvest tool rather than the more efficient scythe, and of the flail which provided winter employment, well into the second half of the nineteenth century exemplify this abundance of human beings.

Cash Crops

In communities dependent upon self-subsistence polyculture, barter and labour services, as a means of exchange of goods and services, were more significant than money, but a means of earning money was nonetheless essential in order to purchase necessities like salt or iron tools which were not always produced locally. Almost everyone was subject to a variety of fiscal obligations, including rents and seigneurial dues and above all to taxes which could not always be commuted to a payment in kind.

This need for money was met by the sale of surplus, of labour, or by the production of market-crops like wine, silk, natural dyes, animals, etc. This and the growth of population encouraged the maximum utilisation of all possibilities. Waste land and forest, for example, were closely integrated into the rural economy, providing wild plants,

50

pasture, and wood for heating and building. Such resources were often vital to the survival of the poor.

Some regions were so well placed *vis-à-vis* major trade routes that agricultural specialisation was possible at an early date. The assurance of food supplies was essential; thus coastal Provence, drawing cereals from the Mediterranean, was able to pay for these by the export of oil, wine and manufactured goods, although for most of the eighteenth century the authorities were concerned at the reduction in food cultivation and sought to restrict the development of vineyards. In coastal Brittany peasants grew wheat for export whilst reserving the inferior cereals for their own consumption. In the Orléans region, due to the Loire, the monoculture of the vine was possible even before the coming of the railway. The most important wine producing areas in the eighteenth century, the generalities of Bordeaux, Languedoc and La Rochelle, were significantly maritime.

High quality wines supported transport costs more easily than did ordinary wines, although these costs served to reinforce their luxury character and limit the range of purchasers. Quality here was the decisive influence on price.

Road transport of ordinary wine was almost prohibited by the high transport costs. Water transport was so slow that the wine often deteriorated in transit. There was a pronounced compartmentalisation of markets in this respect: if ordinary wines could not be transported, they at least enjoyed a quasi-monopoly in their own area because of the difficulty of importing potential competitors. The production of wine varied enormously year by year. In the Côte d'Or, for instance, it fluctuated from almost nothing in some years to 100 per cent above average in others, but more usually it varied 50 per cent above or below average.[5] Local market conditions being inelastic a good harvest resulted in an unsaleable surplus and low prices. Wine sales were in addition extremely sensitive to the level of cereal prices and the availability or not of income surplus to that necessary to purchase food.

Vine cultivation in lower Languedoc had increased since the opening of the port of Sète in 1670, and of the Canal du Midi linking Sète to Toulouse in 1681. Road works, particularly after 1760, further accelerated this development, giving access for more producers to the export routes by canal, river and sea. Less accessible areas continued to distil most of the wine they produced into liquor to reduce its volume and increase its portability. In spite of this development wine did not become the major product in an area which remained a region of subsistence polyculture. The vine was cultivated primarily on hillsides unfit for the cultivation of cereals, and remained essentially a means by which income could be supplemented. In the Cèvennes and northern part of the Vivarais where cereal yields were especially low, wine was produced as a means of exchange by which to obtain bread, but the revenue gained and the supplies of cereals were both too unreliable to permit an abandonment of polyculture.

Especially revealing of the structure of the market in wine is the fact that at the end of the eighteenth century of the thirty-two generalities into which France was divided, only three, Caen, Lille and Valenciennes, which are in the extreme north-west and north, were not wine growing. Save for certain maritime areas even this trade was essentially short distance — an element within polycultural systems.

Livestock

The number of animals was never adequate. The space given to cereals limited too severely the area of pasture necessary for a large animal population. In the north at least the climate was humid enough to permit pasture to grow on the fallow land, and the widespread practice of grazing on all the fields after the harvest added to the resources. These sources of collective pasture had however the great drawbacks of preventing the establishment and maintenance of cultivated pastureland and the possibility of maintaining reserves of pasture for the winter. Without such a system selective breeding techniques could not be employed to improve the quality of the herds. It usually required the agreement of a substantial proportion of the community before land could be withdrawn from collective use, enclosed to protect it from animals, and used for cultivation outside the established rotation system.

Brittany was exceptional in the large area of moorland available for grazing, and in the relatively large numbers of animals which provided milk and butter even for the popular diet. By contrast, in the south the dry climate limited most severely the resources of pastureland. This was only partly counterbalanced by the usual existence of wasteland, and more significantly by transhumance to avoid the summer heat in the plains. This provided upland areas with valuable manure but had the obverse effect on the plains. The animals concerned were mainly sheep and goats who adapted more easily to sparse mountain pasture.

The sheep is a hardier animal than the cow, needing less care, less stable time in areas with severe winter conditions, and providing an especially valued manure. Goats and pigs were the animals of the poor, often providing the only meat they ate. The goats devegetated woods and pastures, but efforts by the authorities to limit their numbers usually failed as they were too prized by the poor for their milk, skins and grease as well as their meat.

The major problem with the animals was to maintain fragile equilibrium between their number and the resources of winter fodder.

Fodder was not transportable over long distances and animal mobility too had its limits. As late as 1840 cultivated fodder represented only 6 per cent of the arable land, compared with the 27 per cent in fallow. A given area of the latter could not sustain nearly as many beasts as the same area producing cultivated pasture. Yet in the backward Ardeche even in 1852, natural pastures formed 89.6 per cent of the total. The predominance of cereals still limited the area given to producing fodder, a great deal of which was of poor quality.

Not only was fodder generally in short supply but the amount varied from year to year. A bad year meant that fewer animals could be kept through the winter. Immediately there were large sales of animals and a corresponding fall in prices, and in succeeding better years, while the losses of animals were made up and slaughtering declined, meat would be in short supply and prices high. Manure supplies and soil fertility would also decline.

The animals, undernourished at best, were susceptible to disease. Veterinary science developed slowly, and was more often than not, in any locality, non-existent. It could do little or nothing to arrest the spread of contagious diseases. The mortality rate among vagabond animals on common and waste land was exceptionally high.

For these reasons there was a reluctance to invest in animals — a poor harvest of fodder, or disease, reduced revenue and capital at one stroke, and reconstitution was a slow and expensive process.

Meat was for most of the population a luxury commodity. Its market was restricted by the low purchasing power of most of the population. Demand, particularly from Paris, was sufficient to encourage only a very limited regional specialisation — in Normandy for example. Agricultural areas close to the cities supplied them with cereals and sheep, incapable of travelling long distances, whilst cows were moved on the hoof from further afield. In most regions stock rearing was little more than an aid and supplement to the cultivation of cereals — sheep being above all producers of manure and oxen and cows all-purpose draught animals, as well as providers of meat and milk.

As long as a localised need to grow cereals existed the margin of evolution for agriculture was restricted. Specialisation within limits set by climate and soils was limited primarily to the type of cereal cultivated. Agricultural systems were characterised by uniformity rather than the variations which might have generated a trade based on complementary products.

The traditional agriculture reflected the needs of each individual community, and the possibilities of the area surrounding it. The reasons for the cultivation of particular crops can be understood only in relation to the total agricultural system of an area and to the system of social relationships and habits there. As there was little flexibility in the system innovations at any point in the structure required basic modifications of greater or lesser degree throughout. Immobility at various points in the structure served to restrain overall change.

Land Ownership and Use

The pattern of agriculture does not simply reflect natural conditions and market possibilities but obviously the decisions of those who own the land, and those who work it.

Large properties were especially common in certain regions — in the north-west, in Normandy, Picardy, and the Île de France, and the Loire region, and also in the valley of the Saône, in the Nivernais, and in the south in Languedoc and the Garonne basin. By contrast they were relatively few in the east, in Brittany, the Massif Central, Pyrenees and Alps. Conversely the degree to which peasants shared in the ownership of the land varied. It is estimated that towards the end of the eighteenth century between 22 and 70 per cent of the land according to region was owned by peasants. Everywhere there were large numbers of small property owners but the real value of this small property varied with the fertility of the soil. To live independently off the product of his land alone the peasant needed to dispose of *c*.10 hectares in Flanders. This is indicative of the limited value of bare statistics of ownership without knowledge of the multiple factors which contribute to determining agricultural productivity.

Soboul has estimated that towards the end of the eighteenth century only about 40 per cent of the rural population — say 8 million of 22 million peasants — were entirely without land,[6] but only a small proportion of the others possessed enough land to achieve genuine independence. Generally their plots were too small, or on inferior land. The wealthier non-peasant landowners tended in practice to possess most of the best land in any area — that of the plains, and river valleys, that closest to the urban markets, where profitability and land values were highest, and residence more attractive — rather than the hillsides where agriculture was extremely demanding in terms of the human labour needed to build and maintain terraces, and consequently less profitable. This tendency increased over time with the desire to maximise revenues.

The Revolution of 1789 and its consequences had only limited effect on the structure of property ownership. It effected, through the sales of confiscated lands and voluntary sales, primarily a transfer of property within the upper classes. Basically the existing agrarian structure was consolidated.

In 1826 the situation was as follows:[7]

	Number of properties	% of total	Area possessed (ha.)	%	Average area (ha.)
Small landowners	5,580,000	89.3	14,800,000	32.5	2.65
Medium landowners	6,633,000	10	21,200,000	46.4	23
Large landowners	34,700	0.6	9,455,000	20.8	273

Although much of the land was owned in large units, far less was farmed directly in large units. The owners of such units preferred to rent it to tenant farmers or else introduce sharecroppers. The distinction between these two forms was not always clear in practice. The charges in both cases were likely to include varying proportions of crops, cash, and a variety of payments in kind and labour. Large-scale tenant farming was predominant only in major regions of cereal cultivation like the Picardy Plain, Brie, Beauce and around Versailles. Landlords were prepared to accept long leases — of up to nine years — of large units of land where the tenant's ability to pay his rents could be presumed, and where he possessed sufficient working capital. Money was in common supply only near towns or routes which encouraged commercial agriculture. Elsewhere, although the need to earn money, particularly to pay taxes, made commercialisation of some products a necessity, commerce remained secondary to subsistence as the motive for production.

Away from commercial circuits peasants were unable to pay rents in any other way than by a share in the crop. Thus sharecropping predominated in from two-thirds to three-quarters of France, especially in the centre, west and south-west. Landowners were generally concerned to maximise their income by letting to as many small tenants as possible. In a period of growing population prospective tenants often competed for the privilege. By the mid nineteenth century in the Pyrenees many sharecroppers were giving two-thirds of their crops to the landowners. Those who possessed capital invested it in land rather than land-improvement. Improving landlords were a small minority compared with the *rentiers* who, without any effort on their part, simply drew increasing revenues from the land. The pattern of landuse in practice reflected the limited development of commercial networks.

An agricultural system should be judged in terms of its capacity to feed people adequately. In this respect French agriculture at the mid point of the nineteenth century was still characterised by its fragility. A political revolution had occurred but not an agricultural one. Although the French population was amongst the best fed in the world at the time, agriculture could still not guarantee security or even sufficient nutrition in years of good harvest. More food was being produced than 150 years earlier and *per capita* diet had improved both in quantity and quality, but a final breakaway from the traditional precarious balance of population and food resources had not occurred. At the end of the July Monarchy, to varying degrees according to the place, its agriculture and social structure, the French countryside was over-populated, to a degree which meant that any shortfalling in the products of agriculture was likely to cause a social crisis.

Living standards were in large part determined by the price of cereals as bread was the basis of most diets. Fluctuations in the supply of cereals consequently determined the general food prices. Demand for a basic foodstuff is inelastic. At various times − if the prospect for a harvest looked bad; after a poor harvest; seasonally, before the harvest and in threshing time, when supplies were running out − prices tended to rise. This was a reflection of the general judgements on the balance of supply and demand affected by the age-old obsession of the masses with famine, and by the speculative activity of the minority of producers who possessed a marketable surplus and facilities for stocking.

One important feature of this process in the eighteenth century was that the fluctuations in prices were of lesser amplitude than previously. Famines, in which people actually died of hunger rather than of disease brought on by chronic undernourishment, disappeared. Even so price fluctuations of the order of 50−100 per cent between the e cyclical low and high were common even as late as the Second Empire.

These national estimates of fluctuations deform reality. 1770, for example, shows up as a year of cyclical high, but in this year maximum cyclical price levels were attained in only eleven generalities out of thirty-two. Prices in the others had reached their high points in previous years or would reach them subsequently. This dispersion of maxima reduces the national increase of prices in 1770 compared with the low point in 1763 to 97 per cent, but if a calculation were to be made on the basis of the maximum price achieved in each generality during the cycle, regardless of the year it was attained in, the average would be 128 per cent. Even this figure fails to take account of seasonal fluctuations which served to reinforce the tendency of prices to rise or fall. Thus, taking prices in the generality of Caen, the increase in prices in the period 1764−70 based on annual average prices was 150 per cent but if the cyclical low is compared with cereal prices in *July* 1770, the rise in prices was 290 per cent.[8]

Fluctuations in prices were greatest in the case of the poorer cereals, the food of the poor, rye, maize, buckwheat − particularly as many normal wheat eaters were thrown back on them in times of shortage.

Paradoxically, food shortages were most likely to occur in the areas in which agricultural techniques were most advanced and specialisation most evident, or in those areas close by which normally relied on the purchase of their surpluses. Price fluctuations were therefore greatest in the north and east, and also in the centre – the regions of continental climate, the more densely populated and the most dependent on cereals. Fluctuations were far less severe in the technically backward Mediterranean area, but which could import by sea and possessed more varied food resources. In the west and south-west price levels were between these two extremes – cultivation of maize reduced dependence on single cereal harvests, and communications by water often existed. The increasing cultivation of the potato in all areas, from around the end of the eighteenth century provided a precious alternative to cereals, the importance of which can be judged from the severity of the 1846–7 crisis when both potatoes and most cereals failed.

Crises could be regional or national. Shortages in one area, in increasing prices, did attract grains from better-off areas, whose prices reflected the state of communications, the efficiency of commerce, and supplies. Everywhere crises of subsistence caused by poor harvest were common, pushing up prices to levels at which the poor found difficulty in buying. In the Ariège, for example, in the nineteenth century, significant crises were recorded in 1812, 1817, 1837, 1853 and especially in 1845–6. Yields were generally so low that at best only a fragile equilibrium existed between supply and demand.

Most peasants were forced to sell something to pay tithes, seigneurial dues, and, even after their abolition, taxes and rents. But relatively few had an adequate marketable surplus. Often, after selling grain immediately after the harvest in order to pay pressing creditors, the peasant had to re-enter the market as a purchaser later in the agricultural year when prices had risen.

Secondly, poor communications, and the absence of rapid and cheap transport, served to preserve an infinite number of semi-closed economies, existing in relative isolation from each other, dependent on their own resources, responding to their own internal pressures, capable of only slow development in the absence of external pressures and resources. As communications and commercial organisation improved, the size of these regional markets did increase and relationships between them became more frequent and regular. The enlargement of the zone of provisioning of Toulouse, Montauban and Castelnaudary, and the increased facility of moving grains from Toulouse to lower Languedoc by canal, are cases in point.

The improvements in communications occurring before the onset of rail construction were however insufficient to end market fragmentation and the consequent variation in agricultural prices both between regions and in the same regions between the seasons. Harvest failure in one region, and the difficulties and high cost of importing

57

foodstuffs to it from areas of surplus, continued to encourage speculation in the necessities of life. Fear, and hope for large profits, led to the withdrawal of food from the market in anticipation of further price rises, thus intensifying the already existing problems of shortage.

The effect of high transport costs on market structures can be seen most clearly from regional disparities in cereal prices. Thus in 1801 the average price in the department with highest prices was 260 per cent above that of the department with lowest prices, although the two were only 700 kilometres apart.[9] In the summer of 1834, when low water on the Saône forced recourse to land transport, cereals costing 11–13 francs in Lorraine cost 16–17 francs at Lyon and 21–22 francs at Nîmes.[10] Eastern France normally produced a surplus of wheat and had the lowest prices in France because it was so difficult to export to areas with higher price levels. High prices in one area would stimulate imports into it and so increase the volume of trade but within limits determined by the purchasing power of a population whose incomes had generally declined at the time the price rise was occurring.

The problem of food supply was even more one of distribution, than of production. The practice of self-subsistence left relatively little food to be redistributed by commerce. In eighteenth-centuryy Auvergne, it has been estimated, that almost all the produce of the peasant holdings, and even half that of large farms, was consumed by the landowners, their families and domestics. The proportion of produce entering trade depended fundamentally on the facilities for communication, since they determined the potential profitability of commercialisation, as well as on the size of the surplus available once those who shared the produce of each farm unit had satisfied their needs.

Those who sold were the producers of a surplus – essentially large landowners, farming land themselves or receiving rents in kind, large-scale farmers, and, before the Revolution, those in receipt of seigneurial dues and tithes. An army of intermediaries engaged in the grain trade, varying from better-off peasants and small brokers *(blâtiers),* who purchased small quantities from proprietors to sell on local and regional markets to consumers, to the less numerous wholesale merchants. It was the latter who engaged in longer distance trade. In the Toulouse area a species of commission agents operated on behalf of the major merchants of lower Languedoc, the millers of Moissac and the exporters of Bordeaux. Here at least the major commercial circuits were controlled by large capitalists operating from such centres as Marseille, Montpellier and Bordeaux. Speculation, for example in the markets of Iberia required large capital and access to information.

In autumn a mass of brokers went from farm to farm buying cereals to sell to the commission merchants at an intermediary centre like

Toulouse, which would in turn deal with the major centres. Large landowners would sell directly to these commission agents, in bulk and at seasonal high prices because they, unlike the small farmer, possessed the storage facilities which allowed them to await higher prices. The consumers who bought were those who did not produce their own food or who produced insufficient to satisfy their needs.

Local market demand was inevitably inelastic. In a time of deficit people would make do with less and transfer their demand to inferior foodstuffs — cereals normally fed to livestock, chestnuts, fruit and vegetables — but as most of them normally lived around subsistence level there was little room for manoeuvre. Conversely, when a surplus was produced, although diet improved, there were limits to the extra food which could be consumed locally, so that if adequate alternative markets were not accessible, in contrast to conditions of shortage and substantial price increase, the presence of surplus often led to large reductions in prices. Market conditions varied between these extremes.

Rather than actual famine, a major cause of price increases was the fear of famine enshrined in the folk-memory. This collective reaction encouraged speculation. In a state of relative over-population which regions found themselves in until the latter half of the nineteenth century, the least crises in the supply of food had extensive repercussions. If normally a large part of the population entered the market to purchase food, and a poor harvest further reduced the number of those who were self-sufficient, the result was a larger population trying to buy food, at the very moment when supplies were reduced. Real income suffered a massive reduction and so in consequence did purchasing power, as a higher than ever proportion of income was devoted to the purchase of food and less to that of manufactured goods. The result was a generalised crisis of the economy.

Besides cereals and wine the major products entering trade were flax, hemp, olives, vegetables, poultry, cattle and dairy products. Most of this trade took place over relatively short distances but involved large numbers of people using carts, pack-animals and their own carrying capacity to take goods to local markets. The existence of some relatively large towns generated inter-regional trade. However, market potential for the producer prior to the development of railways was extremely limited, which hardly encouraged innovations. Transport costs ate up the merchants' profits — thus the intendant of Auvergne in 1750 could not encourage adequate imports into his province and had to employ forced *corvée* labour to transport foodstuffs.

The transport of cereals to the mills and to market and the movement of flour to major urban centres at all times constituted a considerable part of the volume of traffic, but divided into an infinite number of small cart-loads, and impossible to quantify. In the Vaucluse in 1815, for example, there were some 276 mills mainly along the river, but with a few windmills milling mainly grain brought to them by local peasants.

In years of high prices and shortage, merchants were encouraged to extend their normal range of operations. As the relationship between selling price and transport costs was altered, they were attracted to more distant markets. Food shortages were generally regional in character, and this together with the compartmentalised market structure made large variations in prices inevitable. The density of traffic between regions of surplus and those of deficit became substantially greater than was usual. There was an undoubted relationship between grain prices and density of traffic on the roads — increased prices taking perhaps a month to induce activity on the part of merchants and transporters. The distances covered by inter-regional trade were increased from the early eighteenth century by improvements in roads and waterways. It has been suggested that population growth in Languedoc was due more to the Canal du Midi and the more effective distribution of foodstuffs this made possible than by an increase in agricultural productivity.[11]

Improved transport before the rail era did not however change the basic structure of the market. The increase in the reliability of food supply was not enough to end the age-old fear of famine. When food shortage occurred in a particular region, the natural reaction of consumers in localities outside it was to obstruct the movement of cereals from their area to those in which higher prices were being offered, so as to prevent a shortage or increased prices affecting their own market. The demand/supply mechanism so dear to liberal theorists was not allowed to operate freely. Not only the revolution in transport conditions but the accompanying revolution in human mentalities was necessary first.

In the meantime commerce was obstructed by riots and the danger of riots, wherever the poor felt threatened. This was particularly true along the major supply routes to the cities, where traffic was densest. In the case of Paris when its normal regions of supply failed and the zone of supply was enlarged, disturbances were likely over wide areas. Grain in bulk especially was moved by water, so that the main areas of unrest were likely to be the river valleys, and especially those of the Upper and Lower Seine, Oise, Aisne, Yonne, Ourcq, the two Morins Loire, Rhône, Garonne and Canal du Midi. Coastal areas of southern France were relatively fortunate in having access to the sea-borne cereals of the Mediterranean.[12]

For governments concerned especially to avoid public disorders in the towns, a major police operation was required to keep supply routes open. Paris, which in the 1830s required 150–200,000 tons of food a year, was cause for special concern. Administrative measures to some extent had contradictory effects. Prior access to markets was generally reserved to local consumers, and the local administrations, by establishing ceiling prices, acted in restraint of trade in order to prevent starvation and disorder. The freedoms of trade legislated for were difficult to implement. Merchants were forced to scour the countryside to gather grain in bulk, usually offering higher prices than those prevailing on the local market and in so doing reducing supplies to it.

The development of commerce in agriculture depended largely on the growth of urban centres, sale of foodstuffs to which would provide the income necessary to stimulate the demand of the rural population for the products of industry. Dependence on more or less local supplies restrained urban development, necessitated the survival of subsistence agriculture and maintained rural purchasing power at a low level. Until the middle of the nineteenth century this situation prevailed and variations in the price of cereals continued to dominate the economic cycle.

French agriculture, in spite of significant changes which we will now consider, in 1850 in most regions was still primarily producing for self-subsistence, using methods and achieving results which were only very slow to change. If progress did occur, it was insufficient to enable the economy and society to break loose from age-old restraints. Human activity, human psychology and relationships between men were still fundamentally determined by the search for food.

Part II: Development within the Structure of the Ancien Régime

Although fundamental structures remained unchanged, a process of development can be observed during the century preceeding the construction of a railway network. In its beginnings, this was no more than the upturn of the economic cycle. Its uniqueness rests on the fact that it was to be sustained. Sufficient increase in agricultural productivity and improvements in communications, providing the capacity for more efficient distribution, allowed the feeding of a growing population. The slow development of commercial agriculture and increased circulation of money led to increased demand for manufactured goods.

The significance of the railway network was that it permitted progress from this *Ancien Régime* form of slow organic growth, to a more dynamic level of economic activity, occuring within and because of the establishment of new market structures.

This period of change began at some time btween 1720 and 1756 in most regions. Estimates of the scale of increase in agricultural production vary. The statistics available are of limited accuracy given the poverty of sources, and do no more than estimate general tendencies. For the period 1700–09 to 1780–9 estimates of growth varying between 25 per cent[13] and 60 per cent have recently been offered.[14] The choice of a period of crisis as a base rather than that of upturn in the cycle naturally means that even these figures are likely to be exaggerated, especially the higher of the two. Estimates of growth and of rates of growth offering an apparent statistical certainty should be discounted. National averages compiled using a mass of local estimates of unverifiable accuracy are of limited relevance in reference to an economic structure characterised by its compartmentalisation.

To write the history of French rural society in the pre-statistical era is to make conjectures on the basis of a variety of documentary and physical information — ranging from the accounts kept by the wealthy to the terraces constructed by the poor in a desperate effort to bring more land into cultivation. It is to note, using parish records of births and deaths, that the population in most areas was increasing in the absence of the killing famines of the previous century, and to conclude that if the population tended to increase then the supply of food must at last have been more regular and probably increased, given that it was hardly possible for individual diets to be reduced further in quantity or quality.

Population pressure can be seen throughout human history as a stimulant to agriculture improvement. The obvious response to increasing population is to cultivate more land, particularly in a situation where the capital resources necessary for technical innovation are in short supply and labour is plentiful. In Bourgogne, for example, between an edict of 1766 offering tax concessions to encourage clearance of waste land and 1778, an estimated 8–10 per cent increase in the land under cultivation occurred.[15] Such activity was widespread. It is impossible to tell whether it was evidence of the dynamism of a more market-orientated agriculture or simply the age-old response of societies which needed to produce more food to survive. It is doubtful whether simple clearance of land, which often had not been cultivated before because it was inferior in quality, or exposition to already cultivated land did anything to increase yields. The productivity of labour as opposed to total production might in many cases be reduced by this recourse to marginal land.

With the technical resources of the epoch there were limits to the amount of land which could be cleared. In more densely populated areas in the north and east there must have been little land available which was still worth clearing, and a necessary minimum had to be retained as pasture for draught animals. In many areas the only possible response to population pressure was thus technical innovation. Even if it is accepted that the ardour of the few genuine, scientifically minded innovators, and of the agronomists, masked the immobility of the mass cultivators, it would be an error to assume that these latter responded to the challenge of increasing numbers of mouths to feed with apathy. Change through slow evolution is inherent in traditional agricultural structures, but the limits to such a method of change need to be stressed. The peasant, insecure, dependent for food on a small plot of land, had no margin for error. He would consequently, as long as he remained dependent on his own harvest and local food resources accept only such innovations as did not threaten the stability of his polyculture, and which could, without risk, be integrated into it. Agricultural progress, particularly in the south where large-scale farming was less common, occurred mainly through a series of small efforts to ease the problem of subsistence. Security, the main dream of the peasant, seemed to be offered by increasing the area of land farmed or owned rather than investment in more intensive farming. The process of parcellation, which lasted until towards the end of the nineteenth century in some regions, exemplified this intense land hunger.

As population grew, the existence of bare fallow became increasingly objectionable, particularly to the poor. At first, in years in which food was in short supply, and then more permanently, fallow was suppressed in areas in which food resources were under pressure. In the Vaucluse the process was complete by the middle of the nineteenth century. The introduction of maize in the south-west in the eighteenth century reduced the period of fallow to six months and did not upset the existing equilibrium. It provided an extra crop valuable for both humans and animals and had the added virtue of liberating part of the wheat harvest for sale on the market. Its use spread into the Rhône valley, the plains of the Saône, Alsace and even the Loire valley and Paris basin. Maize was important too in improving techniques, since its particular requirements created a general habit of frequent weeding.

This process by which cereal yields were increased resulted, according to one estimate, in parts of Lower Languedoc in an increase in wheat yields from c.10 hectolitres per hectare in 1720 to 14.3 by the end of the period 1725–1825. Significant also was the replacement of the inferior cereals by wheat in many areas. In the areas which would constitute the department of the Ariège wheat formed an estimated 23.2 per cent of the autumnal sowing in 1731, and 46.4 in 1841.

The introduction of the potato evoked a similar process of development. In Alsace this occurred much earlier than in other regions of France, from 1740–70. It was the most over-populated areas of northern and lower Alsace which accepted the potato first, before southern Alsace where population pressure was less intense due to emigration. The rotation of corn and fallow was replaced by that of potato and corn which made a large increase in the food supply, again for both humans and animals – and particularly for pigs, the typical animals of the poor.

The prejudice against the potato was slow to decline. Early varieties had an unpleasant taste and it was long believed that rotation with cereals would compromise the latter, although potatoes had high yields and tended to be more stable in their results. In the Ardèche, for example, two potato crops were possible, one in July-August and the other in November. The temptation to introduce them following failures in the cereals harvests must have been overwhelming and decisive in overcoming resistance, and this seemed to have been the pattern of adoption by the poor. The process was slow in the eighteenth century – the area under potatoes would double in the period 1817–46.[16]

In this manner maize and the potato were introduced into existing agriculture systems and became factors in their further evolution. The nature of this gradual process was such as to provide an increasing guarantee against famine caused by failure of the predominant crop.

Innovation in agriculture has usually been described in terms of the introduction of forage crops to replace fallow, providing more food for animals whilst enriching the soil by the fixation of atmospheric nitrogen. Their use allowed an increase in the number of animals and in the supply of manure, the application of which to the land increased cereal yields. Thus an upward cycle came into existence – more animals, more manure, better soils, larger harvests.

This particular innovation was essentially the work of the more wealthy, and was especially prevalent in the north. Peasants with small areas to cultivate were rarely willing or able to risk their food supply by consecrating part of this land to animal fodder. The whole notion of seeding fields to feed animals offended the basic instincts of men in a subsistence economy. As a result progress was slow. Fallow remained widespread although the means for its suppression were commonly known. To indicate the slowness with which technical innovations were accepted in agriculture it is worth observing that the Agricultural Society of the department of the Vienne, i.e. its bigger landowners, as late as 1861, was still discussing the value of artificial grasses, and that in the Aix area the contracts for leasing imposed a two-year rotation with fallow until the 1920s.

Even in the Paris region, other than in immediate proximity to Paris, change was very far from complete, and the generalisation of fodder crops did not occur before the first half of the nineteenth century, mainly due to the survival of the traditional right of pasture on the fallow. It was only in this period that regional disparities began to become clearly marked, between the Paris region, and other areas in the north and the rest of France — replacing a former equality in mediocrity. The introduction of sugar beet and colza completely upset the traditional three-year rotation. Elsewhere, however, away from accessible urban markets, fodder crops were accepted only to the extent to which they could be integrated within existing systems. In the south-west, made relatively prosperous in the eighteenth century by the introduction of maize there was now neither room nor time in the agricultural calendar for fodder crops. Technical stagnation ensued and relative prosperity turned to backwardness in relation to other regions which did not stand still. More generally, parceleation of the ownership and use of land, and the persistence of customs and rights of usage which protected the poor in the traditional community and provided pasture for all, proved strong obstacles to change.

One conclusion which seems possible at this point is that agricultural societies seem to have developed well into the nineteenth century on the basis of an internal logic: the search for and desire to preserve an equilibrium based on the maximum production of food. Production was organised in response to various pressures: relief, climate, population, urban influences; by men responding to these pressures agriculture changed, but within the narrow limits imposed upon them by the needs of subsistence. Demographic pressure inhibited the taking of risks. Stimuli to innovation acting upon the rural community were essentially endogenous to its structure, and limited in effect.

Changes in the mix of crops and the intensification of land use both served to substantially increase production and per capita output. This was frequently offset in part by the declining fertility of land in areas where pasture and animal manure was lacking — usually regions of small-scale culture like parts of Brittany, of the Massif Central, Alps, Pyrenees and Jura. One can presume that productivity increased, because starvation disappeared, but the growth of temporary migration from these mountainous areas of small cultivation is indicative of the problems of survival the mass of poor peasants faced.

So much more is known about prices than actual production that much of the economic history of all ages is about price movements. It has been estimated that in the period 1726—41 to 1777—89 corn prices rose by 56—60 per cent,[17] due to the influx of Brazilian silver and Mexican gold, and to increased demand. This long period of rising prices ended only in 1817 although intermediary periods of declining prices like that from 1778 in reducing agricultural revenues was to have severe social consequences. What is of interest here is the likely effect on agricultural production of rising prices. These could be seen as stimulating the enterprise of farmers producing for sale in the market, and encouraging more widespread participation in production for the market. Monetary inflation, by causing a general increase in prices other than agricultural, combined with a developing taste for luxury to attract nobles and bourgeois landowners to the idea of increasing revenue by more efficient farming and administration of their estates. Those so stimulated would obviously be men with surplus to sell above the needs of personal and family consumption. The majority of small peasant proprietors were all but excluded from the benefits of rising prices by the demands of seeding, low yields, fallow, the large demands of the manual labourers for bread, tithes, seigneurial dues, rents — all contributed to eliminating him from the market. The small man was in general faced with the need to purchase foodstuffs at increasing prices. In human terms, therefore, if agricultural production was encouraged, price movements were one more factor preserving the misery of the masses.

Meat prices tended to rise somewhat more rapidly than those of cereals, encouraging the development of pastoral farming in regions accessible to urban markets, but again only large-scale farmers had commercial herds. The price of wine, a pre-eminently commercial product rose less rapidly — by an estimated 13—16 per cent between 1726—41 and 1777—89.[18] Demand for wine was limited by its luxury character. For both consumer and most producers it was of secondary importance, save in limited areas of specialisation. It was produced and purchased only after adequate food supplies were assured. Demand for it declined when cereal prices rose and reduced the disposable portion of income. Adaptation by the vine grower to changing market conditions was particularly slow. To pull up vines involved sacrifice of both capital and revenue, and often the land used was good for nothing else. The planting of new vines involved a wait of several years before the first fruits appeared. Extension of the vine should consequently be linked less to rising prices than the development of communications. In Languedoc, for example, the opening of the Canal du Midi in 1681 linking Toulouse to the new port of Sète stimulated production by promoting access to new markets. The extension of the vine is then especially a phenomena of the second half of the nineteenth century, dependent not only on the opening of new markets but on the security of food imports into areas in which specialisation was favoured.

The long increase in prices ended in 1817 and was followed by a tendency to decline which lasted until 1851. This seems to have caused only a slowing in the rates of growth, rather than an absolute decline, and in many cases is likely to have stimulated innovation in an effort to maintain revenues.

The fragility of French agriculture remains evident throughout the eighteenth century and the first fifty years of the nineteenth in the extreme fluctuations of food prices due to low productivity and the at best slim margin between supply and demand. The gains made in productivity were limited and did not offer security or even an adequate diet to the population. Food production remained susceptible above all to climatic factors.

The period 1727–65 was dominated by warm summers and cold winters – by a continental rather than maritime-type climate. This was favourable to cereals production. Good years predominated over bad. This factor more than human action resulted in increased production. Moreover the more frequent availability of marketable surplus over quite a long period encouraged commercial habits and stimulated the more efficient organisation of commerce. This would reduce the severity of the consequences of poor harvests in the period from 1766 when wet or excessively dry summers were frequent and a new period of difficulties began.

It has generally been assumed that there was a tendency for food production to slowly increase from the early eighteenth century. A recent study of Anjou, however, explains the decline of famine, at least in that region, not in terms of the development of agriculture, which stagnated, nor primarily in terms of favourable climatic conditions, but rather by increased and more efficient action by the administration at all levels to distribute grains and limit the effects of poor harvests.

The concern of Government with the adverse effects of poor harvests in terms of human suffering and social unrest was undoubted. The desire to encourage increased production was not always compatible with that of protecting the poor. Thus, under the influence of liberal thinkers, restrictions on the initiative of commercial farmers were reduced. Enclosure was authorised in Haute Normandie and Béarn in 1767; in Lorraine, the Trois Evêches, the Franche Comté in 1760; in Roussillon in 1769; and Languedoc in 1770. Similarly the division of common lands, clearance of wastelands, and drainage of marshes were encouraged. This policy, both as outlined by the central Government and as implemented in the provinces, remained hesitant. For example, general legislation on the right to enclose was not introduced before 1789, and in the Auvergne, successive intendents defended commons as necessary for the subsistence of the poor. The requirement that a majority of inhabitants agree to the division of commons ensured that where, as so often, there was a division of opinion, progress was slow.

The Revolution of 1789 was a victory for the economic liberals. On 5 June 1792 freedom for landowners to use their land as they wished was proclaimed. However, the decree of 25 September 1791 gave recognition to collective practices enshrined in custom. The legislation of the Revolutionary period did no more than accelerate, and this to a limited degree, the tendencies already evident in an evolution begun early in the eighteenth century. Like earlier legislation it represented and contributed to the growth of a climate of opinion, at least amongst wealthier landowners, in favour of change.

The most obvious gain of the poor was the abolition of feudal dues and the tithe, although the latter in particular was often re-incorporated into rents. It is impossible to judge the extent to which this led to an increase in the marketable surplus available to small cultivators, or whether it was simply consumed by them.

Most significantly the Revolution did not alter farm structures. A certain redistribution of property occurred — from the Church and nobles to the middle-class and peasants — but farm sizes, technology and market structures remained unaltered. The position of the small man most reluctant to innovate was strengthened. Parcellation of the land was intensified by the new civil code. Legislation ending collective restraints on enclosure was still commonly resisted as an assault on popular interests and age-old rights.

The Revolution did little to stimulate agriculture. Civil strife and war obviously had deleterious effects. Legislation was often irrelevant. There existed a gulf between official conceptions, between liberal economic theories, and the realities of rural life. Attitudes in the villages remained dominated by the state of spirit of the *Ancien Régime* born of the psychosis of fear of famine. The principles of economic liberalism affirmed in 1789 could have only limited effects whilst transport costs remained so high as to exert an effective restraint on the development of trade. It was market structures which determined the character and ability of agriculture and rural structures to change. It was the slowness of market structures to change, the absence of a dynamic, stimulating element which restricted men's horizons and their ability to wish for something different. If from the eighteenth century numerous books on agronomy were published, these were not read by peasants or even by more than a minority of the socially dominant group which linked the village to the outside world. Even in the middle of the nineteenth century the departmental agricultural societies generally included only a minority even of large proprietors. In general the economic and social context remained unpropitious for innovation.

Investment in technical improvement was only likely where markets and profits were assured, above all near urban centres, few of which were large. Urban growth was restrained by, amongst other factors, the difficulty of ensuring food supplies. Poor transport facilities inevitably restrained demand by localising it. Diet was determined essentially by what could be obtained locally and conservative eating habits served further to restrain innovators. The town was, nevertheless, of great importance as a dynamic influence on the countryside. The growing prosperity overseas commerce brought to many Breton towns for example led to the replacement of buckwheat and millet in the diet of the urban poor by the more nutritious rye. In the larger towns, in Rennes and Nantes, by the end of the eighteenth century this was being replaced by wheat. These changes in demand affected agricultural crop patterns. Another effect of urban demand was the continued development of market-gardening — most obviously around Paris, but also around places like Avignon and Carpentras. From these central places the development of the techniques of intensive cultivation, of irrigation, manuring and new rotations, slowly spread. Potentially profitable agriculture close to urban centres attracted investors living in them who provided much of the capital for innovation. These men were particularly susceptible to rising prices.

The geographical limits to such urban influence should be emphasised. Undoubtedly substantial improvements were made to transport facilities before the construction of railways, but most of the development even of roads occurred during the railway era. Commercial activity increased as the eighteenth century progressed. The volume of traffic on roads and waterways grew with growing security of movement, increasing urban demand and better transport facilities. Substantial increases in expenditure on road works evinced the growing awareness of the importance of communications. Progress was not constant. The period of the Empire was one of declining usability for all save strategic routes, but the law on local roads of 1836 brought to its culminating point a period of development substantial compared with earlier periods.

It has been calculated that the average transport costs of wine from Bourgogne from the 1750s represented from one-fifth to one-sixth of the price of the merchandise, whilst it would have tripled or quadrupled in the seventeenth century. This fact was decisive in stimulating trade and investment in the land. The construction of the Canal du Midi linking upper with lower Languedoc was a major factor in the avoidance of famine in this region in the eighteenth century, permitting export of cereals from an area of surplus to one of habitual deficit. In the Calvados the development of cattle raising in the first half of the nineteenth century can be linked to the development of a network of more effective local roads. Due to physical improvements in the system of communication transport costs rose less rapidly than the general cost of living. Even so it is necessary to re-affirm the negative aspects of the transport situation. The physical obstacles, the slowness of movement, the high costs, the variation in these costs with seasons and supply and demand were great uncertainties in the profit calculations of merchants.

The economy and society of the *Ancien Régime* were above all characterised by the dispersal of communities close to their food supplies, the limited contacts between them, the narrow horizons open to men, the limited effectiveness of pressures and stimuli to change. Strong forces encouraged conservatism and caution.

Crop patterns changed only slowly because of the organic interrelatedness of their constituent elements, and also because the existing pattern seemed to represent the wisdom of past generations. They had been developed by an empirical process and could be modified only when alternative elements were seen by the peasant to constitute an improvement. The break with the past took time, involving as it did a break with tradition and the rejection of psychological and moral pressures to avoid change and risk.

A strong feature of peasant mentality was the desire for security as it was understood in a particular epoch. Further, their apparent inability to combat the adverse forces of nature, particularly climate and epidemic, created feelings of fatalism and passivity. For an under-nourished population lacking energy and initiative the basic aim must be survival and this would result in the absence of long-term perspectives, and acceptance of conditions that kept them alive, however bad they might be.

Due to the fear of famine created by low productivity and enforced regional autarky peasant resistance to change was inevitable. The need for innovation was a characteristic of other social groups, and was even then limited. An innovator who wished to opt out of the rotation systems and common pasture would probably meet resistance from his neighbours, who lacked capital resources and who were unaware of the possibilities offered by investment, resistance based on a fear of the consequences of a reduction in the area under cereals. The peasants struggled to preserve collective rights and instinctively rejected the theory that a proprietor had absolute rights in his property. There was an intense consciousness of the common interests and customary rights of the community.

Only a small minority of the wealthier peasants, the large-scale farmers and proprietors had the economic and intellectual power necessary for innovation. A variety of factors reduced the potential innovating rôle of the wealthier landowners. In a period of population pressure revenue could be increased simply by subdividing their estates and renting to the maximum number of small tenants. The effort, the capital investment, and the risks involved in innovations were unnecessary. The custom of short leases was a factor which did not encourage the tenant to make improvements. To protect the land against exhaustion in this situation, where tenants might be encouraged to take as much as possible out of the land before their leases ran out, tenancies were hedged around with all sorts of restrictions. The habitual clause found in contracts was the stipulation 'cultivater suivant les usages du pays'.

Through leases which in effect reinforced the practices of the past large landowners often acted as a strong conservative force in respect of agricultural techniques, especially in the regions where sharecropping predominated and where surveillance by the landlord or his agent was particularly close.

Population pressure also exerted a conservative influence by providing a large labour force which competed for employment andl enabled employers to keep wages at low levels. The existence of cheap labour, and also the social pressures demanding its employment, encouraged the survival of a labour intensive rather than capital intensive system. Even the replacement of the sickle by the more efficient scythe for harvesting was rarely possible. It is significant that the rapid acceleration in the improvement of hand tools, and the simultaneous introduction of harvesting machinery, occurred only when employers found that because of emigration from the countryside labour supply was declining and labour costs increasing.

This situation developed only from the 1850s, and prior to it investment in agriculture by all social groups tended to be in land rather than techniques. Much of the capital available was attracted to other forms of investment such as commerce, the purchase of office, state loans — or in luxury spending. Even in areas of large-scale farming there seems generally to have been a lack of capital for agriculture. The Revolution probably reduced investment in new techniques when, by abolishing tithes and feudal dues, legislation reduced the concentration of income and the potential for dynamic action by the wealthy. This had the effect of speeding up the process of small-scale innovation by a multitude of peasant farmers whilst slowing the process of large-scale structural adaptation.

The most significant sign of a structural change in the economy was the moderation of the crises of agricultural underproduction. Converse the most significant sign of the slowness of change was the survival of these crises, and the fact that although in the bad years the population suffered less, in general their living standards were, if not declining, not appreciably improving in the years before the middle of the nineteenth century.

Part III: Structural Transformation

From the middle of the nineteenth century a combination of factors served to effect the most significant structural changes in the history of French agriculture. These factors were the improvements in communications, a more rapid rate of urbanisation and increasing, but also a changing, demand for the products of agriculture.

During the Restoration and particularly after the law of 1836 on local roads substantial efforts were made to improve both national and regional links, but this was not enough to permit a transformation of the pre-industrial character of most of the French economy. Markets remained too restricted. It has been estimated that in the eighteenth century food could not normally be transported more than 15 km. from its place of origin because of high transport costs. By 1830 the range of movement had been substantially increased to 50 km., but this was far less than the estimated range of 250 km. achieved by 1855 when the rail network remained incomplete.[19] Despite improvement in the road surfaces, as long as road transport remained dependent upon animal-power rapid and massive transport of goods in a regional or extra-regional context was impossible.

At least in theory the difference in price for the same product in two markets should not exceed the cost of transport between them. With the development of the railways transport costs were substantially reduced and price differences between market places with them. For the first time the economic mechanism favoured by liberal economists could function. Inter-regional competition, and rapidly even international competition became possible and the previous often massive price variations between markets were evened out. Compartmentalisation was at an end.

This transformation can be clearly seen in the case of cereal prices. In 1800 when wheat was 11 fr. per hectolitre in the Marne, it was 46 fr. in the Alpes-Maritime; in 1817 the maximum differences were between 36 fr. in the Côtes-du-Nord and 81 fr. in Haut-Rhin. In 1847, after significant improvements of the waterways and roads the maximum gulf was still 20 fr. between the 29 fr. of Aude and Ariège and the 49 fr. of Bas-Rhin. From 1860 however this never reached 4 fr. and remained generally between 2 and 3 fr.

The official rail tariff for the transport of cereals was 0.14 fr. per ton, per kilometre in the 1850s, with a proviso for reduction to half this figure when cereal prices went above 20 fr. on the regulating market at Gray. In practice special rates reduced costs to between 0.025 fr. and 0.06 fr. per ton even in normal times.

It was noted that with these transport costs the mere rise of 1 franc on a particular market was now enough to stimulate merchants within a radius 2–300 km., who were rapidly informed by press and telegraph, to enter this market, whereas formerly a 20 fr. gap might not have been enough, given slow transmission of information, slow and difficult transport, high costs, and insecurity on the roads. Or, to take a more specific example, in 1847 when a hectolitre of wheat cost 27 fr. at

Marseille, it would have cost 14.75 fr. to transport it to Vesoul (Haute-Saône) by road and water. For this operation to be profitable wheat at Vesoul must be sold for at least 42 fr. In 1868 however, when the cost of transport by rail was 2.95 fr. per hectolitre, the price at Vesoul needed to be only 30 fr. for the merchant to make a profit.[20]

It was significant that the riots against high prices and the transport of cereals, a cause of popular protest since time immemorial, disappeared in the 1850s at the same time as the seasonal and annual fluctuations in food prices were substantially evened out. The fear of dearth, such an important determinant of popular action came to an end, when for the first time in human history supply and demand could be rapidly balanced. Consumers were no longer dependent on local meteorological conditions.

During the Second Empire the network created was designed to satisfy national rather than local needs. Lines were constructed primarily in areas in which traffic was intense, and only with the inception of the Freycinet Plan from the late 1870s did the railway penetrate the more isolated areas of the Alps, Massif Central and west.

Accompanying this development of a rail network was a notable effort to improve local roads. The railway substituted itself for the road only where it served the same link, and on roads giving access to railways traffic grew more intense. Road improvements were particularly important in the poorer regions with less dense rail networks.

The changing character of cyclical crises was indicative of the changing economic structure of France. The amplitude of variations in the price of foodstuffs rapidly declined and with this the consequences of harvest failure on purchasing power and commercial and industrial activity. With the creation of national and even international markets increasingly responsive to demand the *Ancien Régime économique* came to an end.

As early as 1847 the Paris-Orléans line proved the value of bulk, rapid and cheap transport of cereals. In places having access to it demand was balanced by supply from early in May that year. Other areas were not as fortunate and experienced the full effects of the poor cereal harvest of 1846. Imports from abroad did increase to previously unheard-of levels. Prior to 1845 imports of grain and flour had never exceeded 3 million hectolitres. The poor harvest of 1846 led to imports of 5 million and the figure rose to 10 million in 1847.[21] The growing volume of imports from America and Russia undoubtedly restrained speculation and price increases. These new sources of supply were now added to the previous main suppliers, the Sardinian states, Turkey and Germany.

Throughout these years, however, the existence of a sliding scale of tariffs inhibited the activity of merchants, who were afraid that a decline in prices on the home market would expose cereals already purchased abroad to higher tariffs than expected on arrival in French ports.

If the activity of the Paris-Orléans in 1847 had been a sign of things to come, the activity of the railway companies was far more evident following the harvest failures of 1853 and 1855. The deficits in these years were as serious as that of 1847, but the effect on prices and on general levels of economic activity were nowhere near as serious. Already it was clear that the basic structure of the economy and its mechanisms were being fundamentally transformed.

In 1855 home production of cereals for human consumption was around 72 million hectolitres. Imports of some 10 million hectolitres were required to cover the deficit, but due to the still incomplete rail network and the restraint imposed by the tariff system this provisioning took about eight months to complete. Prices on the regulating market at Gray rose to 31.10 fr.

In 1861 it was necessary to import 13½ million hectolitres but the transport network had improved to such an extent that provisioning was completed before the end of the year and the prices never attained 30 fr. The suppression of the sliding scale in 1860 and its subsequent removal facilitated mercantile activity. By 1879, following a series of bad harvests (1875–9), 29,800,000 hectolitres could be imported without difficulty. By then the continued pressure of imports on domestic prices was stimulating demands from agricultural interests for a return to tariff protection, which was accorded in 1885.[22]

The extension of the area of supply by cheap and rapid transport ended dearth, by permitting movement from areas of surplus to those of deficit at home, and by means of import from abroad. Previously the main beneficiaries from such movements had been areas on navigable waters, but now the benefit was generalised. In 1867, for example, following an abundant cereals harvest in Hungary, it was possible to profitably market part of the surplus in France. The consequences of localised shortage and also of localised glut were minimised and price fluctuations were evened out. By 1861 an estimated two-thirds of the total consumption of cereals was being transported by the six main railway companies.[23]

During this same period of transport revolution, agricultural productivity was being substantially increased. Due to the growing application of fertilisers, and increase in the supply of manure, cereals yields improved by about 50 per cent nationally between 1850 and 1880.[24] The acceleration of the rate of replacement of bare fallow also occurred and can be seen in the following figures:

Declining extent of bare fallow
1840   6,763,281 hectares
1852   5,705,217
1862   5,147,762

This decline contributed to an increase in production, even though marginal land was increasingly abandoned, and land formerly under cereals was converted to other uses. Improvement of soils also permitted a more rapid continuation of the movement from inferior to superior cereals. Thus wheat production increased in the following manner:

1840   5,586,786 hectares
1852   6,984,712
1862   7,456,000
1873   6,966,419 (Loss of Alsace-Lorraine)
1882   7,191,144

Whilst lacking in absolute accuracy the statistics provide a fair reflection of tendencies.

The cyclical crisis was transformed from that of the *Ancien Régime* dominated by agriculture to a more modern type over which financial and industrial influences predominated. The consequences were not simply economic, but with the termination of the fear of famine a fundamental change was induced in the psychology of the poor.

Although of less general significance than the consequences for cereal market structures, improved communications transformed those for other agricultural products.

Prior to the establishment of a rail network, the markets, for ordinary wines, at least were limited. Dependence on local markets led traditionally to cycles of the type good crop, low price; poor crop, high price, i.e. varying supply meeting with inelastic demand. The latter too tended to vary inversely with the price of more essential foodstuffs.

In Bourgogne the cycle 1846—54 was the last of this classical type Increasingly from 1858—9, abundant crops did not lead to the collapse of prices; indeed in 1861, 1865, 1870 prices rose. Price levels were now determined by national and not local market conditions, and during the 1860s demand was stabilised at a high level. With the enlargement of the market, the reduction of fluctuations in foodstuff prices, gradually improving living standards, demand became more regular. Wine lost its character as a semi-luxury as growing quantities of cheap wine were marketed. Consumption at Paris rose from 860,000 hectolitres in 1840, to 3,901,000 in 1872, whilst national annual consumption per head increased from 51 litres in 1840 to 60 in 1859,

68 in 1865, 75 in 1866 and 77 in 1872.

In response to this the area under wines increased:[25]

1850	1,972,340 hectares
1852	2,190,909
1862	2,320,809
1875	2,582,716

In the whole of Languedoc in 1800 there had been only 65,000 hectares under vines, but in the Hérault alone in 1869 there were 226,000.

In the case of Bourgogne the opening of the Paris-Dijon line in 1851 had given access to new markets and ended the regional isolation characteristic of an *Ancien Régime* situation. Similar consequences had been experienced along the Loire with the opening of the Paris-Orléan-Tours line in 1843–6 and would be experienced in the Bordelais with the completion of the Tours-Bordeaux line in 1853, and in the Midi from 1858.

In the case of fine wines, distinguished by their individuality, dependence on local production continued — the cycle abundance = low price ended with enlargement of the market, but not that of shortage = high price.

The differential tariffs offered by the railway companies had almost as much effect on market structures as did the sheer existence of cheap transport. Tariffs that were digressive with distance, especially favoured the access to markets of the distant producers. They immensely strengthened the competitive position of the wines of the Midi in other regions of France. Only phylloxera postponed the establishment of a highly competitive market, and the decline of the *vins ordinaire* of the more marginal vine cultivating areas.

The cultivation of the vine in the Paris area declined at an even earlier date because of the attractiveness of the Paris market to distant producers. In the Oise valley for example the area under vine declined from 2,285 hectares in 1852 to only 811 in 1862.[26]

For other areas, for example Bourgogne, the first effect of the railway was to enlarge markets and thus increase prices in the zone of production. The railway reached the Bourgogne before it reached the south, giving a period of prosperity which would not survive the further development of the railway network and the extension of competition. Even when competition from the wines of the Midi was physically possible both in the Paris market and particularly in the Bourgogne itself, the effects were at first limited. Rail links existed as early as 1856 but consumer taste is conservative and commercial networks have to be established. Thus the octroi records of Dijon show significant competition only in 1867, when a poor crop in Bourgogne forced a temporary change in habits on consumers, which became permanent, though at a rate slowed by the effects of phylloxera in the south. The advantage which northern vine growing areas had obtained from proximity to the Paris market was eroded, and competition ensued even in their home markets. Price competition gradually broke down consumer habits.

The vine was increasingly restricted to areas in which it produced wine of remarkable quality, or in large quantity. The south was favoured in the latter respect by its more suitable natural conditions. In the north quality was the only protection now that offered by isolation had been broken down. Here price competition was of little importance. In an area like Bourgogne the wines of Chablis might profit from the new market conditions, but inferior wines could not survive for long. In general all the land suitable for high-quality wines was already used, so that the alternatives for vine growers were eventually reduced to cultivation of another crop or abandonment of their land which might anyway not be suitable for anything other than the vine. Efforts were also made to improve techniques of cultivation and reduce costs. The introduction of the plough into the vineyard in an effort to reduce the labour force was one element in this; another was to seek increased yields, a tendency which, occurring on a national scale, would in time lead to over-production.

These various effects of rail construction were reinforced by those of disease. From the period of 1851–3 oidium had caused many small-scale vine growers to abandon its cultivation, which continued to have effects in many areas until the early 1860s. Phylloxera had far more severe consequences. It first appeared in Gard in 1863 and spread at first slowly – to the Hérault only by 1869. Then its rate of expansion speeded up – by 1877 the whole Midi, Jura, Bourgogne and slowly Champagne were affected so that a crop of 60 million hectolitres in 1873 had fallen below 30 million in 1885. It took fifteen years to spread from the Midi to Bourgogne and gave the latter area a respite from competition.

In many areas, already in a poor competitive position, vines killed by phylloxera were not reconstituted. Land values, especially for hill soils, unfit for anything other than vines, often declined drastically.

The remedy was to graft resistant American plants onto the existing vines. This required great effort and expense, and new techniques were also advisable for permanent protection against disease. The new requirements for capital investment inevitably eliminated many of the smaller men, although earlier prosperity and the savings it had permitted enabled large numbers of them to adapt.

The new conditions of production and marketing made wine production of necessity an increasingly specialised process. Cultivation

77

of the vine in the south moved from the hill-sides onto the plains, where soils were better and labour costs likely to be lower. Often it replaced cereals, for the first time removed from their pre-eminent rôle in the agricultural economy. Only fine wines, protected by their distinctive characteristics, survived and remained where they had always been grown, just as they would survive the crises of over-production production which increasingly reduced the price of inferior wines, and the revenues of their cultivators.

In no other sector would the changes in the agricultural economy be as substantial as in that of the vine. The map of cultivation had been transformed, as had the conditions of production where the vine survived. The changing of the structure of the market had enforced specialisation both on individual cultivators and on a regional basis.

The facility with which livestock could be transported together with freedom from the previous dominant need to cultivate cereals did much to encourage regional specialisation. The increase in the number of cows was especially significant:[27]

1840	9,936,538
1852	10,093,737
1862	12,811,589
1873	11,721,459 (loss of Alsace-Lorraine)
1882	12,997,854

Regions in which wheat grew badly — cool, humid and well-watered places — and those suffering from a labour shortage were particularly attracted to pastoral farming. Animals had always been present but their number restricted by the needs of a self-subsistence polyculture. Now the Charolais, Bourbonnais, Jura and Alps were able to specialise in meant production, whilst areas closer to urban markets concentrated more on dairy produce. An isolated area like the Haut-Bugey, formerly so poor, was able, due to improved road-rail links to specialise in the production of Gruyère cheese. In many areas the effects of the railways were indeed spectacular. Before the opening of the Paris-Brest line 900–1,000 cows per year left the department of Mayenne for Paris. By 1868–75 the average had attained 7,000. Production of Roquefort cheese, 1,500 tons in 1850, tripled by 1890 due to the stimulus offered by easier access to markets once the Tournemire-Roquefort rail link was created.[28]

As living standards improved meat consumption increased, and it lost much of its luxury character. Fluctuations in its consumption declined. Increased demand made animals a more attractive form of investment. This can be seen in the adoption of selective breeding techniques and the rapid improvement in breeds, and in the extension of cultivated pasture. Nevertheless livestock production remained susceptible to large variations in production costs, the number of animals continuing to vary significantly over time, because of the difficulties of transporting forage, a bulky crop.

The old local breeds of cows suitable to a subsistence economy in which their prime function was to provide manure or as work animals, and which were a risky investment due to the prevalence of disease in them, tended to disappear. Even though stable conditions remained generally poor and tuberculosis was common, livestock weights increased. In the Ille-et-Vilaine the average weight of a cow in 1840 was 150 kilos. By 1882 this was 215. In the same period milk yield increased by one-third. Nationally the picture was even better with an average increase in this period from 240 to 321 kilos [29] for cows and 413 to 447 kilos for oxen which increased their effectiveness as work animals, though in many areas they were being replaced by horses.

If, in the case of cattle the tendency was generally towards increase in number, not all areas benefited to the same degree from the extension of markets. Thus in the Calvados, its previous geographical advantage of proximity to Paris was reduced. In the face of growing competition the Pays d'Auge turned increasingly from meat to dairy produce.

The statistics available for number of sheep show a different trend.[30]

1840	32,141,430
1852	33,281,592
1862	29,529,678
1873	25,935,114 (loss of Alsace-Lorraine)
1882	23,809,439

A variety of factors contributed towards this decline. In many places where sheep had been an accessory to other products, or simply allowed to roam waste land the decline in the area of the waste, and of fallow, the increasing number of cows, the cultivation of the vine or fruit trees on formerly bare hill-sides — in the Rhône valley for example — all left less space for sheep. From the 1860s the price of wool fell drastically in the face of competition from Argentinian and Australian suppliers. Between 1860 and 1890 a decline from 6 fr. to 1.50 fr. per kilo was recorded. This encouraged either the abandonment of sheep or a move from emphasis on wool production to that of mutton. This occurred in the Beauce where merinos were crossed with south downs, and in the Seine-et-Marne by crossing with the Dishley breed. Numbers declined in spite of the success of this crossing.

In the case of pigs an increase in number of these traditional animals of the poor is evidence of improvement in popular living standards. Between 1840 and 1873, and in spite of the territorial losses, numbers increased from 4,910,721 to 5,755,656 and average weight from 91 to 120 kilos.[31]

Already in 1863 the six major railway companies were able to transport over 4 million head of livestock, including 1½ million to the Paris market. Paris not only in respect of meat prices but agricultural prices generally, increasingly assumed a predominant rôle in the determination of national market prices.

Where the cost of transport was high, then demand was necessarily localised; and this largely determined the character of production. Conversely if transport costs were reduced to a negligable factor then, at least in theory, the agricultural geography would be determined solely by natural factors, with specialisation determined by soil structures and climate rather than the location of customers.

The new market structure created by the railways permitted price competition between the products of regions previously too isolated from each other. As well as providing new opportunities for producers, it also increased competition. Most obviously this was true in areas which previously had enjoyed a semi-monopoly in the supply of particular markets – the area close to Paris for example. In 1830 the zone provisioning the city with fruit and vegetables was only 50 km. in circumference. By 1855 it had been extended to 250 km., taking in, for example, Normandy and Tourraine. Products whose price fell by half' on the Paris market now sold at the place of production where formerly there had been only negligible demand for them, at perhaps double the former price. The consumer at a distance and the producer benefited; the consumer at the place of production paid more.

To some extent loss of monopoly was compensated for by the overall growth in demand. In addition competitive pressures did not develop overnight. The techniques for transport of perishables remained inadequate until the development of refrigeration from the 1890s. The products most immediately affected by changed market structures were thus wine and cereals. It took time for producers to be able to respond to new market possibilities – for example it took at least three years to establish a vineyard. Large areas and many peasant farmers remained impermeable to change. Isolated by distance or psychology from new ideas and possibilities, excluded or choosing to remain outside the more integrated market structure which had come into being, they held to the old ways. The rapidity with which particular sectors of industry were able to respond is especially illustrative of the greater rigidity of agriculture structures.

Producers in all areas gained a new freedom from the certainty that basic foodstuffs in short supply could be easily obtained from other regions or continents. Products that were produced only with great effort and at high costs – if the cost was ever counted – could be obtained from elsewhere, and the local producers, with a stimulus of access to wider markets could concentrate on producing that which best suited local conditions. Only once the obligation to be independent had ended was subsistence polyculture no longer a necessity.

The improvement of communications created societies more *open* to external influences than ever before. This was the vital factor in stimulating change, and in particular the provision of access to markets which provided a 'clear incentive' to the producer to increase his output 'beyond the level of community demand', i.e. to consciously make the change from subsistence-orientated to market-orientated agriculture, and to increase production and productivity.[32]

More and more manufactured goods entered the village, like clothing, cheaper and better in quality and more fashionable than anything produced by local craftsmen. These new tastes had to be paid for. Money became more and more a necessity, and thus agriculture even in the most isolated areas became part of an exchange economy.

The adaptation of existing agricultural systems to new market conditions took time, and did not occur everywhere at the same pace. It depended on such factors as existing farm structures, the availability of capital, commercial organisation and awareness, or else the pressures for change induced by the growth of competition or changing labour supply conditions. It was not simply a technical problem but one requiring a favourable social structure.

The transformation was most rapid and complete in areas which previously had been characterised by an intensive polyculture – the Paris region, Nord, Alsace, Rhône valley and Mediterranean plains, in areas of stock-breeding like the Charolais and Normandy, and areas of vine cultivation. Often it required a crisis to force the reorientation of the existing system. Thus Avignon was reached by rail in 1855 but in the Comtat Venaissin the construction of irrigation systems for vegetable production developed only after 1880 when the successive crises of the madder, silk and phylloxera had destroyed the traditional resources.

Regions, especially in the south, where family farming predominated (whether on land owned or rented) were not as open to the penetration of market forces as those where relatively large farms employed hired labour. In the latter profit rather than subsistence was the motive for production, and techniques as well as products were selected in an effort to maximise profitability. Greater responsiveness to changing market conditions was evident. In the former where the least efficient were only slowly eliminated by the inability to make ends meet, the overall social and farm structures were in consequence slow to change, and technical innovation slow to occur.

Nevertheless the signs are that from the 1850s to the early 1870s profitability encouraged investment, although this was restricted by increasingly favourable investment opportunities in other sectors of the economy. The development of a banking network did more to channel capital away from the land than provide agriculture with needed resources. The traditional tendency to invest in more land rather than improved techniques also remained strong amongst the peasantry.

To a degree agriculture did become more capital intensive. Cheaper transport made the more extensive use of mineral fertilisers possible. Although at more than 40 km. away from the railway lines transport costs still remained prohibitive. In large areas with poor soils, in Brittany, the Massif Central, Gatinais, Vosges, Bresses, Landes and Gascony, waste land was brought into cultivation often to provide fodder crops and wheat replaced rye. In effect a chemically new soil was created, transforming the agriculture of these poor areas. Without railways phosphates could not have been transported from the Ardennes, Boulonnais and Somme, or, from the ports, nitrates from Chile and guano from Peru. In the decade 1868—78, encouraged by special rail tariffs the bulk transported increased from 627,000 to 1,218,000 tons.[33] The effects of this development should not, however, be exaggerated. The application of fertiliser depended on technical knowledge and availability of capital and small-scale farmers often possessed neither.

More generalised improvements were those which occurred dramatically in the hand tools used. Only from 1850s did the scythe replace the sickle as a harvesting tool in most areas of France. It became increasingly important to increase labour productivity, as at the same time agriculture became more intensive and the supply of labour declined due to emigration from the countryside.

The adoption of machinery was a slower and more restricted process, both because of the capital required and the difficulty of employing machinery on the small farms into which so much of France was divided. For the latter reason threshing machines were introduced more easily than reaping. Although harvesting machines were introduced in the Paris region from the 1860s they did not appear in large numbers elsewhere before the 1890s. In 1887 there were only 35,000 reaping machines in France.

The introduction of new crops, particularly those supplying fodder, the increases in the number of animals, and in organic fertiliser supply — these were changes which could be applied generally throughout the country. Mechanisation, and the application of mineral fertilisers on the other hand required capital, large-scale farming, and the pressure for change provided by diminishing labour supply.

The extent to which the small farmer had survived and the degree to which he continued to be able to survive were the main limiting factors on structural changes. In many areas the old property structure did change: medium-sized farms gained at the expense of both the small, where emigration occurred, and of the large, whose owners, stricken by rising labour costs and falling prices were attracted to alternative investments. But the prosperous years of the Second Empire also permitted many small men to buy land. The innovations in agriculture made it possible for them to increase yields, reliance on family labour to ignore labour costs, and willingness to accept low returns by remaining at the traditional low living standards. The survival of polyculture, particularly where the division of land into a number of plots with a variety of soils made a monoculture unwise, sheltered them from commercial crises. The high tariffs introduced in 1882 would reduce the pressures for change and facilitate the survival of traditional peasant farming.

The structure of French agriculture prevailing before the railway era, and all its consequences, the way in which land, labour and capital had been combined in the various regions, served to place limits on the potential for adaptation to new commercial possibilities. Thus improved transport facilities did not attenuate regional divergencies. Areas which were already relatively advanced due to previous easy access to markets were able, because concentration of farms, accumulation of capital, and commercial organisation had already occurred to an important extent, to respond more easily to changes in market structure and by technical innovation to maintain relatively high levels of productivity and competitiveness.

Prior to railway development certain areas of specialisation had existed, facilitated by the easier communications on the plains and in the the river valleys. Subsequently it was possible to intensify such specialisation and develop the network of exchange.

Improved communications and the growth of urban demand favoured areas where pasture, vine and horticulture could be developed. These were products for which demand grew rapidly as living standards improved and which were not subject to such an intense foreign competition as were cereal producers. The market prices of the latter products tended to decline; those of the former to rise. In area after area farmers faced a new problem: formerly production had generally been for subsistence and to meet the needs of a local market, but now it was increasingly necessary to compete, which meant, in order to compete successfully, either minimising production costs or else differentiating the product by its superior quality. Thus ensured food supplies and the growing awareness that a better, less harsh existence was possible led to the slow abandonment of marginal land. The effort required to construct and maintain terraces on hill-sides seemed for the first time to be wasted. In Provence, the poorest land, that furthest away from habitations was abandoned — in contrast the cultivation of the plains flourished — as new markets encouraged horticulture and made investment in irrigation profitable.

Cereal cultivation obviously remained important both for animal foodstuff and bread, and was not necessarily a proof of archaism. Cereals were simply integrated within transformed agricultural systems but in a less dominant rôle than previously. The increase in their yields facilitated both this process and the transfer of land to other uses.

Due to the railways, and in spite of the limits to change, a definite restructuring of French agriculture occurred from the 1850s, characterised above all by the growth of specialisation. Within the life-span of a single generation substantial changes took place in the human condition. To the rural population the material world must have seemed less hostile, and resignation to their age-old circumstances less necessary. The new market forces had the effect of subordinating the countryside more directly to the towns than ever before, causing the structures of the agricultural world to change rapidly, but in response to external factors rather than internal. Prior to the railway epoch innovation in agriculture had been largely a response to demographic pressure within the rural community, the peasant himself serving as the dynamic agent. Now, increasingly, as urban products flooded the countryside, this and the growing urban demand for food would more closely determine crop patterns, whilst urban commercial organisations would dominate marketing.

To attribute the transformation to the railways alone would be exaggeration, but they were the major factor for change, the novel element in this situation. They alone permitted a balancing of supply and demand and the elimination of the traditional crises. In response to new commercial opportunities production grew significantly faster than population. Supplies of foodstuffs increased, and the quality of diet was improved by the development of meat, dairy, vegetable and fruit production.

A period of rapid change was grafted on to one of slow growth, and with it a revolution in human material conditions and mentalities occurred. Due to the transport revolution a new type of economy came into existence, and that of the *Ancien Régime*, characterised by inadequate food supplies, massive price fluctuations and the resultant fear of famine, disappeared in France. On the basis of these fundamental changes in food supply the transformation of society as a whole accelerated.

Notes

1.   Labrousse, F. *et al., Histoire économique et sociale de la France,* II, p. 99.
2.   Toutain, J.C., *Le produit de l'agriculture Française de 1700–1958,* 1961.

3. Le Roy Ladurie, E. and Goy, J., 'Première esquisse d'une conjoncture du produit décimal et domanial' in *Les Fluctuations du produit de la dîme,* 1972, pp. 369–72.
4. Morineau, M., *Les faux-semblants d'un démarrage economique: agriculture et démographie en France au 18e siècle,* 1971.
5. Laurent, R., *Les vignerons de la Côte d'Or au 19e siècle,* 1958, pp. 192–3.
6. Soboul, A., *La société Française dans la seconde moitié du 18e siècle,* 1964, p. 65.
7. Based on Dupeux, G., *La société française,* 1966, p. 117.
8. This follows closely Labrousse *et al.,* op. cit., pp. 407–9.
9. Bairoch, P., *Révolution industrielle et sous-développement,* 1969.
10. Rivet, F., *La navigation à vapeur sur le Saône et le Rhône,* 1962, p.116; Dauzet, P., *Le siècle des chemins de fer en France,* Fontenay-au-Roses,, 1948, p. 52.
11. Frêche, G., 'Etudes statistiques sur le commerce céréalier de la France méridionale au 18e siècle', *R.H.E.S.,* 1971, p. 224.
12. Follows closely Lévy-Leboyer, M., *Les banques européennes et l'industrialisation internationale dans la première moitié du 19e siècle,* 1964.
13. Labrousse *et al.,* op. cit., pp. 361–2.
14. Toutain, op. cit.
15. de Saint-Jacob, P., *Les Paysans de la Bourgogne du Nord au dernier siècle de l'ancien régime,* 1960, pp. 263–4.
16. Pautard, J., *Les disparités régionales dans la croissance de l'agriculture française,* 1965, p. 100.
17. Léon, P., *Economies et sociétés pre-industrielles,* II, p. 196.
18. Ibid.
19. Clark, C. and Haswell, M.,. *The Economics of subsistence Agriculture,* 1964, p. 192.
20. Rénouard, D., *Les transports de marchandises par fer, route et eau depuis 1850,* 1960, p. 43.
21. Levasseur, E., *Histoire du commerce de la France,* II, 1912, pp. 731–2.
22. Ibid.
23. Lavollée, C., 'Les chemins de fer français', *R.D.M.,* 1866, p. 26.
24. Dupeux, G., *Aspects de l'histoire sociale et politique du Loir et Cher,* 1962. p. 220.
25. Fromont, P., 'Les chemins de fer et l'agriculture', *A.F.,* 1948, p. 70.
26. Brunet, P., *Structure agraire et économie rurale des plateaux tertiaires entre la Seine et l'Oise,* Caen, 1968, p. 362.
27. Armengaud, A., *Les populations de l'est-acquitain au début de l'époque contemporaine,* 1961, p. 273.
28. Sorlin, P., *La société française, 1840–1914,* 1969, pp. 32–3.
29. Armengaud, op. cit., p. 274.
30. Ibid., p. 273.
31. Ibid.
32. Clark and Haswell, op. cit., p. 213; Bouvier, J., 'Le mouvement d'une civilisation nouvelle' in Duby, G. (ed.), *Histoire de la France,* III, 1971, p. 91.
33. Rénouard, op. cit., p. 44.

Further Reading — Agriculture

Agulhon, M., *La vie sociale en Provence intérieure au lendemain de la révolution,* 1970.
Ardant, G., *Theorie sociologique de l'impôt,* I, 1965.

Armengaud, A., *La population française au 19e siècle*, 1971.

Armengaud, A., *Les populations de l'est-aquitain au début de l'époque contemporaine*, 1961.

Armengaud, A., 'La question du blé dans la Haute Garonne au milieu du 19e siècle', Etudes vol. XVI, *Bibliothèque de la Révolution de 1848*, 1954.

Augé-Laribe, M., *La révolution agricole*, 1955.

Baehrel, R., *Une croissance: La basse–Provence rurale (fin du 16e siècle–1789)*, 1961.

Bairoch, P., *Révolution industrielle et sous-développement*, 1969.

Bardet, J.P., *et al.*, *Le bâtiment. Enquête d'histoire économique 14e–19e siècles*, I, 1971.

Bastié, J., *Le croissance de la banlieue parisienne*, 1964.

Bergeron, L., 'Problèmes économiques de la France napoléonienne', *R.H.M.C.*, 1970.

de Bertier de Sauvigny, G., *La Restauration*, 1955.

Blanchard, M., *Les chemins de fer de l'Aude (1840–58) – Essais historiques sur les premiers chemins de fer du Midi Languedocien et de la vallée du Rhône*, Montpellier, 1935.

Blanchard, M., ibid., *Les premiers chemins de fer autour d'Orléans (1829–60)*.

Boserup, E., *The conditions of Agricultural Growth*, 1965.

Bougeatre, E., *La vie rurale dans le mantois et le vexin au 19e siècle*, Meulan, 1971.

Bourde, A.–J., *Agronomie et agronomes en France au 18e siècle*, 3 vols, 1967.

Bouvier, J., 'Le mouvement d'une civilisation nouvelle' in Duby, G. (ed.), *Histoire de la France*, III, 1971.

Bozon, P., *La vie rurale en vivarais*, 1963.

Brunet, P., *Structure agraire et économie rurale des plateaux tertiaires entre la Seine et l'Oise*, Caen, 1968.

de Cambiaire, A., *L'auto-consommation agricole en France*, 1952.

Caralp-Landon, R., *Les chemins de fer dans le Massif Central*, 1959.

Caron, P., *Histoire de l'exploitation d'un grand réseau. La compagnie du chemin de fer du Nord, 1846–1937*, 1973.

Chatelain, A., 'Problèmes ruraux en Bugey au milieu du 19e siècle', *R.G.L.*, 1959.

Chatelain, A., 'La lente progression de la faux', *A.E.S.C.*, 1956.

Chevalier, L., 'Les fondements économiques et sociaux de l'histoire politique de la région parisienne', Unpublished doctoral thesis, Paris, 1950.

Chevalier, M., *La vie humaine dans les Pyrenées Ariègeoises*, 1956.

Clark, C. and Haswell, M., *The Economics of subsistence Agriculture*, 1964.

Clause, C., 'L'industrie lainière rémoise a l'époque napoléonienne', *R.H.M.C.*, 1969.

Clout, H.D., and Phillips, A.D.M., 'Fertilisants mineraux en France au 19e siècle', *E.R.*, 1972.

Cobb, R., *The Police and the People*, 1970.

Crouzet, F., 'Agriculture et révolution industrielle', *C.H.*, 1967.

Dauzet, P., *Le siècle des chemins de fer en France*, Fontenay-au-Roses, 1948.

Demangeon, S., 'L'approvisionnement de Paris en fruits et légumes', *A.G.*, 1928.

Désert, G., 'Les paysans du Calvados au 19e siècle', *A.N.*, 1971.

Désert, G., 'L'agriculture et les paysans sarthois au 19e siècle', Levy-Leboyer, M. (ed.), *Un siècle et demi d'économie sarthoise* (1815–1966), Rouen, 1969.

Desmarest, J., *Evolution de la France contemporaine. La France de 1870*, 1970.

Dion, R., *'Orléans et l'ancienne navigation de la Loire'*, *A.G.*, 1938.

Dubuc, R., *'L'approvisionnement de Paris en lait'*, *A.G.*, 1938.

Duby, C., Review of D. Faucher's 'La vie rurale vue par un géographe', *E.R.*, 1963.

Dupeux, G., *La société française*, 1966.

Dupeux, G., *Aspects de l'histoire sociale et politique de Loir et Cher*, 1962.

Durand, A., *La vie rurale dans les Massifs volcaniques des Dores, du Cézalier, du Cantal et de l'Aubrac*, Aurillac, 1966.

Faucher, D., *Le paysan et la machine*, 1954.

Faucher, D., 'La révolution agricole du 18e–19e siècle' in *La vie rurale vue par un géographe*, Toulouse, 1962.

Ibid., 'Réflections sur la méthode'.

Ibid., 'Les systèmes de culture'.

Ibid., 'Les jardins familiaux'.

Ibid., 'De quelques incidents en France de la révolution agricole'.

Faucher, D., 'Routine et innovation dans la vie paysanne', *J.P.N.P.*, 1948.

Faucher, D., 'Les pre-alpes du sud', *R.G.A.*, 1947.

Faucher, D., *L'homme et le Rhône*, 1968.

Fel, A., *Les hautes terres du Massif Central. Tradition paysanne et économie agricole*, 1962.

Festy, O., 'L'agriculture pendant la révolution française. Les conditions de production et de récolté des céréales. Etude d'histoire économique

1789–1795', 1947.

Forster, R., *The Nobility of Toulouse in the 18th Century*, Baltimore, 1960.

de Foville, A., *La transformation des moyens de transport et ses consequences économiques et sociales*, 1880.

Freche, G., 'Etudes statistiques sur le commerce céréalier de la France méridionale en 18ᵉ siècle', *R.H.E.S.*, 1970.

Freche, G., *Les prix des grains, des vins et des légumes á Toulouse (1486–1868)*, 1967.

Fromont, P., 'Les chemins de fer et l'agriculture', *A.F.*, 1948.

Fussell, G.E., 'The Agricultural Revolution, 1600–1850' in Kranzberg, M., and Pursell, C.W. (eds.), *Technology in Western Civilisation*, 1967.

Galtier, G., *Le vignoble du Languedoc mediterraneen et du Roussillon*, Montpellier, n.d.

Garrier, G., *Paysans du Beaujolais et du Lyonnais 1800–1970*, 2 vols, Grenoble, 1973.

Gibert, A., 'Le vignoble français', *R.G.L.*, 1949.

Gonnet, P., 'Sondages à travers l'économie française; le cas de la côte d'Or' in Labrousse, *Aspects de la crise et de la dépression de l'économie française au milieu du 19ᵉ siècle, 1846–51*, 1956.

Gonnet, P., 'Contribution a l'étude du traffic routier au milieu du 19ᵉ siècle' in *Actes du 90ᵉ Congrès*, III, 1966.

Goubert, P., 'Les techniques agricoles dans le pays picard aux 17ᵉ et 18ᵉ siècles', *R.H.E.S.*, 1957.

Goubert, P., 'Recherches d'histoire rurale dans la France d'ouest (17ᵉ et 18ᵉ siècles)', *B.H.S.B.*, 1965.

Goubert, P., *L'Ancien Régime*, I, 1969.

de Goursac, M., *Les transport agricoles en France*, 1907.

Guichard, P., 'D'une société répliée á une société ouverte: L'évolution socio-économique de la région d'Andance, de la fin du 17ᵉ siècle á la Révolution' in Léon, P. (ed.), *Structures économiques et problèmes sociaux du monde rural dans la France du sud-est*, 1966.

Higonnet, P.L.R., *Port-de-Montvert—Social Structure and Politics in a French Village, 1700–1914*, Cambridge University Press, 1971.

Houee, P., *Les étapes du développement rural*, I, 1972.

Janne, H., 'Tradition et continuité dans les sociétés en évolution rapide', *C.I.S.*, 1968.

Jardin, A., and Tudesq, A.J., *La France des notables*, I, 1973.

Jones, E.J., and Woolf, S.J. (eds.), *Agrarian Change and Economic*

Development, 1969.

Jouffroy, L.-M., *Une étape de la construction des grandes lignes de chemin de fer en France: le ligne de Paris á la frontière Allemagne,* 3 vols, n.d.

Jouffroy, L.-M., *L'ère du rail,* 1953.

Juillard, E., *La vie rurale dans la plaine du basse-Alsace: Essai de géographie sociale,* 1957.

Klatzmann, J., *La localisation des cultures et des productions animales en France,* 1955.

Labasse, J., 'La circulation des capitaux en France au 19e siècle', *I.H.,* 1955.

Labrousse, E., *La crise de l'économie française á la fin de l'ancien régime et au début de la révolution,* 1944.

Labrousse, E., *Aspects de l'évolution économique et sociale de la France et du Royaume-Uni de 1815–1880,* 1949.

Labrousse, E., *et al., Histoire économique et sociale de la France,* II, 1970.

Labrousse, E., *et al., Aspects de la crise et de la dépression de l'economie française au milieu du 19e siècle, 1846–51,* 1956.

Laurent, R., *Les vignerons de la Côte d'Or au 19e siècle,* 1958.

Laurent, R., *L'Octroi de Dijon au 19e siècle,* 1960.

Laurent, R., 'Une source: Les archives d'Octroi', *A.E.S.C.,* 1956.

Lavollée, C., *Les chemins de fer français, R.D.M.,* 1966.

Lebrun, F., *Les hommes et le mort en Anjou aux 17e et 18e siècles,* 1971.

Lefebvre, G., 'Répartition de la propriété et de l'exploitation foncières á la fin de l'ancien régime', *Etudes sur la Révolution française,* 1963.

Ibid., *'La vente des biens nationaux,.*

Lefebvre, G., *Les paysans du Nord pendant la Révolution française,* Bari, 1959.

Lefevre, A., *Sous le second Empire: chemins de fer et politique,* 1951.

LeGoff, T.G.A., 'An 18th Century Grain Merchant Ignace Advisse Desruisseaux' in Bosher, J.F. (ed.), *French Government and Society 1500–1850,* Essays in Memory of Alfred Cobban, 1973.

Lemarchand, G., *Le féodalisme dans la France rurale des temps modernes,* A.H.R.F., 1969.

Leon, P., *Economies et sociétés pre-industrielles,* II, 1970.

Lequin, Y., 'Les grands traits de l'évolution agricole á Plozouet Ex (Finistere) depuis la fin du 18e siècle', *R.G.L.,* 1967.

Le Roy Ladurie, E., *Histoire du climat depuis l'an mil,* 1967.

Le Roy Ladurie, E., Les rendements du blé en Languedoc, Proceedings of the 3rd International Conference of Economic History, Munich 1965, 1969.

Le Roy Ladurie, E., and Goy, J., 'Première esquisse d'une conjoncture du produit décimal et domanial. Fin du moyen-âge/18ᵉ siècle' in *Les fluctuations du produit de la dîme*, 1972.

Letaconnaux, J., 'Les transports en France au 18ᵉ siècle', *R.H.M.C.*, 1908–9.

Levasseur, E., *Histoire du commerce de la France*, II, 1912.

Lévy-Leboyer, M., *Les banques européennes et l'industrialisation internationale dans la première moitie du 19ᵉ siècle*, 1964.

Ligou, D., 'Review of A. Poitrineau' La vie rurale en Basse-Auvergne, *R.H.E.S.*, 1967.

Livet, R., *Habitat rural et structures agraires en Basse-Provence*, Aix-en-Provence, 1962.

Luxembourg, M., 'La vie agricole dans la basse vallée du Gers', *R.G.P.S.-O.*, 1934.

Maistre, A., *Le canal des deux mers. Canal royal du Languedoc 1666–1810*, Toulouse, 1968.

Mandrou, R., *La France aux 17ᵉ et 18ᵉ siècles*, 1967.

Marchilhacy, C., *Le diocèse d'Orleans au milieu du 19ᵉ siecle*, 1964.

Marres, P., 'La modernisation de l'économie du bas-Languedoc et des Cévennes méridionales', *S.L.G.*, 1954.

May, M.-G., 'Le chemin de fer de Paris à Marseille. Etude de géographie économique', *A.G.*, 1930.

Mendras, H., *Sociologie de la campagne française*, 1959.

Meyer, J., *La noblesse bretonne au 18ᵉ siècle*, 2 vols, 1966.

Moreau, J.P., 'La vie rurale dans le sud-est du bassin parisien entre les vallées de l'armançon et de la Loire', I.H., 1955.

Morineau, M., *Les faux-Semblants d'un démarrage économique: agriculture et démographie en France au 18ᵉ siècle*, 1971.

Morineau, M., 'Budgets populaires en France au 18ᵉ siècle', *R.H.E.S.*, 1972.

Morineau, M., 'Histoire sans frontière: prix et révolution agricole', *A.E.S.C.*, 1969.

Pautard, J., *Les disparités régionales dans la croissance de l'agriculture française*, 1965.

Philipponneau, M., *La vie rurale dans le banlieu parisienne. Etude de géographie humaine*, 1956.

Pinchemel, P., *France: A Geographical Survey*, 1969.

Pitié, J., *Exode rural et migrations intérieures en France. L'exemple de la Vienne et du Poitou-Charentes*, Poitiers, 1971.

Poitrineau, A., 'L'alimentation populaire en Auvergne au 18ᵉ siècle' in Hémardinquer, J.J., *Pour une histoire de l'alimentation*, 1970.

Poitrineau, A., , *La vie rurale en basse-Auvergne au 18ᵉ siècle*, 1965.

Price, R.D., 'The Change from Labour Abundance to Labour Shortage in French Agriculture in the 19th Century', *E.H.R.*, 1975.

Remond, A., *Etudes sur le circulation marchande en France aux 18e et 19e siècles*, 1956.
Renouard, D., *Les transports de marchandises par fer, route et eau depuis 1850*, 1960.
Rivet, F., *Le navigation à vapeur sur le Saone et le Rhône*, 1962.
Rosier, B., *Structures agricoles et développement économique*, 1968.
Rougerie, J., 'Le Second Empire' in Duby, G. (ed.), *Histoire de la France*, III, 1972.

de Saint-Jacob, P., *Les paysans de la Bourgogne du nord au dernier siècle de l'ancien régime*, 1960.
Seigneur, P., *La vie économique du Vaucluse de 1815 á 1848*, Aix-en-Provence, 1957.
Slicher van Bath, B.H., *The Agrarian History of Western Europe*, 1963.
Soboul, A., *La société française dans la seconde moitié du 18e siècle. Structures sociales, cultures et modes de vie*, 1964.
Soboul, A., *La France á la veille de la Révolution*, I, 1966.
Sorlin, P., *La société française, 1840–1914, 1969*.
Sperber, M.,'Tradition et culture de masse', C.S., 1966.

Tardieu, S., *La vie domestique dans le mâconnais rural pré-industriel*, 1964.
Thuillier, G., *Aspects de l'économie nivernaise au 19e siècle*, 1966.
Tilly, L.A., 'The Food Riot as a Form of political Conflict in France', *J.I.H.*, 1971.
Toutain, J.C., *Le product de l'agriculture française de 1700–1958*, 1961.
Toutain, J.C., *Les transports en France de 1830 á 1965*, 1965.

Vidalenc, J., *La société française de 1815 à 1848*, vol. I, Le peuple des campagnes, 1970.
Vigier, P., *La seconde république dans le région alpine*, I, 1963.

Walter, G., *Histoire des paysans de France*, 1963.
Wolkowitsch, M., *L'économie régionale des transports dans le centre et le centre-ouest de la France*, n.d.

3 INDUSTRIAL DEVELOPMENT

Patterns of Change

The general characteristics of the ec   omic structure of France until
the middle of the nineteenth century have been listed as:

1. The predominance of the agricultural sector and within this of
   the cultivation of basic foodstuffs, with a poor harvest causing a
   general crisis of the economy.
2. The inadequacy of the means of transport resulting in massive
   price fluctuations and in general economic disequilibrium.
3. The predominance within the industrial sector of the production
   of consumer goods and particularly textiles.[1]

The essential point being made is that prior to the development of a
railway network and in spite of isolated developments of advanced
productive techniques, the economy of the *Ancien Régime* survived.
This by no means denies that industrial development occurred nor that
France was throughout most of this period an industrial power second
only to Britain. It is to maintain that structural change was extremely
limited and that growth occurred primarily through the production of
more of the old products by means of an extension of the existing
methods of production rather than by technical innovation. This was
also the pattern of development in much of British industry, but the
balance between innovation and routine in France was more firmly
weighted in favour of the latter.

In most areas industry had been born in isolation, serving local
needs and using local raw materials, wool, flax, leather, minerals, etc.
To meet local needs productive activity needed also to be localised, in
the countryside as well as the town. Production and distribution were
assured essentially by a mass of artisans, many of whom served directly
a multiplicity of individual customers, but with also a large, and
growing, dependent sector, working for and controlled by merchants
who supplied raw materials and distributed the finished product. The
development of this commercial capitalism was of fundamental
importance in the growth of production.

Until about 1750—60, industrial equipment could fairly be
described as medieval in character. In this respect there was little
difference between town and country. What differentiated urban from

92

rural industry was not the size of the workshops or the type of equipment but the numerical concentration of workers in a town and their full-time devotion to their trade.

Generalised growth is evident in the industrial sector from around 1730, although some sectors, for example, the Lyon silk industry, and Amiens textiles, had been sheltered from the severe depression which began towards the end of the seventeenth century. This variation is symptomatic of the isolation of geographical regions and the feebleness of exchange between them.

The artisanal workshop can be conceived of as being essentially static in outlook, preoccupied with maintaining its present situation. Although in decline, the urban corporations, with their desire to control quality and entry into trades, reinforced this tendency throughout the eighteenth century.

Increased production could most rapidly and cheaply occur through the extension of rural industry, employing semi-peasant labour, and with the exception of dispersed innovations from 1760 and especially 1780, this was how increases in production were secured. A particular advantage was the relative ease with which adaptations to fluctuations in demand could occur.

Rates of growth seem to have been particularly high in certain industries and in certain regions — poles of growth can thus be isolated, although for this period the weakness of their linkages with the rest of the economy should be stressed.

In textiles, if woollens remained dominant, the more rapid rate of development of cotton was evident, since it was an industry less inhibited by structures evolved in the past and able to use imported techniques. The carding and spinning enterprises of the Duke of Orleans at Orléans and the establishments at Mulhouse and Thann in Alsace for printing on cloth are examples, but their significance should be limited to that of harbingers of a future development. In metallugy at Le Creusot, and coal-mining, especially Anzin, similar examples of technical innovation and concentration of production developed but they too were exceptional and their contribution to total production minimal. Concentration was more likely to take the nebular form evolved, for example at Abbeville, where towards the end of the eighteenth century van Robais employed in textiles about 1,800 workers in the town and 10,000 others in the countryside. Commercial capitalism thus continued to dominate industrial.

The Revolutionary period disrupted industrial activity due to a lack of internal stability and the loss of overseas markets, and, more significantly in the long term, through the consolidation of the economic situation of the small peasant. This inhibited overall structural change. The economic growth of the period 1802—10, that is before the decline of the Empire, was in large part due to recuperation from the earlier period. Relatively few enterprises were efficient enough to gain from the possibilities of the enlarged Europe and its markets. This whole period was thus one in which industrial growth slowed.

One calculation of annual growth rates during the troubled periods 1781–90 to 1803–12 provides an estimate of 1.98 per cent contrasting with a figure of 2.86 per cent for 1802–12 to 1825–34, and of 3.52 per cent (the highest for the nineteenth century) for 1825–34 to 1835–44.[2] Subsequent high growth, particularly for the period 1815–20 (one estimate is of 3.70 per cent per annum),[3] can be conceived of as compensating for the stagnation of the closing years of the Empire, followed by a slowing down of the rate of growth to an estimated 3.05 and 1.46 per cent in the next two quinquenia,[4] with a renewed increase in activity, again not sustained, from around 1830,[5] terminated by a major crisis of complex character lasting from the mid-1840s until 1851.

One significant feature of this growth was that it did not change the fundamental characteristics of French industry. There was undoubtedly a continuing tendency towards concentration, a tendency characteristic of a small number of especially dynamic enterprises, but production remained dominated by small and medium-sized enterprises, able to survive and continue to use archaic techniques because of the protection assured to their local markets by transport difficulties. Modern forms of concentrated production were exceptional and coexisted with the typical establishments of a pre-industrial economy. As late as 1851 the census revealed three million workers employed in workshops compared with 1½ million in 'grande industrie' – defined significantly as establishments employing more than ten people.

It seems likely that industrial modernisation was delayed due to a number of interrelated factors, including poor communications, inadequate raw material and power supplies, the slowness of agricultural development and of the increase in demand from the rural population. In terms of the value of production and numbers employed, agriculture, and secondarily building, the sectors least characterised by innovation, remained dominant and within the industrial economy, the predominance of consumer goods industries was clearly maintained.

The characteristics of a modern economy have been described as the predominance of the industrial sector; the existence of cheap and rapid means of transport creating a unified market; and the predominance within the industrial sector of producer goods industries and especially metallurgy.

Industrial development in France occurred slowly. No single period can be descibed as that of 'take off', but there were nonetheless periods in which developments occurred which had a decisive effect in altering the basic structure of the economy.

The chronology of growth in the nineteenth century can be described as follows: 1815 to 1846, slow regular growth with fluctuations of minor importance; 1847 to 1851, a major crisis; 1852 to 1857, very rapid growth, succeeded by depression in 1858 and 1859, with slow growth, interrupted by the war of 1870–1 and its consequences, between 1860 and 1882. Growth in the year 1882 to 1896 was very slow, followed in the period 1897 to 1913 by somewhat faster growth.[6] The single period in which growth occurred at a rate comparable to that of other industrialising countries, i.e. 1852–7 was decisive in causing the fundamental structural change which assured subsequently the dominance of industry proper over artisanal production. If growth rates during this period were statistically not so very much higher than during the prosperous periods of the July Monarchy, there was an evident acceleration of development in key sectors like railway construction, mining and metallurgy. During the longer period 1830–60 rapid development occurred in the coal and metallurgy industries but only railway construction, which itself vastly increased the demand for their products, could, by transforming the transport infra-structure remove the major restraint on further growth. The significance of the political decision in 1852 to proceed with rapid railway construction should not be underestimated.

To some extent, railway development must be integrated within an existing process of growth which had already stimulated the metallurgical and engineering industries to such a degree that they possessed the capacity and technology to provide most of the material necessary for railway equipment, but without any doubt the creation of a railway network was a major factor in stimulating the further concentration of production by which capitalism became industrial rather than commercial.

The railway ended the isolation of more or less closed local economies. By unifying internal markets it accelerated the circulation of raw materials and finished products. It permitted a massive extension of mechanisation and of credit systems, the two other features, along with the railways themselves, of what has been called a 'triple revolution'.[7]

In sum, it favoured the extension of large-scale production by making it possible for the consumers in any particular locality to chose between the products of local industry using archaic techniques for small-scale production, and the goods of often superior quality produced in factories at generally lower cost.

Growth and the development of concentration did not however occur in a uniform manner. Rates of growth varied between industries and within the same industry over time. The significance at particular times of particular industries with above average rates of growth, which served to stimulate economic activity throughout the economy, should be noted. These 'poles of growth', by their purchases of goods and services from other industries, partially conditioned their sales and consequently the volume and cost of their product, as well as their profitability; also by the sale of their own products they affected the costs and profits of other industries. By proving the validity of new techniques and so encouraging their wider adoption, such relatively advanced industries played an important rôle in the process of innovation.

A series of industries with above-average rates of growth have been identified:[8] the cotton industry from 1786 to 1840 and again in 1880 to 1890; woollens from 1880 to 1890; silk, 1807 to 1850 and again in 1870 to 1890; sugar, 1807 to 1830, and 1900 to 1910; coal, 1786 to 1870; metallurgy, 1830 to 1910; and chemicals 1860 to 1900.

During the key period at the middle of the nineteenth century the textile industry was not a major factor in growth. Indeed, throughout the century it evinced far less dynamism than a number of other industries. The average annual growth rates between 1815 and 1913 show this — coal-mining grew at 4.2 per cent, primary metallurgy at 3.5 per cent, transformative metallurgy at 3.4 per cent, chemicals at 4.2 per cent, textiles at only 1.5 per cent. From 1835—44 to 1845—54 and 1845—54 to 1855—64 metallurgy grew at rates of 4.3 per cent and 7.1 per cent per annum and coal at 4.3 and 6.1 per cent,[9] evincing clearly the acceleration of the process of industrialisation. If industrialisation started with textiles, it could only be sustained by developments in the spheres of coal, metallurgy and engineering.

Whilst stressing the significance of the structural change which occurred around the middle of the nineteenth century, it would be unwise to ignore the limits to it. If the balance within the economy had shifted in the direction of modern concentrated production, the more traditional industries like textiles, clothing, leather, building, woodworking in 1870 still represented 85 per cent of the gross product, compared with the 10 per cent of more modern industries like fuel and minerals, metallurgy and engineering.[10]

The former were industries characterised by a multitude of small firms, each representing a feeble investment of capital. The census of 1872 clearly reveals this continued coexistence of traditional and modern sectors.

Census 1872	Employer	Worker
Extractive industries	14,717	164,819
Large-scale industry	183,227	1,112,006
Small-scale industry	596,776	1,060,444
	794,720	2,337,269

Industrial growth was undoubtedly slowed by the slowness of change in traditional sectors like textiles and of course agriculture. In the former and throughout artisanal production, the continued development of commercial concentration helps explain the ability to survive and also the fact that in a situation of relatively high raw material costs, and relatively low labour costs, the dispersal of production had a certain rational basis. It was the case, however, that if on the basis of such a structure the artistic trades emphasising the quality of their product were able to survive, large sectors of the textiles and clothing industries, by far the largest employers of labour, were in rapidly increasing difficulties. Vertical integration of the productive process and effective control of the elements of production became a necessity if costs were to be minimised and competition with factory production possible. Rural industry was able to survive for as long as cheap labour permitted the maintenance of sufficiently low costs to make it competitive. Migration from the countryside becoming intense during the Second Empire both reduced the reserves of labour, and increased the bargaining power of those workers who remained.

The effects of the American Civil War, the war of 1870 and especially the agricultural crisis of 1882—96 were to create an adverse economic situation which demanded investment in modernisation to increase productivity and lower costs. This can be seen as the final blow to the dualistic structure of French industry.

In many respects the average French enterprise continued to appear small and under-equipped, producing at higher costs, than enterprises in other industrial nations. This is indicative of the limited elasticity of the existing structure. It remains the case however that the decisive break with the economy and consequently the society of the *Ancien Régime* had occurred around the middle of the nineteenth century. A dynamic industrial sector had then been created and the pre-conditions for its continuing growth established. Industrial enterprises, which to survive must 'liquidate the past through depreciation and assure the future by investment',[11] which were consequently committed to growth, had been created, on a scale, particularly in the area of heavy industry, sufficient to allow them to play a dominant economic rôle. If to modern eyes the rate of growth achieved — averaging 2.56 per cent per annum for industry in the nineteenth century — appears low, placed in the context of that century, and contrasted with the lack of sustained growth in previous epochs, this development, and indeed that of the whole long period of growth from *c.*1730, appears of remarkable significance in the history of humanity, part of a contemporaneous process of social transformation, affecting agriculture as well as industry, and all aspects of human life.

Some of the detail of economic development can best be filled in by a consideration of particular industries.

Building

The most important non-agricultural activity in the traditional society, at least in terms of the numbers employed, was the building industry. Only around 1870—90 was it surpassed in this respect by textiles.[12] Paradoxically, this is one of the least studied of industries.[13] It has been estimated that during the First Empire 720—730,000 workers were employed in building — c. 3.8 per cent of the active population. By 1851 building workers represented c. 4.24 per cent of the active population, and by 1866 this had risen to 4.99 per cent, to which might be added a further c. 1.30 per cent employed in annexed industries like quarries, brickworks, tile and cement production. As much as 30 per cent of the industrial labour force in the 1860s was employed in building and related industries after which a certain decline occurred reflecting the end of the initial phase of industrialisation and urbanisation.

This importance was not uniform throughout France. An examination of the relationship between the building labour force and the total adult male labour force has revealed a variation between 2 per cent to over 14 per cent according to departments, with a fundamental division between the north, with a high proportion, and the rest of France. The figure for the department of the Creuse, where according to the 1851 census 27.9 per cent of the adult males were employed in building work, is easily explained by the importance of seasonal and temporary migration from this impoverished area. During the Second Empire, around 35,000 workers left their homes each year for building sites in Paris, Lyon and elsewhere. Migrant labour only declined in importance in the last third of the century as migration tended to become permanent, the building industry less seasonal, and conditions in the Creuse itself changed.

Until this last third of the century, and even then, change occurred only slowly, the character of enterprises remaining artisanal. Little technical change occurred, limited capital was necessary, and small-scale organisation remained possible. In 1851 there were on average 2.27 workers for every entrepreneur, with the highest number, 6.57 in the department of the Seine.[14]

In Paris itself there were in 1860 5,378 entrepreneurs with 71,242 workers, an average of 13 workers per enterprise. For France as a whole the 1871 census revealed 173,454 employers employing 446,837 workers, i.e. still less than three workers each.[15] If, even in the towns, enterprise was on a miniscule scale, in the countryside many buildings were constructed by their proprietors with specialists employed perhaps for some of the more difficult stages. Given the significance of do-it-yourself construction work the total volume of construction activity is especially difficult to estimate.

Technical progress in the building industry faced its most fundamental obstacle in the shape of high transport costs. In 1816 in the Caen plain, where roads were relatively good, the cost of a cubic metre of worked stone increased by 60 per cent when transported for 17 km., and 80 per cent for 21 km. The consequence of this was that wherever possible local materials were used.[16] There thus existed everywhere numerous brickworks and producers of tiles, lime, and cement, vital to the local building industry but each producing on a very small scale for exclusively local needs.

Improvements in the conditions of road transport had only a marginal effect on the supply of building materials. Railway development ended dependence on local materials. It put into the hands of the craftsmen employed better quality materials, often at lower prices. It resulted also in a relative uniformity of basic building materials. Stone and brick more resistant to temperature replaced puddled clay in many places. In areas like the Massif Central thatch was rapidly replaced by tiles imported from elsewhere.

The level of building activity depends on a complex of factors. It is obviously related closely to the general degree of prosperity — thus the growing revenues of large landowners and farmers in the eighteenth century and the desire for more comfortable housing stimulated activity. Until the second half of the following century the stimulus came primarily from agriculture, and the cycle of building activity tended to follow that of rural revenues. The complaints of many observers make it plain that the response to the growth of urban population was slow to occur.

The annual rate of growth of the building industry during the nineteenth century has been estimated at $c.$ 2.1 per cent, a figure close to that of industry as a whole. This growth was not regular but occurred as a succession of phases of intense activity followed by depression. There were in effect three phases of particularly intense construction corresponding to the first ten years of the Restoration period, of the Second Empire and of the Third Republic when minor phases of depression did little to affect the general trend. The period of the July Monarchy and of the liberal Empire saw a significant reversal of the previous tendency.[17]

In the larger cities, and particularly in the second half of the nineteenth century, activity was stimulated by rapid population growth which led to increases in rents and stimulated investment in building. It was closely linked to the overall rate of population growth and of urbanisation. Once the demand for housing had been at least partially met, a temporary situation of overproduction might exist, causing a decline in rents and in investment. Competing investment opportunities also affected levels of investment in buildings, with effects felt increasingly from the 1860s.

The transport revolution, as we have seen, made possible improvements in the quality of housing. Increased prosperity had similar consequences. Yet, particularly in the countryside, modes of life were slow to change, depending as they did on human habits and decisions as to priorities. As horizons expanded, as part of the general improvement in living standards, so however the quality of housing did improve.

Textiles

1. Cotton

Another major industry in the pre-industrial economy was textiles. The most significant development within this sphere was the growth of the cotton industry. Until the 1840—50s the demand for cotton products and consequently the structure of the industry was largely determined by the fragmented character of potential markets.

Alsace and the Nord were the areas in which mechanisation was most advanced. In Alsace, high quality, and relatively high costs of production meant that transport costs made up a relatively small portion of final selling costs. Consumers were not amongst the poorest part of the population and demand was in consequence less volatile. In the Nord, a large local market existed in a densely populated area possessing good regional communications, although demand remained more susceptible to fluctuation in consumer income. By contrast, in Normandy, communications were poor, and the industry depended on a smaller local market. Production too was primarily of cheaper clothes for workers and demand fluctuated especially widely with movements in food prices. To a very large extent diversity within the cotton industry reflected varying conditions and types of demand.[18]

Two factors seem to have exerted a decisive influence on the location of the cotton industry: power sources, and labour costs. From the 1750—60s in Upper Alsace, following the establishment of cotton print production at Mulhouse, spinning and weaving were introduced into towns like Sainte-Marie-aux-Mines where the water-power, pure water and the cheap labour of the Vosges valleys could be used. A similar combination of factors attracted the industry to the Beaujolais, Lyonnais, Dauphiné, Pays de Caux and Norman bocage.

Wherever population densities were high supplementary employment in industry was necessary, seasonally, where ownership of land was widespread or often permanently in towns into which migration from the countryside had occurred. This helped make possible the growing concentration of production in factories in the Nord for example, whilst on the western littoral from Cholet to Angers a more sedentary population combined working the land with domestic industry.

At the turn of the century, the mechanisation and concentration of the cotton industry was most clearly evident at Paris, with three other main poles of growth around Rouen, Lille and Mulhouse, each with its particular rhythm and form of growth reflecting the combination of local resources. High labour costs led rapidly to the migration of the industry from Paris.

In a situation of fragmented markets, and, from 1817, of depressed agricultural prices, it was essential to keep costs, and particularly those of labour, the main item in costs, low. This alone would permit the maintenance of profitability and capital accumulation. In the latter respect, and consequently in terms of technical improvement and the quality of production, Alsace was able to establish an early advantage by borrowing Swiss capital, capturing the most profitable sectors of production and subsequently by re-investment of a large proportion of profits so as to preserve this lead. Thus whereas in c.1840 Rouen remained the main cotton spinning centre with 38 per cent of the national spinning capacity, Mulhouse possessed 29 per cent, compared with only 8 per cent during the Empire.

Other areas tended to depend rather on the advantage of cheap labour especially when machinery and fuel were expensive and capital supplies more restricted. Because of inferior equipment and dependence, especially in weaving, on unsurveilled seasonal rural labour quality often suffered. This was particularly the case in regions like Normandy or the Dauphiné and, as inter-regional competition grew, these areas met with great difficulty. In the cast of the Dauphiné, handicapped also by distance from the Channel and North Sea ports, the industry virtually disappeared.

The wide range of efficiency between textile regions is especially striking in the eighteenth and first part of the nineteenth centuries. Poor communications and the effects this had on market structures evidently restricted competition. Mulhouse for example had to pay around 40 fr. per ton for the transport, by road, of raw cotton from Le Havre, which significantly increased costs of production and reduced competitiveness.

Generally this was a high cost industry, incapable of competing in international markets. The survival of the familial structure of enterprises restricted the possibilities of capital accumulation. The often extreme division of labour and of risks had the same effect, slowing capital accumulation at a time when, for technical reasons, larger investments were required. Thus in 1835 in the Rouen area there were

450 cloth manufacturers, 300 spiners, 60 dyers, 60–70 printers. In Normandy landowners often constructed mills to use the water-power available on their land, and then rented them to industrialists who installed the machinery. In the *arrondissement* of Rouen, and this at mid-century, about 45 per cent of the labour force in spinning worked in enterprises employing over 100 workers, but often, even in these, machinery was archaic, and labour efficiency consequently low, with one worker to 200 spindles compared with one to 800 in modernised enterprises. Weaving here, as elsewhere, remained a rural activity, with workers dependent on the manufacturing centre, dispersed throughout the nearby valleys. The situation was the same around Saint-Quentin, for example, where some 75,000 rural workers were employed and similar even in the more advanced Nord and Alsace.

Rural industry had developed primarily because of the availability of cheap labour, and additionally, in the eighteenth century, because of the absence of Government and guild regulation in the countryside. It declined in the early nineteenth century only where affected by the loss of overseas markets. Elsewhere the development of mechanised cotton spinning had maintained a large demand for rural weaving. From the 1850s, the simultaneous occurrence of the industrialisation of the weaving processes, intensified competition from urban based industry and the massive wave of migration from the countryside which reduced the supply of labour and increased wage levels in rural areas, served to reduce the advantage of cheap labour, and brought about the rapid disappearance of rural industry.

Concentration in both spinning and weaving took initially a commercial and financial form. Subsequently, and primarily to increase quality control, production in both sectors was concentrated in one building at first using old techniques but often with the use of power. The continued use of water-power resulted in the dispersal of production and restrictions in size until the introduction of the steam-engine intensified the tendency towards concentration.

Even with these limiting factors, the statistics available indicate the rapid development of cotton production. During the first half of the nineteenth century cotton spinning represented the most dynamic and most modern element of the industrial scene, with important stimulating effects on various other industries, and in particular mechanical engineering. Raw cotton consumption rose in the following manner:

Annual averages (in thousand metric tons)[19]

1781–90	4.0
1812–14	8.0
1815–24	18.9
1825–34	33.5

1835—44	54.3
1845—54	65.0
1855—64	74.1
1865—74	85.9

By the end of the eighteenth century most of the techniques which were to revolutionise textiles production had already been discovered. Actual innovation, however, even in this the most dynamic of industries was rather slow. Most rapid to spread was the spinning-jenny, introduced in England around 1765, and in France in the early 1770s. By 1789 it was in general use, particularly in Normandy and Picardy. It was manufactured mainly by Englishmen operating with French Government subsidies, and had the great advantages of low cost and simplicity of operation. Although jennies were often gathered together in mills they could be used at home, and without power. Their introduction caused relatively little upheavel in the existing domestic industry and yet substantially increased labour productivity and reduced costs of production. It has been estimated that whereas the spinner using a spinning wheel could produce 1½—2 livres of spun cotton per day, using a machine with 40 spindles it was possible to produce 70—80 livres.

In contrast, the water-frame and the mule-jenny, introduced in France towards the end of the 1780s, spread far more slowly. In 1780 for example there were 900 mills in France compared with 20,000 in Britain. Both offered further increases in productivity but the former in particular was a large and heavy machine requiring installation in mills and large capital investments. The mule-jenny was more widely used because, although requiring mills, it was small and lighter and required a smaller investment, but only during the July Monarchy was cotton spinning completely mechanised and the quality of thread remained inferior comparable with the of English producers. Throughout the intervening years continual improvements were made to this machinery. The humble mule-jennies with 60 spindles common in the Dauphiné from the 1820s were soon replaced by more powerful machines with 120, 140 or over 200 spindles, and with automatic reeling and twisting. Even so this type of modification seems generally to have occurred more slowly than in England.

Self-acting machines became common only towards the end of the 1840s, beginning at Mulhouse in 1844. Their greater power needs tended to offset the attraction of labour economies especially when plenty of cheap labour was available. The crisis with which the 1840s culminated, by bringing down prices and intensifying competition, stimulated their introduction.

Weaving was even more backward. The flying shuttle, invented in

England in the early 1730s both reduced the demands on the worker and made weaving more rapid and regular. It appeared in France as early as 1747 but became widespread only early in the following century, being adapted at Roubaix around 1820, in Normandy around 1825, and in Alsace c.1830. The power-loom was only slowly introduced, even in England, and the process was yet more gradual in France, due to the expense and the failure to adapt it to the production of light cloths until c.1830. Weaving kept pace with the more advanced mechanisation of the spinning processes by extending its use of the resource of rural labour. Over-population, and lack of alternative employments created a docile labour force, whose low wages maintained the capital costs of production at a low level and so created a disincentive to modernisation, apparent even in relatively advanced departments like the Nord. Around Rouen in 1837 a spinning industry mounting 317,000 spindles provided thread for some 52,650 weavers dispersed over a wide area.

The power sources used in textiles were significant factors in determining location and scale of production. Thus many Alsatian and Norman producers, due to the lack of local coal resources, and the cost of steam-engines, continued to use water-power. Even in 1847 in Normandy 58 per cent of the power used was developed by water-wheels (2,325 of 4,017 horse-power). The introduction of steam-engines was especially rapid in the Nord because of the availability of local coal. In 1824 69 were active; in 1844 570, of which 281 were in the *arrondissment* of Lille where much of the cotton industry was situated. Reflecting this rapid technical progress it has been estimated that between 1834 and 1845, while production in spinning in the department increased by 50 per cent, and quality improved, the labour force declined. The concentration of production was also evident in the industry. At Lille in 1859 the largest cotton spinning establishment, that of Henri Barrois, employed about 300 workers, but 150 was more normal. However in 1832 there had existed at Lille 50 cotton spinning mills with an average of 3,600 spindles each, whilst by 1849 there were only 27 with an average of 8,550.

The process of change, already rapid from the Restoration, in the Nord favoured by large local demand, and around Mulhouse by high quality, was stimulated by the severity of the economic crisis from 1846 and the intensified competition this engendered. Subsequently the construction of the railway network caused a permanent increase in internal and international competition, the latter further stimulated by tariff reductions. The American Civil War and the substantial increase in raw material prices it caused also contributed significantly to this process of modernisation and concentration. These developments were evident in the rapid decline of rural industry, in the closure of many small units of production and in the accelerated rate of technical improvement. Thus where in Rouen in 1859 6,420 power-looms had been employed, by 1869 the number was 60,510. In the spinning sector, the effort to reduce costs can be illustrated by the introduction of self-acting spindles in the Haut-Rhin, and the corresponding decline of mule-jennies.[20]

	Self-acting	Mule-jennies
1854	108,000	–
1864	706,000	504,000
1875	1,315,000	70,000

The railway, by facilitating access to national and international markets, helped to reduce the costs of raw cotton and coal and make the French cotton industry more competitive, more capable of competing in enlarged markets. Steam replaced water-power, and machines in factories finally displaced looms in cottages. The intensification of competition required continual modernisation which could be carried out only by large firms.

2. Wool

Technical innovation in the woollens industry was slower than in cotton. The jenny was introduced on the eve of 1789, but save around Amiens its use was not common, and it took until the 1870s to eliminate spinning by hand. One explanation offered for this slowness was that profit margins in the industry were too low to finance investment. The threat of competition from England was also less of a stimulation than in the case of cotton, given the relevant slowness of mechanisation of woollens there. In both countries this was in large part due to the delicate nature of woollen threads. The desire to make use of the availability of cheap labour was an added factor.

As in the case of cotton the mechanisation of weaving was slower than that of spinning. The flying shuttle was in general use by about 1817, but hand-weaving was hardly challenged before the period of the Second Empire. The expense of power-looms, of supplying power and providing factory buildings remained a powerful disincentive only overcome by the intensification of competition and the growing shortage of rural labour. A similar picture prevails of the mechanisation of the preparatory processes — combing and carding machines spread only from 1825–30.

Again comparable to the cotton industry was the pattern of advanced and backward areas. Amongst the advanced can be included Roubaix, Reims and to a lesser extent St Quentin and Elbeuf, with a few factories, including some of the most advanced, in Alsace. The backward were especially in the south at such places as Lodeve, Carcassone and Castres. Productive capacity was increasingly· concentrated in the former at the expense of both the rural areas surrounding them and of the less efficient centres.

The overall growth of the woollens industry is clearly evident. It used an estimated 39,000 tons of domestically produced wool at the beginning of the eighteenth century, and 43,000 tons at the end, whilst at the same time imports increased from 1,500 to 12,000 tons. By 1850 the industry was consuming around 90,000 tons of wool per year and in 1870 160,000 tons with domestic production significantly remaining at 50–60,000 tons throughout this period. The decline of production by around 45 per cent during the Revolution should be noted as a factor having far-reaching effects on the locational structure of the industry.

In contrast with the recently implanted cotton industry, woollens was an age-old feature of subsistence societies making use of local resources. In some areas it still retained this character, with peasants using their own wool to produce their own clothes and selling any surplus in the local markets. In some cases merchants had organised the trade, and throughout the eighteenth century this rural industry continued to expand. The first restraint on this expansion was the loss of markets during the Revolutionary and Imperial wars, and the subsequent slowness in adapting to changing markets and failure to improve both quality and techniques. A more permanent threat was technical progress in the north, which increasingly threatened the traditional woollen industry of the north-east, of Berry, Dauphiné and the Midi still clinging to the advantages of cheaper wool and labour.

Efforts were gradually made to improve production in most areas. In the Dauphiné from early in the nineteenth century the contraction of rural production and concentration in the centres with more advanced techniques was evident, but only at Vienne was this to be successful in the long run and there mainly through the development of specialised products not meeting with direct competition from those of the north.

The putting-out system became increasingly less remunerative for both merchants and workers, but the efforts to concentrate and modernise were generally on too small a scale and too limited to be successful. This was indeed true of the whole industry. Around 1820, Reims, one of the leading centres had only five or six large producers, compared with 300 small workshops and large-scale employment of rural labour. Even in 1870 in the Roubaix-Tourcoing complex, probably the most modern, there were some 300 enterprises.

Outside the north an even more archaic situation prevailed, which could survive only for as long as poor communications offered a certain protection. This shield was of declining efficacy as road development increased, and was finally destroyed when the railways came, bringing the woollen and cotton clothing of the north, superior in quality and lower in price into the most isolated regions. A precipitant decline in the situation of the woollens industry outside the relatively advanced producing areas in the north occurred from 1850—60, affecting places like Castres, Mazamet, Bédarieux, Lodève, Ganges and the rural areas surrounding them at the same time as contributing to the destruction of rural weaving in the north itself.

3. Silk

The first half of the nineteenth century was the great period of expansion of the silk industry. Output estimated at an annual average of 900 metric tons in the period 1781—90 falling to 600 during 1801—14, grew as follows:[21]

1815—24	1,200
1825—34	1,500
1835—44	2,400
1845—54	4,000
1855—64	4,400
1865—74	4,800

This growth was reflected in the number of looms operating — at Lyon 7,000 in 1814 increased to 42,000 in 1832 — and in the development of the rearing of the silk worms and the preparatory functions. These latter were spread throughout the Drome, Isère, Ardèche, Vaucluse and even Gard, whilst weaving was centred in Lyon and to a lesser extent Avignon.

The most significant technical development in the silk industry was the propagation of the Jacquard loom from the second decade of the nineteenth century. By about 1830 about a third of the looms in use were of this type, and they remained dominant even in the 1870s. Use of water-power in order to reduce labour costs developed from the 1830s but in many cases this need was avoided by the dispersal of the industry into the countryside, a tendency encouraged by growing social tensions and violence in Lyon.

An industry which exported up to three-quarters of its products was especially susceptible to fluctuations in demand. Its strength was its generally superior quality and responsiveness to changes of fashion. This concern with quality restrained the dispersal of the industry because of dependence on the skilled workers grouped at Lyon. It also, in part, explained the peculiar structure of the industry, both there and at

Avignon. Small enterprises were more easily able to adapt to the incessant variations in fashion. In 1835 at Lyon there were some 8,000 independent workshops employing about 30,000 skilled workers and apprentices, with supplies of raw material and sales organised by some 500 merchants who effectively controlled the industry.

As in so many other spheres significant concentration was little evident before the period of the Second Empire. Then, due to the intensification of competition in international markets, in part caused by the less dependable quality of silks produced in the countryside, to the loss of markets during the American Civil War, and to the disease prevalent amongst the silk worms and the increase in raw material costs the struggle for survival at Lyon itself became more bitter.

4. Other Textiles

Most archaic of all the branches of textiles were the production of hemp, lace and linen. The latter was the last of the major branches of textiles to solve the problems of mechanical spinning — the de Girard method was patented in 1810 but used only after 1830.

The main flax growing areas were Flanders, Brittany, Southern Normandy and Anjou. In 1821 it was grown in some 40 departments. Cloth production was essentially rural and domestic, but even by this date the industry had faced a major blow in the shape of the loss of of colonial markets. Previously, in the 1780s the lower Maine area had exported perhaps two-thirds of its output. Growing competition from cotton products accelerated this decline, particularly in the pre-railway period in the Flanders region where the two entered most directly into competition. Cotton products were stronger, more supple, better looking and offered better protection against the weather.

A variety of means of increasing competitiveness were introduced, reducing even further the rewards for labour, such as concentration of workers using the same techniques in factories in order to regularise production, and, particularly from the years 1840—45, mechanisation. The competition of urban with rural producers grew increasingly intense in all regions and the disappearance of the latter more rapid. In the north, for example, the linen weavers of the Lys valley and Abbeville declined in numbers whilst concentration and mechanisation occurred at Lille, Armentières, Valenciennes and Hazebrouck.

Thus, in all sectors of the textile industry a similar process of structural change occurred involving the concentration and mechanisation of production to meet increasingly intense competitive pressures.

Metallurgy

One of the most remarkable features of economic development in recent times has been ironmongery of all sorts. It seems probable that from the early nineteenth century the demand for iron and iron products was increasing as part of the growth of the traditional economy and particularly of the improvement of agricultural tools.

The greatest single purchaser of metallurgical products was the State, mainly in the shape of military equipment. To ensure its needs the State encouraged modernisation and technical improvement, but as fluctuating military procurements could not guarantee a stable level of demand, and due to a lack of alternative clients, the development of large-scale production was restrained.

The major problem was that of transporting the finished product. Transport costs significantly increased prices and so restricted the potential marketing area of large producers. Thus, in 1829 it cost 46 fr. to move 1 ton of iron from Le Creusot to Paris, i.e. 10 per cent of the selling price of 470 fr., and until the late 1840s the continuing general inadequacy of transport conditions meant that up to 50 per cent of the price of finished products, according to the places of production and sale, was made up of transport costs.

Iron production was generally dependent on restricted local markets, and used local water, minerals and forest resources. The smallness and isolation of the markets, and the limited availability of resources encouraged routine. Local markets were effectively protected from competition by their inaccessibility to outsiders.

The stimulus to change came from competitive pressures in the few areas in which real competition existed — along such commercial axes as the Saône and Rhône valleys, or in the Paris market to which a number of metallurgical regions had access by means of river and canal. Change in market structures consequent upon improvement in transport conditions extended markets, and particularly with railway development intensified competition for them. Progressively, but with growing rapidity from the 1840s the structure of the industry itself was transformed.

The enlargement of the market, and its unification stimulated efforts to increase production, to improve techniques and quality and reduce prices, establishing a competitive situation in which small rural producers could not survive for long.

The demand for rails, particularly when the major networks were being constructed, in the early 1840s and in the years 1853–64, and subsequently the growth of demand for iron from engineering and shipbuilding and the building industry, created a new type of iron market, at first alongside the traditional market, which only large-scale producers could supply. These demands stimulated the first really extensive modernisation of the iron industry.

By the end of the Second Empire 17,400 km. of railway line were in use over which ran 4,900 railway engines, 12,000 carriages and 122,000 goods waggons. From 1872 steel rails replaced iron. The ability of already established iron and engineering capacity to respond to these new demands is indicative of how significant earlier developments in these industries were, and of how aware of the new possibilities some enterprises rapidly became. In 1842 of 646 locomotives in use only 162 had been imported. In 1856 the proportion of imported to French-produced locomotives was 105 to 1,902.

The general economic importance of railway company orders was due to their volume, and their comparative regularity given a constant need for renewal. Of equal importance was the demand for high quality. The first two characteristics permitted economies of scale, and the third led to improved quality and falling prices.

These railway orders represented until the end of the century over 10 per cent of the total volume of orders for metallurgical products. Their relative importance was particularly significant during the years 1855–64 which can be seen as a decisive period of structural change in the industry. Favouring, as they did those enterprises best able to adapt to meet the new demands, and to compete in terms of price and quality, railway orders accelerated the process of concentration. Railway orders were of less significance in the development of engineering but contributed to overcoming such problems as lack of power in machine-shops, the scarcity and cost of well cast iron, and the limited demand for machines.

Declining iron prices and the growth of competition had been evident from around 1820. Even then furnaces in the Vienne region were unable to compete in the Dauphiné itself with iron from better-equipped establishments at Le Creusot and St Etienne, which had the advantage of local coal supplies and large, low-cost production. The decline of archaic producers was restrained by the fragmentation of markets and also by the willingness of the more efficient producers, in the absence of foreign competition, and except in time of crisis, to accept the high price levels set by the less efficient and thus earn a supplementary profit. Price competition was much restrained by these various factors. In periods of crisis, by contrast, large producers reduced prices, and so extended their normal zone of operations and invaded the markets of the less efficient. A gradual weakening of the position of archaic units occurred with each crisis, and the gradual extension of competition.

This slow process was accelerated by railway construction and the effects of tariff reductions, particularly the commercial treaty of 1860 with England. This latter ensured that the internal prices of modern producers would at least be at a level competitive with those of potential foreign competition, and incidently too low for ill-equipped internal producers. If many iron-masters were afraid that the Treaty would ruin them that it did so was not in many cases directly due to an influx of English metal but to the possibility and its effects on the internal pricing policies and the technical development of the modernising French producers. Due to easier communications, industrial centres like those of the Haute-Marne using local wood, water and ore resources to produce high quality but expensive iron now faced competition even in local markets from cheaper iron produced in regions using coal and coke as fuel.

In 1850 it cost 127 fr. to produce one ton of pig-iron using charcoal, and 108 fr. using coke. By 1860, due to increasing wood costs, the two price levels stood at 149 fr. and 107 fr. respectively.

The first constructions of railways stimulated iron production in the particular areas involved. Only subsequently, as the network was extended, were localities distant from the actual place of construction able to supply it. So paradoxically the early years of railway construction served to revive or stimulate the traditional small-scale metallurgy. They provided one of those periods in which demand exceeded supply and the inefficient producers could share in the general growth. New enterprises fully engaged in the railway market, only competed in traditional markets when railway demand slackened, as in the crisis years from 1847, or more permanently in the 1860s once the major networks had been completed. As late as 1860 many important works were supplied with pig-iron which they could not produce themselves in sufficient quantity, or of the quality required for transformation into steel, by small rural producers. But by then capacity had been expanded and quality improved, leaving the small producers to rapidly disappear in the decade 1860–70. The primitive Catalan forges in the Pyrenees which had achieved their maximum production as late as 1853 and then enjoyed a recovery in 1860–1 when the Pyrenean railway network was being constructed were finally killed by the replacement of cementation by puddling in steel manufacture from 1850, the introduction of the Bessemer process which closed the market for high quality pig-iron, and by the establishment of coke-using furnaces in the Ariège valley in 1867–8 which captured the local market for agricultural tools. Catalan iron costing 275 fr. per ton could not compete with establishments producing coke-iron at 180–200 fr. per ton.

Until as late as the early 1860s, traditional charcoal-using metallurgy can be said to have benefited from the general increase in economic activity, at a time, however, when the competitive position of large enterprises was continually being strengthened. Charcoal metallurgy was progressively abandoned, first along the railway lines which brought cheaper products. Some establishments survived, using the coal which could now be transported cheaply to them, and transforming their techniques, often to specialise in products like high quality steels at Montluçon. Those which remained isolated by poor communications had no opportunity to do even this.

Changing market structures and technical conditions had an evident effect upon the location and structure of the industry.

Limited demand, technical conditions and resource location had required the dispersal of production. This was partly offset at all periods by a certain concentration of ownership, much of it ephemeral where forge-masters simply rented establishments, and some more durable as in the case of the establishments de Wendel slowly accumulated from 1704. This was a centralisation of ownership and control, whilst the units of production remained dispersed.

This process was accelerated during the Revolutionary-Imperial period by closures and changes of ownership consequent upon emigration (noblemen and religious houses having owned many furnaces and forges) and the extension of markets due to the supression of internal customs barriers and the needs of war.

The slow development of competitive pressures led to the gradual closure of the least economic producers and the concentration of production in the more efficient units and/or those better located for access to markets. Large units also possessed the very great advantage of sufficient capital to buy coal-mines and forests, guaranteeing themselves against fluctuations in the prices of the fuels which made up such a large part of total costs, but with the disadvantage of immobilising a great deal of capital.

Towards the end of the Restoration and especially in the boom years of 1835–8, and 1845–7 a new progress was evident with the creation of important mining – metallurgical complexes at Fourchambault, Châtillon-Commentry, Decazeville and Alais. These combined a certain geographical concentration with continued dispersal over a fairly extensive area, with both coal and charcoal-using plants. In other cases concentration remained at the level of ownership. Thus the Boigues Family controlled a large number of separate producing units throughout Berry and the Nivernais.

Growing demand in the 1830–40s particularly for rails in the north where the first major line of the future network was completed in 1846 resulted in the injection of capital into established ironworks like Le Creusot, and in the north the creation of new works at Denain, Anzin, and Maubeuge.

Whereas in 1828 an estimated 24.35 per cent of all basic iron was produced by the ten largest enterprises, by 1845 the ten largest produced 37.5 per cent of the total, and by 1860 the eight largest supplied 53 per cent. This is clearly indicative of the fact that growth in the iron industry was primarily that of large not medium or small enterprises, and of those using the new technologies. The future belonged to a small and declining number of companies, which through price and market agreements divided the main market between themselves, to those which could accumulate the capital to go beyond the stage of concentration to that of integration of the metal-making process, and which possessed the resources to introduce the new steel-making processes and to take advantage of the establishment of a national market during the Second Empire.[22]

Geographical concentration, much less integration, had hardly been possible at an earlier date primarily because of transport difficulties which forced the use of local resources and dependence on local markets. The availability of hydraulic-power conditioned the geographical location of much of the industry, especially of forges using the traditional tilt-hammer. The apogée of these forges in the southern Vosges, Haute-Marne, Châtillonnais, Franche-Comté and Dauphiné can be fixed in the 1830s.

By 1840–50 iron ore and coal resources were, in many areas, inadequate for works producing on a large scale — in the Nivernais Fourchambault was abandoned. Even though the transport costs of raw materials had been reduced, and at some traditional centres, e.g. Commentry, local coal deposits could be combined with ore brought in by canal and rail, growing competition made good location and minimal transport costs important. Production was thus concentrated increasingly at Le Creusot, Hayange, Denain, Anzin and St Etienne — all coal-field sites increasingly dependent on foreign ore supplies. Elsewhere metal-making survived both by improving techniques and specialising in high quality products.

The question of technical change has been left until the end in the hope that the reasons and the pace of innovation will be more easily explicable following the discussion of changing market structures.

The limits to demand were also the main limits to technical innovation. Few modern enterprises could be created before communications were improved, and even where the market potential existed it was often difficult to raise the necessary capital. Moreover, the whole spirit of the small enterprises, their inertia, routine, desire for security and independence served as barriers to further investment.

The technical difficulties of change should not be underestimated. From the fifteenth and sixteenth centuries to the late eighteenth there had been little technical innovation. The forge-master and his skilled workers possessed a technical expertise, usually transmitted from father to son, entirely empirical in character. Thus even if the new techniques developed in England were known the scarcity of workers trained to use them and the consequence of this for the quality of the product made innovation perilous. Similarly the English techniques had to be adapted to local minerals and coal, and a more scientific approach dependent upon chemical analysis of products and materials introduced to calculate the correct mixture for the furnaces. Industrial chemists and engineers had to be trained in sufficient number to replace the master-workers.

In short, combined with apathy and lack of capital was a real uncertainty, lasting until the new techniques had clearly proved that they could ensure at least as good a return on capital as the old.

For these various reasons the process of change in metallurgy was slow. In 1789 pig-iron was almost entirely produced in furnaces or Catalan forges using charcoal. The only major exception was Le Creusot, founded in 1785, with government support and employing the latest English techniques, which used coke and steam-engines. During the Revolutionary-Imperial period this type of innovation seems to have almost ceased, in spite of rising wood prices, and the consequences for profit levels when charcoal costs made up about 60 per cent of the cost of iron.

Rising fuel costs did however stimulate continual small-scale innovation, e.g. efforts to improve the shape and construction of furnaces and increase their capacity to ensure more economical use of charcoal, but not involving any fundamental technical progress. This would continue to be a feature of the charcoal iron industry as long as it survived. Some of the techniques designed for application to new coke-using establishments such as the injection of hot air to reduce fuel consumption could be, and were, in this case from the middle 1830s, applied in charcoal furnaces, helping to maintain their competitiveness.

Without doubt rising wood prices also encouraged the use of coke. This stimulus was not as great in France as in England, where the wood shortage had been greater. France was not as fortunate in possessing ore deposits near those of coal, or as good communications. The location and nature of coal deposits prevented their large scale and rapid use. The cost of transport of coal to iron ore or vice versa was often prohibitive. Coal prices were, even at pit-heads, high in comparison to the English because of the slowness with which coal production was expanded and the low productivity of mines. This plus poor communications did not promise the regularity in supply which large ironworks required unless large amounts of capital were to be tied up in stocks.

Forge-masters at a distance from waterways, or not situated near coal had little choice but to continue using charcoal, making efforts to economise in its use, and, if they possessed sufficient capital, to purchase forests and avoid competitive bidding for wood. This was the

114

situation at Fourchambault in the late 1820s when coal, which cost
0 fr. 60–0 fr. 75 per metric quintal at pit-heads in the Loire, cost
3 fr. at Fourchambault. Of its furnaces dispersed in the Cher and
Nievre, three used charcoal exclusively, and seven a mixture of charcoal
and coke which ensured some economy. As late as the 1850s 1,300
woodcutters were employed, plus a large number of men employed in
transporting the wood.

Establishments near coal deposits like Le Creusot, Alais and
Decazeville or favoured by good communications like Vienne and the
Loire basin, did use coal. Their numbers were increased as
communications improved, for example by the Commentry-Montlugon
complex following the construction of railways and the Canal du
Berry. Thus an evolution occurred: 2 furnaces used coke in 1819,
29 of 408 in 1830, 41 of 462 in 1840, 120 or 591 in 1856, 141
of 413 in 1865,[23] or in terms of production of pig-iron[24].

	(1000 metric tons)	
	wood	coke
1836	262	38
1845	246	138
1850	229	176
1860	316	582
1864	224	876

The increase during the 1850s was particularly marked and
reflected the new market structure created by the railways, and the
new possibilities for innovation they had created. Before this period
even if it would have been possible to construct the large furnaces the
new processes required to make them economical, it would not have
been possible in most cases to have supplied them economically with
the quantities of ore, coal, flux, capital and labour they required.

The introduction of the use of coal in forges was more rapid. Here,
providing supplies of pig-iron were adequate, English techniques could
more easily and with limited capital cost be introduced. The puddling
process, which involved stirring molten metal and rolling rather than
hammering to remove defects and obtain the desired shape, introduced
in a number of large ironworks in 1819–20 could, even where coal
supplies were inadequate, form the basis for partial innovation,
combining charcoal furnaces and coal-using puddling furnaces with
hydraulically operated rollers. Even in 1830 when only 9 per cent of
pig-iron was produced with coke 50 per cent of iron was produced with
coal.

115

Iron Production (1,000 metric tons)[25]

	wood	coal
1850	73	173
1860	96	436

Such partial innovations maintained in many areas a large market for pig-iron produced with charcoal, for example in the Haute Marne where the nearest coal basin was 270 km. away at Sarrebrück or at Fourchambault with a forge dependent on ten dispersed furnaces. In fact of 232 furnaces constructed from 1822–40 only 60 used coke.

Consumer preference for charcoal-iron slowed change. Its quality was believed to be superior to that of coke-iron, and purchasers often specified use of charcoal. By the 1850s, however, this difference had declined.

The maximum number of charcoal furnaces was reached in 1838, although their total product continued to increase until 1846. After 1840 the progress of coke accelerated. New furnaces used coke or at least a mixture, whilst the proportion of coke iron in total pig-iron production increased more rapidly than the number of furnaces, given that the average coke furnace produced by the 1850s about 6,400 tons, per annum compared with the 1,000 tons of the charcoal furnace. By the 1840–50s, as competition intensified, this particular technical change must at last have appeared definite. The coke-fired blast-furnaces allied to the steam-engine, for the first time permitted iron production on a mass scale.

Use of the steam-engine to create a blast and provide power gave a new dimension to ironworks. It dictated the concentration and close co-ordination of the various processes for producing iron. The major engineering and constructional problems its use created were solved, as at Imphy in 1825, by constructing the entire works around the 100 horse-power steam-engine.

Technical development generally called for the growing concentration of production. The use of one machine tended to lead to another. The process accelerated once access to markets and competition for them were increased. By 1846, Hayange, then probably the most modern establishment in France, was operating 5 coke furnaces and one charcoal, 4 sets of rollers for sheet-iron, one power-hammer, 9 reverberatory furnaces and 16 puddling furnaces, with mineral circulating in tipper trucks. This sort of development required easy access to considerable deposits of coal and ore, technical knowledge, large investments and accessible markets.

The introduction of the Bessemer process for steel-making in 1858 by the Jackson brothers at their Saint-Seurin works (Dordogne) and then successively at Imphy, Assailly, Terrenoire (1862) and Le Creusot

(1870) marked a further important stage in the development both of the structure of the metallurgical industry and the organisation of industrial enterprises. By 1878 there were twenty-four Bessemer converters operating. The process involved the injection of oxygen under pressure into liquid cast-iron to burn off carbon and silicium. Previously steel had been produced in Catalan forges using local high-quality ores. Then in 1814 the cementation process was introduced using Catalan-produced pig-iron, near Albi and at St Etienne, and in 1844 the crucible method in the St Etienne area.

The Bessemer process and the concurrently developing Siemens-Martin process with a reverberatory furnace which permitted, if at high cost, better control of the steel-making process and better quality, for the first time allowed large scale and relatively cheap steel production. The introduction of the Thomas Gilchrist process from 1878 extended this development by permitting the use of Lorraine ores with high phosphoric content.

In effect a whole new industry had been established due to the creation of a mass market and substantial investment in technical innovation. In a very short time the jump had been made from an artisanal to industrial production of the most modern kind. In many ways, by the end of the Second Empire iron and steel companies like that of Le Creusot symbolised the new capitalism. Numerically they were a small minority but their economic significance and the influence their directors, integrated into the small group of great financiers, exerted, was substantial.

These new enterprises broke of necessity with the traditional conception of the rôle of the entrepeneur. The transformation of techniques of production and the enlarged dimensions of the company required a transformation of the techniques of administration, closer control of accounting and financial procedures, a new emphasis on marketing and the employment of a relatively large group of managerial personnel. The problems of controlling a large enterprise employing a large labour force, of co-ordinating the supply of huge quantities of raw materials, complicated production processes, and sales in increasingly diverse and widespread markets, were very different from those faced by the traditional iron-maker.

Compared with the development of the cotton industry that of metallurgy was of wider significance for general economic development in terms of its forward and backward linkages with the rest of the economy. This was probably the case in England, but it was even more so in France where broad structural change in the economy was not possible until the railway development of the 1850s.

In supplying rails, increasingly cheaper metal for mechanical and constructional engineering, in the demand it set up for coal and capital the effects of metallurgical development were pervasive.

Power

The most common form of power in the traditional economy was that provided by water-wheels. These were not definitively supplanted until the 1850s, and even as late as 1845 hydraulic installations provided about 150,000 horse-power, approximately three times that generated by steam. The geographical location of much of the metallurgical and textile industry was determined by the need to be sited along waterways. In 1845 the cotton industry employed 462 hydraulic machines compared with 243 steam-engines, the silk industry 435 compared with 143. The limitations imposed by this form of power were obvious: excessively low, high or frozen rivers could impose a halt on production.

The Newcomen engine, as perfected by Watt, offered a technical solution to these difficulties, and one, constructed in France by the Perier brothers was installed at Le Creusot in 1785. Further diffusion of this power source was however slow — even Le Creusot continued for some time to use both water-wheels and steam-engines.

By 1810 there were some 200 steam-engines in France. But even in the relatively industrialised Nord, only the mine pumps at Anzin were moved by steam-power. Progress had been interrupted by the Revolution and would only resume after 1815 when English experience was again available. The number in use increased as follows:[26]

Year	Number of machines	Horse-power
1830	625	10,000
1839	2,450	33,000
1845	4,114	50,000
1848	5,200	60,000
1852	16,080	75,500
1862	17,000	205,000
1875	32,000	401,000

The slowness with which the employment of steam-engines increased in the early part of the century can be explained by a number of factors. Often the cost of the innovation was either prohibitive or only reluctantly accepted. For the ironworks at Imphy in 1825 a 100 horse-power steam-engine cost 136,000 fr., to which ought to be added the cost of transporting it there (12,000 fr.), associated construction work (142,000 fr.) and the fashioning and putting in place of connecting rods (118,000 fr.). Early engines were often unreliable and repairs to them were always expensive and resulted either in a work stoppage or the use of alternative power sources which were expensive to maintain in readiness.

Another limiting factor was fuel cost, particularly in areas without local coal supplies, and in the absence of an adequate transport network. Thus at Mulhouse, coal costing 15 fr. per ton at the pit-head in Rive de Gier cost 50—53 fr. in 1831. An enquiry in 1834 in the Nord revealed that the main obstacle to the spread of steam-engines was the transport cost of fuel, and this in a department which in terms of both local coal resources and communications was better off than most. Even so in 1843 the Nord with its 7,700 horse-power generated by steam, and the Loire with its 6,500 horse-power, i.e. the two main coal-mining areas, generated one-third of the steam-power in France, though still mainly for draining mines.

The introduction of steam in the Nord was moreover encouraged by the flatness of the land. In more undulating regions, where falling water generated greater power it was a more efficient power-source which could be employed with relatively little capital cost. Although in comparison with steam, water-wheels remained relatively inefficient, improvements in their design and capacity continued, and from the 1830s the installation of turbines designed by Fourneyton — the most successful of which generated 220 horse-power — encouraged enterprises to retain hydraulic power that much longer.

Inevitably as the scale of production increased, and dependence upon water-levels became more unacceptable the large units turned from water to steam-power. The change became almost a pre-requisite of concentration. This is evident in tracing the development of power sources in metallurgy.

The industry was characterised by the coexistence of sources for some time. As late as 1842 2,857 hydraulic machines provided 84 per cent of the motive force consumed but by 1861—5 the number had been reduced to 934 generating 13,693 horse-power compared with 1,369 steam-engines of 31,417 horse-power. 70 per cent of the power consumed was developed by steam-engines (compared with only 40 per cent for French industry as a whole).[27]

In the case of metallurgy, techniques for the recuperation of heat had reduced the costs. The achievements of the railway network from the 1850s and the large reduction in the cost of transporting coal permitted a far more general diffusion of the steam-engine than had previously been possible. Then, and only then came to its end, a civilisation founded on wood and water.

Coal

Coal resources were developed far more slowly in France than in Britain. The shortage of wood was not as serious, and the supply of water-power was far greater. Poor communications limited the market for those mines which were developed thus 'France neither needed nor found it possible to develop the resources quickly'.[28]

There were, however, from quite early in the eighteenth century complaints from wood users about the increased scarcity and rising price of wood. This has been seen as the decisive factor in the development of the Valenciennes field. Coal slowly replaced wood as fuel in glass-, pottery- and brickworks. In the early eighteenth century it was already in use in some forges in the Gier valley although for smelting on an industrial scale it was not introduced until 1785 at Le Creusot.

It seems probable that the complaints of entrepreneurs about wood scarcity were exaggerated. If scarcity existed it was on a limited regional basis in parts of Champagne, Franche Comté and Bourgogne, although rising prices were general.

Scarcity and price rise only slowly reached such proportions as to stimulate a transfer to coal, and this in spite of increases varying between 50 and 100 per cent between 1816 and 1843, caused for many establishments by the enforced widening of their area of provisioning and the general consequences this had for costs. At the ironworks of Rive-de-Gier a quintal of charcoal cost 3.50 fr. in 1790, 7.80 fr. in 1830, and 8.25 fr. in 1842 at a time when technical change demanded the use of increased quantities.

The empiricism and routine of mining entrepreneurs and consumers, particularly in the field of metallurgy, the proximity of iron ore resources in most areas to forests rather than coal, the continued availability of large unexploited wood resources, the problems and cost of transporting coal, the unsatisfactory quality of much of the coal mined, all served to restrain substitution.

At Carmaux in the eighteenth century transport costs so restricted markets that the owners of the coal-mines constructed a glassworks to consume its coal, transport costs forming a small portion of the total cost of glass. In a sense coal had to be transformed into glass to permit movement. As in other areas of the economy the stimulus to innovate was muted, and it was only the development of the railways that accelerated change, in this case by providing coal at competitive prices to all places with access to the rails. The *octroi* records of Dijon reveal the substantial increase in use both in industry and as a domestic fuel that this made possible.

The major problem limiting the extension of the use of coal was transport cost. Currents of circulation for any commodity depend upon the existence of markets and means of transport. Even after the development of canals in the 1840s only the Paris and Lyon regions could with facility be provisioned with coal along with the lower reaches of the Seine and Loire, and to a lesser extent Gironde and Adour. These areas were able to import English coal, or coal from the Nord transported by coaster from Dunkirk, although at prices much higher than pit-head prices in French coal producing areas. Transport costs prevented penetration inland. Earlier improvements in canal and road links, along with measures such as the 1761 *arrêt* exempting coal from internal customs, had stimulated production, but only the railways could provide facilities for regular bulk transport. Until then most coal was consumed in the locality of the mine and manufacturers and cities not near mines used little. Coal, which in 1838 cost 8 fr. per ton at Belgian pit-heads cost 37 fr. at Charleville, 45 at Sedan, 50 at Rethel, 65 at Reims and 87.50 fr. in the Haute-Marne, its furthest point of penetration. In 1830, in the Loire basin, it has been calculated that coal doubled in price when transported 48 km. by road or 100 km. by water.

The first railways were constructed precisely to help overcome the previously insurmountable problems of transporting coal. In 1827 a line from St Etienne to Andrèzieux on the Loire, using horse traction was opened. Due essentially to the construction of the line from Alès to Beaucaire on the Rhone, production at Alès, which had been 45,000 tons in 1835 grew to 415,000 tons by 1845. For the mine at La Machine the horse-drawn railway to the Loire completed in 1843 replaced transport by pack-animal or ox-cart, and even then the fact that the river was navigable only in periods of high water during autumn and spring meant that large stocks were accumulated during other seasons. A complete network using steam locomotion was the only answer, with effects on coal consumption and overall economic development which might be suggested by the rapid reduction of coal prices at Marseille from 45 fr. a ton to 25 fr. once rail links were created.

The development of the rail network had important consequences both for the structure of the market for coal and the organisation of the industry. Previously, because of variations in mining conditions, prices had varied considerably between the major coal-fields. Transport costs had been too high to permit movement from areas of low to areas of high price.

As communications improved so competition for markets was extended — for example the small mines of the Centre which traditionally had provisioned the Paris market by use of the rivers Loire and Allier faced from early in the nineteenth century the competition of canal-borne coal from the better-equipped mines of the Nord producing at lower costs. With the development of rail the zone of competition was extended into areas close to the mines of the Centre themselves. The more efficient producers, due to the lower cost of their product, extended their geographical market at the expense of the less efficient, once transport costs were reduced. Thus hopes for a wider market proved unreal for most mines. For others it proved a vital stimulus, their production increasing in direct proportion to the extension of the rail network. The producers of the north were moreover favoured by preferential rail tariff policies because there, unlike in the Massif Central, the railways were competing with the canals for traffic. The stimulus afforded by the increased demand consequent upon the growth in industrial use of coal, and by competition for markets, from British, Belgian as well as internal producers, resulted in efforts to increase the scale and reduce the relative cost of production. Larger and more frequent injections of capital became necessary. Demand, and high coal prices, rising especially steeply from 1852 to 1856–7, encouraged investment in technical improvement. Both consumers and producers benefited from new price structures. In 1847 coal cost 50 fr. per ton at Paris. In 1875 it cost 39 fr. despite the increase in pit-head prices only 10 fr. to 15.90 fr. The consequences of this was to stimulate both demand and supply. Previously techniques had usually been primitive. Whenever possible strip-mining had obviated the need to construct mine shafts but growing demand exhausted surface seams. Mere scratching of the surface with seasonal peasant labour became increasingly inadequate, and was replaced by deep mining. Sub-surface techniques, however, changed little. In the second half of the nineteenth century, production depended essentially on human effort. Significantly, even if geological conditions were better in what was by then the major French coal-field – that of the Nord – they were clearly inferior, and productivity lower than in the Ruhr.

Since 1744 the State's rights over the subsoil had been clearly affirmed, but successive governments had usually protected the interests of landowners by making small concessions to them. A law of 1838 encouraged amalgamation but during the Second Empire it remained government policy, in granting concessions, and through refusing to allow amalgamations, to maintain the fragmented structure of the coal industry in the hope that effective price competition would ensue and reduce general industrial costs. To an important extent archaic, small-scale production survived, but at the side of increasingly large enterprises which symbolised for many the modernisation of the French economy.

The Anzin company was one of the latter sort, founded in 1757 by both the landowners and those granted subsoil concessions. At that time the company controlled 16 pits, employed 1,500 workers, 200 horses and 5 steam-engines and extracted 100,000 tons of coal a year. On the eve of the Revolution a labour force of 4,000 extracted 300,000 tons (out of a French total of about 1 million tons). The period of Revolution and Empire was one of stagnation caused by war, uncertainties concerning ownership, and the competition of Belgian coal. Subsequent growth was especially favoured by its relative closeness to Paris, the major centre of consumption, and reinforced by the opening of the Canal de Saint Quentin in 1810. It was one of the ten companies which in 1840 produced 55.5 per cent of France's total production. Fifteen produced 62.86 per cent. These figures indicate an important degree of concentration. In the basin of the Nord, 5 companies produced 99.3 per cent by value of the production of that area, with one, Anzin contributing 71.8 per cent and by virtue of this determining pricing and wage policies for the whole basin. In the basin of the Centre 4 companies produced 84.6 per cent, in that of the Midi 2 companies 79.1 per cent, and in that of the Loire, the most important coal basin at the time — where 3 companies produced only 40.54 per cent of the total, concentration was at its least intense.[29] During this period besides the Nord which produced almost one-third of the French total and the Loire basin (over half) other basins were of only regional importance. But the contribution of mines like Alès in the Gard, Epinac, Blanzy, Le Creusot in the Bourgogne and Nivernais, the mines of Tarn and Aveyron including Carmaux, of Commentry in Bourbonnais, of Ronchamp and of the Moselle in the east, was of great economic significance, especially for regional development. It should be remembered that due to transport difficulties they were the only source of coal permitting industrialisation in their regions. Industrial development was most rapid in these areas of relatively cheap coal which thus played a significant rôle in determining location both of industry and population. Figures of coal consumption in manufacturing industry and gasworks in 1847, calculated as an average per head of population, clearly reveal this. For France as a whole, 147 kilograms, but for Ariège 10.5, Dordogne 14.8, and Tarn 63.5.[30]

By 1851, nationally the 10 largest companies produced 71.13 per cent of the total, a figure which subsequently fell as the Government acted in 1852 to prevent the establishment of a quasi-monopoly by the Compagnie des mines de la Loire, and as mining activity was extended in Lorraine and in the Pas-de-Calais. These new mines were, however, technically advanced. The overall economic significance of the northern fields was increased by the development of the Pas-de-Calais, which of itself accounted for half the French output by 1886.

Coal productions grew as follows:[31] (in million metric tons)

| 1811 | 0.8 | 1820 | 1.1 |
| 1815 | 0.9 | 1825 | 1.5 |

1830–4	2.0	1855–9	7.6
1835–9	2.9	1860–4	10.0
1840–4	3.5	1865–9	12.7
1845–9	4.4	1870–4	15.4
1850–4	5.3		

By 1910–17 it averaged 39.9 million metric tons per annum. In 1869 when production had reached 14 million tons, it was also necessary to import 6–8 million tons, compared with 2–3 million tons in 1850. The rate of increase of imports was in fact higher than that for national production.

These figures showing the massive increase in use of coal, particularly during the latter part of the nineteenth century reveal that 'the tempo of industrial life had changed suddenly'. The cost of coal was of vital significance in the industrialisation of France. The development of coal-mining was part of the general growth of the economy, stimulated by this, and vitally necessary to its continuation, and particularly to the structural change which resulted in modernisation.

Industrial Geography

The economic geography of France was to be in many ways transformed by the emergence of factory industry using coal to provide motive power. This, combined with the improvement of communications permitted concentrated production to supply enlarged markets.

Even in the eighteenth century some areas had possessed less industry than others, mainly as a reflection of varying endowments in the vital resources of wood and water. This was the case in the Mediterranean south with no forests, most of the Massif Central, already stripped of forests, and the Paris basin. Each region adapted itself as best it could to meet demand using the factors of production locally available.

Enterprises with limited capitals, protected by poor communications from competition, did not have to be too concerned about costs. If raw materials and power resources existed then production was generally possible. Subsequently as trade grew more intense and competition developed it became essential to reduce costs by increasing productivity. The factors of production had to be put to more effective use and rapidly the resources available in many locations began to appear inadequate. New techniques could only profitably be introduced in optimum situations.

Although this process of the geographical concentration of the production of particular goods did not occur to the same extent as in Britain, it nevertheless resulted in a change and displacement in the significance of some industries and of some regions. Major technical innovations did not transform to the same extent the whole national economy. Investments tended to be concentrated in the more attractive sectors and regions — in geographical zones of growth from which change spread.

From the middle years of the nineteenth century if isolated industries survived along the valleys of the Loire and Rhône, in Languedoc and lower Normandy, there were four main industrial areas: in the first place the Paris region with its artistic trades, food preparing industries, clothing, building and small-scale metallurgy; in the departments of the north and Ardennes textiles, mining and small-scale metallurgy; in the Siene Inférieure and Eure, textiles; and along the eastern border of the Massif Central including also the Saône-et-Loire, Rhône and Loire, textiles, mining and metallurgy. Most of this development occurred north of the line of the Loire. The census of 1866 revealed that 28.8 per cent of the working population was employed in industry but that in the north this rose to 52 per cent, in the Seine to 50 per cent, in the Ardennes to 47 per cent and in the Bas-Rhin to 47 per cent. The decline of the south to the profit of the north is an important aspect of the concentration of production, and of the emergence of enormous regional disparities within France.

In the eighteenth century this relative underdevelopment of the south was far less evident. As well as textile towns like Castres, Mazamet, Lavelanet, Agen and Montauban which served also as centres for dispersed rural industry employing wool, silk, hemp, linen and even cotton, there were commonly manufacturers of rope, hats, pottery, tanning, shoe-making, and flour milling. This was small-scale production but its structure, and techniques were no more archaic than elsewhere in France.

Underdevelopment was especially a product of the first half of the nineteenth century. The wars of the Revolution and Empire and the loss of markets which ensued undoubtedly had a very damaging effect on industry in the west and south-west, in Languedoc and the Mediteranean region. The decline of the Atlantic ports, of Nantes and Bordeaux and of industrial activity in their hinterlands caused a ruralisation of large areas especially in the Garonne valley, Brittany, and Normandy. This decline was due not only to the loss of markets during the wars but also to more a permanent shift towards northern Europe of the main lines of communication. The south, and especially the south-west, open to the sea in the eighteenth century, now stagnated whilst industry developed more rapidly in the north and east.

For some time the old industries and existing industrial structure survived. They retained their internal markets for as long as their geographical isolation existed. Artisanal production continued in the main urban centres, and along rivers, using water-power and local raw materials and often inextricably mixed with agricultural life. Survival was possible because isolation provided protection from competition, but failure to adopt new techniques, the absence of the necessity to do so as long as existing market structures survived, meant that once a railway network had been constructed the slow decline evident from the first decade of the nineteenth century would become more rapid save in a few favoured sectors.

Something akin to a vicious circle existed in the earlier part of the century. Poor communications and limited supplies of raw materials had made the south a repulsive milieu for modern industry; because the existing artisanal industry required small markets it meant that technical innovation was not indispensable to it. Industrial forms were adopted to a social context and to market structures, but when improvement of communications rapidly changed the latter competition from more efficient producers drove out of existence many small units before they had time to adapt, before they could accumulate the necessary capital, expertise and will-power.

As the reign of coal and steam began, the traditional resources and their organisation became rapidly outmoded. By the beginning of the twentieth century Languedoc had lost most of its importance as an industrial area, with the exception of a zone around Marseille and in the Rhône, into which easy import of raw materials was possible. In the Dauphiné, from the first two decades of the nineteenth century, industry began to move from the mountains to the plain, from the water-power to the coal and capital resources of the St Etienne and Lyon regions.

The industries of the Massif Central declined as its resources became obsolete. Industry began to move to the north and to Lorraine in the last third of the century and within the Massif there was an evident re-location near to the railway lines.

The relative significance of Normandy as an industrial region similarly declined. In the eighteenth century the province had been one the most industrialised areas of France due to good ports, its proximity to Paris, water-power and wool. The years of war had similar effects to those in the south, and again stagnation and relative decline turned to rapid de-industrialisation from the 1850s, due, it has been suggested, not only to changing market structures, but an undynamic ethic created by demographic stagnation.[32]

In contrast with these areas of decline, and in large part at their expense, other areas were undergoing fairly rapid industrialisation.

In Paris, if there was a premature development of a modern textile industry in the period 1796–1810, this, in spite of the existence of a large market, was not sustained. The high costs of land, rents and wages provoked its dispersal to the provinces. Until after the

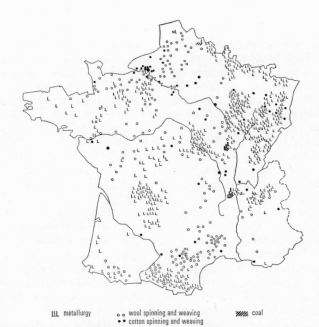

LLL metallurgy   ∘∘ wool spinning and weaving   ▨▨ coal
                    •• cotton spinning and weaving

Map 6 Localisation of Industry in France about 1780
Source: Ch. Moraze, *Les Français et la République*, A. Colin, 1956

▨▨ coal   ▌ metallurgy   • cotton   ▫ wool

Map 7 Localisation of Industry in France about 1880
Source: Ch. Moraze, *Les Français et la République*, A. Colin, 1956

middle years of the nineteenth century, large-scale production remained rare in Paris. Small workshops producing basic necessities and luxury goods proliferated, the latter benefiting from the concentration of skilled workers. In spite of this apparently archaic situation, and indicative of both the limited degree of industrialisation and the industrial significance of Paris was the fact that in 1840–5 Parisian industry produced about 40 per cent, in terms of value, of French production.[33] Particularly from the 1860s the attractions of Paris as a market, the growing centralisation of financial life, of commerce, and of the communications system led to a rapid and considerable concentration of industry in the suburbs and Paris region more generally.

In other regions, and in particular in the Nord and in Alsace this process of concentration was evident even earlier. Both possessed the advantages of available capital, from earlier commercial activity, and in the case of Alsace from links with Swiss banks, and also of cheap labour due to rural over-population. The process of development was similar in both regions, with the development of integrated industrial systems beginning with textile development, modernisation requiring the use of steam-power, the development of coal resources, of machine building capacity, and of iron industries — that is the development of a number of linked industries progressing in part because of reciprocal influences. These were typical poles of growth.

More light can be thrown on the development of industrial geography by considering the development of particular industries.

Textile production had existed wherever the necessary raw materials were available. From late in the eighteenth century the traditional linen and woollens industries began to face competition from cotton. The wars of the Revolution and Empire closed many of their overseas markets, with disastrous effects on some of the western areas in which the rural economy was based on a close association of agriculture and industry.

Progressively, and with greater rapidity only from the 1830s and especially the 1850s there tended to occur a displacement of textile production towards the north-west, north and east. As competition became more intense production declined elsewhere. The woollen centres of the Midi, Dauphiné and Berry, for example, met growing competition from the technically more advanced producers of Roubaix, Sedan, Aubusson, Elbeuf and Reims. This concentration was due to a variety of technical failings which have already been considered, and to changes in the market structure, stimulating larger scale production which required new sources of power, coal in particular, and increased dependence on overseas suppliers of raw materials which were both cheaper and of better quality. This dependence is obvious in the case of cotton, but similarly the woollens and linen industries became increasingly dependent on foreign sources, the former on Argentina and Australia and the latter on Russia and Belgium. Established textiles producing areas close to the coast tended therefore to be favoured. The other major factor was the existence of cheap labour, migrating to the developing factory towns like Lille and Mulhouse, after following an initial professional formation in rural industry. From the 1830s there was a growing public awareness of the development of new modern industrial complexes, and especially of the ensuing social problems.

A similar geographical concentration of production was evident in metallurgy. In the 1780s the major metallurgical regions were lower Alsace and Champagne: on the edge of the forests of the Ardennes and Argonne and on the wooded plateau of the upper Marne; in Franche-Comté along the rivers falling from the Jura and Vosges; in Lorraine, Bourgogne, Berry and the Nivernais. The decisive locational factors were the availability of water for power, wood for fuel, and iron ore. Elsewhere, however, small furnaces and forges supplying purely local needs were common.

By the 1830s a shift was already evident to coal producing areas. In the crucial period of railway construction in the 1850–60s, although iron production increased in all regions under the stimulus of growing demand, the competitive pressures set up tended to enforce integration of production both to increase total production and productivity, and demand a location which reduced the transport costs of raw materials to a minimum. Economic pressures thus stimulated the concentration of both textiles and metallurgy in coal-field areas.

This concentration of industry at relatively few favoured points caused a de-industrialisation of the countryside, but obviously promoted the more efficient use of resources. Its completeness should not be exaggerated, but the changes occurring from around 1830, and especially as a consequence of railway development, were nevertheless decisive in shaping the industrial character and economic structure of France.

In respect of industrial geography the location of coal supplies and the transport revolution led to the disappearance of a number of small industrial centres and of some industries from particular areas, and the creation in other areas of poles of growth to which industries were drawn because of their own needs and because of linked processes of production. In the latter respect industry produced industry at Lyon, Paris, areas in the north, upper Alsace and along the lower Seine. In the west and south, away from port areas, in part because the new transport infra-structure was developed there more slowly, but mainly because of

129

the lack of resources, de-industrialisation occurred, which greatly accentuated the disequilibrium between the two parts of France.

Communications and Market Structures

Industrial location is a function of the nature of demand and of the facility for supply. A link between the two, determining the character of each, is provided by the transport infra-structure, and it is the development of transport which to a large extent made possible and determined the shape of the structural changes in the French economy, and which brought the economy of the *Ancien Régime* to an end.

Awareness of the need to improve communications for both commercial and strategic reasons was evident throughout the eighteenth century, and significant improvements were made. The 1792–1815 period was, in this respect as in so many others, in the economic sphere one of stagnation when only strategic routes were maintained. In the subsequent period, that immediately prior to the construction of railways, substantial canal and road works further developed the creations of the previous century, and made possible, especially in the more favoured regions like the north, the beginnings of industrial modernisation.

By and large, however, before the railway era and its accompanying road developments, markets remained small and relatively isolated, demand limited, and producers disseminated in small units throughout the country, dependent on local resources of raw materials, labour and capital. Even at the end of the eighteenth century 85 per cent of the population lived in the countryside. The demand of this population for industrial products was limited by poverty, and because of geographical isolation it was met primarily by local producers. If economic growth be conceived of as a 'self-reinforcing interaction between agriculture and industry in terms of the demands of each',[34] it should be remembered that although this was a period in which the total agricultural product and the areas under cultivation were expanding under population pressure, agricultural productivity remained basically stagnant before the 1840s. Regional disparities do not obscure a generalised poverty. Average income from agriculture could not therefore rise much, if at all. The limits to the participation of most of the population in sales on the market resulted in a minimal circulation of the money whose possession was necessary to permit the purchase of industrial products.

The clear tendency of prices to rise from early in the eighteenth century to 1817 stimulated increased production in agriculture and increased the revenue of those who were able to benefit from substantial participation in commerce. The purchasing power of a small minority of large landowners and farmers was increased. But rising prices had a reverse effect on the consumer power of the mass of wage earners and peasants who generally bought more food in the market than they sold. The appropriation of much of the economic surplus by a small proportion of the population in the form of agricultural profits, rents, tithes, profits of law, etc., if it facilitated capital accumulation and a certain amount of investment in industry, stimulated demand for luxury goods rather than the products of the mass-consumer goods industries whose techniques were susceptible to mechanisation.

The causes of increase in internal demand can perhaps be seen from the case of the Dauphiné. Here the period 1720—40 was one in which good summers and good harvests were rare, agricultural surplus small and demand limited. But in the second half of the century harvest failures became rarer, and as a consequence there was more frequently a surplus for the peasants to sell, the money being used to buy textiles and the products of forges. This situation made demographic growth possible, and through this and increased prosperity stimulated industrial growth, but only within the narrow limits allowed by low agricultural productivity and the continuing difficulties in the area of marketing. These defects in the structure of the market economy limited both the pressure and the incentive to innovate.

Before the development of railways, the means of transport were all characterised by slowness, feeble carrying capacity, irregularity and high costs. Costs were further increased before 1789 by the existence of internal customs barriers, although the basic problem would have existed anyway. Yet industrial growth did occur, and most precociously in the sector of cheap textiles production which is most dependent on mass demand. In part this was due to external demand. At the fair of Beaucaire, in which exporters played a prominent rôle sales increased from 14 million livres in 1750 to over 41 million in 1780. Even taking into account the rise in prices this reflected a considerable increase in trade. With the exception of port areas however, exchanges occurred over shorter distances. Markets were local and practically independent of each other. Each had its own fairly complete array of trades, and each experienced not only an economic but a social stagnation, its tastes and needs changing only very slowly.

The question of market structure and the organisation of trade is a basic one. Without changes in these spheres industrial growth is hardly possible.

In most communities the exchange of goods and textiles was, to a considerable extent, by means of barter. Organised commerce was built on a time-space conception very different from ours, which changed only very slowly. Trading occurred at regular markets in larger villages, a number of annual fairs in almost all of them, and more regularly through small-scale merchants and peddlers. Larger-scale traders brought into a given market area those goods it could not produce itself. The volume of trade tended to grow from early in the eighteenth century. This and the growing zones of action of many producers indicate that a certain, however limited, improvement in transport facilities was occurring. Freight rates from Paris to Lyon for example declined by 13.3 per cent between 1715 and 1769, and by 33.3 per cent on the Lyon-Orléans route. Rising prices contributed towards making transport costs a less burdensome item of total cost. It was on the flat northern plains where water and road transport were easier and, moreover, in competition, that this particular hurdle was most diminished and a more coherent market began to take shape.

The increase in demand brought about by population growth and changing market structures was not so rapid that it could not be met by a mere extension of existing production techniques. In the case of the Lyon silk industry for example the first half of the nineteenth century, as had been that of the eighteenth, was characterised by extension rather than innovation in production, and this was closely linked to the development of commercial capitalism. Entrepreneurs adapted slowly to changing market situations in the manner most obvious to them.

To sum up, the market remained primarily rural, and demand was limited by poverty in the absence of radical structural change in agriculture before the second half of the nineteenth century. To some extent the city tended to replace the fair in its market rôle and demand became more diversified. Urban populations welcomed cottons as an improvement on coarser clothes, and this, together with external trade, had some effect in stimulating the more dynamic sectors of the textile industry. But urban demand shared the same limiting factor as rural: the overwhelming poverty of the majority of the urban population – a situation which was scarcely relieved before the 1850s.

Although the volume of internal commerce was always much greater than that of external, the importance of the latter should not be ignored. It was, at least before the Revolution, the most dynamic sector of the economy. It has been calcuated that external trade between 1716–20 and 1787–9 grew by something in the order of 400–450 per cent, with, on the eve of the Revolution, colonial trade contributing over half.[35]

It was in external trade that the first signs of recovery from the crisis of the end of the seventeenth century were seen, with the foundation of trading companies like the French East Indian Company in 1717–19. Most external trade at this date was with other European countries, and as late as 1775 this was true of 63.2 per cent of the total traffic, but the balance was shifting towards a growing dependence on the colonies. At the same time there seems to have occurred a slowing down in the rate of growth which is clearly evident from around 1760–70, at a time when the reverse was true of English trade and perhaps due to growing competition in international markets. External trade had an undoubted stimulating effect on the French economy and particularly on the development of a rural textile industry. The effects of its growing demand should be considered in comparison with the very slow growth of internal demand.

The effect of the Revolutionary and Imperial wars was to reduce the significance of oceanic trade, and increase dependence on internal demand. To a more substantial extent than previously the demand for industrial products tended to follow the level of agricultural prosperity. The importance of external trade should not however be totally discounted. Trade with the rest of Europe remained important and continued to grow. The sectors of industry included in this trade were forced to modernise their techniques to be competitive, and in turn forced competitors on internal markets to innovate.

A major cause of economic stagnation continued to be the limited geographical areas of markets for mass products. The creation of larger markets stimulated innovation designed to increase productivity and competitiveness by reducing the costs of production.

From the 1830s due to canal and road construction, especially in the north, and in particular from the early 1850s, rapid progress was made towards the establishment of an unified internal market. The work was not finished until the completion of the Freycinet Plan, but already in the 1850s the main centres of consumption like Paris were linked with the main industrial areas. Railway development was of far greater economic significance for France than for England. The geographical area was much more extensive and less well served by water-borne means of transport. However, for essentially political reasons the building of a rail network was delayed. By 1851 there were less than 3,000 km. of railway, and much of this in discontinuous sections divided among many companies. Between 1852 and 1856 the main lines of a coherent network were laid down, and by 1870 there were nearly 20,000 lines in operation. Subsequent construction included many small uneconomic lines, which had however the virtue of ending the isolation of many rural communities.

In 1850 4,271,000 tons of merchandise were moved by rail. In 1865 the figure was 44 million. The volume of road and canal traffic continued to grow although the pattern of movement on them was altered. The railway network was complemented by a telegraph network extending for 41,000 km. by 1870. These developments made possible improvements in the organisation and massive increases in the scale of commerce, and in the demand for industrial goods.

'The railway was the instrument which allowed the capitalist system

133

to spread freely, to extend its influence to all forms of human activity and to impose itself in quick succession on all parts of the country, causing all the remains of older economic structures to collapse.'[36] The statement is somewhat exaggerated, but makes a valid point. The construction of the railway network itself required the accumulation of capital on an unprecedented scale. Never before had so many workers, and clerks and engineers been gathered together, so much metal manufactured, buildings constructed, and building materials produced. The stimulus was enormous and so were the effects. Transport costs were substantially reduced and regularised, instead of fluctuating with the supply and demand for the means of transport. The use of coal and modern techniques was extended both because this now became a practical possibility and because of the establishment of new competitive pressures once the barrier of isolation was removed. Every improvement in communications tended to increase the number of consumers who could be reached by particular enterprises. This extended the geographical range of action, and primarily benefited the more efficient producers who could increase production and compete successfully with the previous suppliers of newly accessible areas.

For the less efficient producers it often became impossible to continue to produce, once market isolation ended. Local consumers abandoned many local products for cheaper goods produced elsewhere. Only consumer inertia, and in some cases the superior reputation of products permitted the survival and in some cases, e.g. Thiers cutlery, extension of sales once the railway had arrived. This creation of a national market created new conditions for producers to work in which for many required rapid modernisation.

In spite of inertia a rapid and extensive change occurred in market structure and consequently the industrial geography of France. More substantial and rapid flows of goods and capital, men and ideas were made possible by the railway and telegraph. A process of selection was under way in which the more dynamic enterprises gradually drove the less efficient out of existence.

Increasingly all geographical areas, and all products, found themselves in a competitive situation in which selling price was the essential factor, as the protection afforded by isolation disappeared. Differential tariffs established by the railway companies to favour transport in bulk and over long distances intensified the capacity of the new form of transport to break down existing market structures.

Improved communications generally stimulated the commercialisation of agriculture. Thus the whole process of structural change in industry and agriculture, in the French economy as a whole, is best conceived of as an interrelated, broad, contemporaneous process, linked to the changes in transport. The declining price of machine-produced goods, especially textiles, the increasing market participation of the rural population, the intensification of agricultural production, the spread of new 'wants' in a population with wider horizons, all served to reduce self-production. The generation of larger surpluses which increased productivity implied, and the more favourable terms of exchange between agricultural and industrial products made possible the accumulation of money for purchases.

Of great significance in the increase of demand were the changes in demographic structure. The population of France had grown from about 18 million in 1700 to about 25 million in 1789 and to 38 million by 1870. It stagnated around 38–9 million between 1865 and 1914. The population grew by only 10 per cent between the censuses of 1851 and 1911, compared with 36 per cent between 1801 and 1851, which itself seems to have been a slower rate of growth than in earlier years. This slowing down limited the growth of internal demand, but of greater importance than numerical growth in stimulating demand is the quality of life of the population, the demand for improvement in its living standards.

Demand was, for one thing, increasingly urban based. In 1851 25.5 per cent of the total population had been classified as urban; in 1861 28.9 per cent; in 1871 31.1 per cent; and in 1881 34.8 per cent.

In the period 1840–80 the urban population rose by about 780,000 per quinquennium. Industry and its workers were replacing the country-side as the major markets, especially as from around 1855 workers, real income tended to increase after a long period of stagnation.

The whole process of growth was visible especially in the new rhythm of commerce, now linked to the inter-connected development of railway, telegraph and banking networks which speeded the circulation of money and simplified the monetary techniques, as for example by the 1865 law on cheques. With a more fluid monetary foundation, and the growing numbers of shopkeepers, wholesale merchants, commercial travellers, and the first chain stores replacing the traditional fairs and pedlars, commercial structures were clearly transformed in the period from 1860–80 and in their turn served to more effectively generate and satisfy demand than earlier forms of commerce.

The changes consequent upon increased demand were immense. The transformation of market structures accompanying the revolution in transport permitted a change in the character of the French economy, permitted industrialisation and effectively ended the *Ancien Régime économique*.

It should not be forgotton though that the structure of the economy had not been completely transformed. The balance had moved decisively in the direction of modernisation but not entirely.

Market imperfections remained the main retarding factors, slowing the diffusion of new techniques. Industrial companies, especially in metallurgy, often engaged in price alignment and the division of markets, whilst competition was further reduced by a common unwillingness on the part of the more efficient producers to squeeze the less efficient out of existence. They preferred instead, at least when demand was high, to accept the high price levels set by the latter.

War and fear of war, served to reduce business confidence, to cause unemployment and reduce demand. The consequences of the American Civil War on the international economy, the national crisis of confidence following Sadowa in 1866 and the expectation and final occurrence of the France-Prussian War were all important in reducing the dynamic for change. The development of agriculture was slower than in England. Migration from the land was most intense, paradoxically, from the more dynamic agricultural areas, leaving large areas of inefficiency, underemployment of labour and reduced rural purchasing power. The habits of life in relatively closed economies, and the patterns of demand created did not disappear overnight. Deeply rooted regional and social tastes made for unhomogeneous markets restricting the potential effects of price competition.

Both consumer inertia and the growth of overall levels of demand for many goods, which the more efficient producers were not always able to satisfy allowed for the survival of many archaic producers.

Economic Cycles

By evening out fluctuations in agricultural prices through the creation of an international market, the transport revolution had the effect of reducing the fluctuations in demand from the rural population for industrial products.

Although substantial variations in the purchasing power of the rural population continued to affect industrial activity, from the 1850s and unlike in any previous period of human history, economic crises were no longer primarily agricultural in character.

The progress of economic change in France can to a large degree be charted in relation to the evolution of crises. Ernest Labrousse revealed, to historians, what had been clear to contemporary observers, namely that agricultural prices tended to dominate economic activity generally in an exchange economy of the type prevailing in France until the middle nineteenth century, i.e. characterised by the high cost of transport, the predominance of bread in the popular diet. According to Labrousse, in this situation the whole economic cycle was dominated by variations in the price of cereals.

Where cereal prices rose by about two-thirds, as they did for example between the seasonal low of 1788 and the maximum of 1789, or by three-quarters, as in the case of rye (a major item in the popular diet), this, coupled with the fact that because of the system of land ownership the vast majority of the population, even rural, found their incomes declining at a time when as consumers they were faced with increased prices, brought about a lessened demand for the products of industry.

The crisis began in the countryside but rapidly affected both rural and urban industries. Each industry reacted in a manner reflecting its particular market structure and the severity of the crisis in its area. Most markets being local in character a description of crises in national terms can be misleading in hiding the countless variations between regions small in area. The analysis of economic crises and their effects, like that of demography, ought perhaps to be conducted essentially at a micro-regional level. To take one example, the industrial crisis of 1819 was due to high cereal prices, but whilst these affected the demand for the products of the Norman textile industry, that for the high quality products of Alsace remained more stable. Most severely affected by crises were the textiles and building industries, by far the most significant industrial employers of labour. In textiles, as demand declined production would be reduced fairly rapidly. Given the small amount of capital invested, the overheads payable when equipment was not being used were minimal, especially in rural industry. Often the merchants organising the 'putting-out' system owned no equipment and now simply postponed distributing raw materials. In both town and country employment declined. The wages of those lucky enought to remain in employment were reduced. Urban incomes, and consequently demand in urban markets, were reduced, whilst the income from rural industry on which so much of the rural population depended declined to a proportionately greater extent, at least where they were producing for internal markets. The building industry seems in its fluctuations to have been even more hypersensitive than textiles. The variation in activity between the maximum and minimum has been calculated for the crisis period of 1847–51 as 70 per cent at Paris, 48 per cent at Caen, 40 per cent at Castres, 30 per cent at Le Mans, 28 per cent at Dijon, and 24 per cent at Toulouse.

During any single crisis, some regions or industries enjoyed a relatively sheltered position reflecting local economic conditions. Ports engaged in importing foodstuffs were an obvious beneficiary of the crisis situation. Harvest failure, in requiring imports of food, tended to cause balance of payments difficulties and reduce internal monetary flows. From this and the lack of confidence bank credits were reduced

137

creating a generalised financial crisis. Recovery came when food supply improved and prices fell. It was not immediate because much of the population remained impoverished and indebted.

This is a simplified picture of cyclical economic movements designed to identify the most significant factors. There were other causes of industrial crisis. The failure of industrial crops or diseased animals increased raw material prices and the price of goods whilst demand was consequently reduced. Sugar, linens and leather are obvious examples of industries dependent upon agriculture for raw materials.

War, even where, as in the eighteenth century, rarely resulting in invasion and physical destruction of factors of production; disrupted markets and affected business confidence. During the Revolution and Empire this was especially evident. Balance of payments difficulties, military needs and hoarding contributed to causing a deflationary situation in 1802–7 and 1812–15 which was complicated by occasional harvest failures, for example in 1811–12.

Thus, besides fluctuations due to cereal harvests, there were those due to political and financial causes, although these were often interlinked. Autonomous commercial crises were of limited significance. Monetary supply, credit, the activity of banks and speculators were all factors in the situation, but in the period c.1730–1850 monetary supply was not a deflationary factor of as much significance as earlier, whilst economic concentration, although developing, had not yet created a market and financial structure susceptible to national and international crises of confidence, and in which mistaken investment decisions in a highly capitalised, leader-sector of industry, could by means of overproduction engender a more general crisis. In short nothing had occurred to fundamentally transform the classical mechanism, in which what counted were, on the supply side, variations in the cost of production due especially to the price fluctuation of textile raw materials, and on the demand side, the age-old crises of subsistence.

Change is more evident in the post-1817 period than earlier. As previously, and for the same reason, i.e. the slowness of structural change in the economy, agriculture and the price movements of agricultural products dominated economic activity. The period has, however, been labelled that of an intermediary economy in which industrialisation was occurring more rapidly than before and economic crises bore increasingly the imprint of causes typical to the modern industrial economy. The crisis of 1867–8 was to be the last in which harvest failure had generalised effects on the economy of the type we have described. The effect of movements of grain prices on the demand for textiles, for example, appreciably declined from the creation of the basic railway network in the 1850s.

The chronology of crisis in the Dauphiné described by Pierre Léon illustrates this process of transition from the economy of the *Ancien Régime* to that of an industrial society.[38] Here the crisis caused by the poor harvest of 1827 was intensified by a crisis of industrial over-production developing from 1825–6, that of 1828–32 similarly, whilst in the crisis of 1837–42, the commercial element took first place amongst causes. This crisis began at a time when food prices were low and followed the financial and commercial crisis of 1836 in England which affected sales by May 1837, indicative of growing dependence on wider markets. This crisis was increased by an agricultural crisis from 1839–40.

Léon contrasts the crisis of 1829 with that of 1839–40. In the first a restriction of credit due to loss of confidence aggravated a crisis of a traditional type, but was of limited significance because with an undeveloped banking network manufacturers and merchants depended only to a limited degree on bank credit. In the latter case, because the relationship between banking and industry was already clearly more developed, the effects of a restriction of credit consequent upon an international financial crisis beginning in America were far more serious.

The industrial region of the Nord during the two decades from 1830 illustrates a similar development. The frequency of crisis is striking. Ten of the eighteen years of the July Monarchy were years of difficulty. Also striking is the fact that although these crises can in part be related to international economic developments, the relationship between bad harvests and industrial crisis remains clear – thus 1830–1, 1839–40, 1845–6. Cyclical movements peculiar to industry gradually complicated the structure of crises.

The crisis from 1846 can perhaps be described as the last major crisis of the pre-industrial economy in France. The *Ancien Régime économique* ended with a bang; with a crisis combining harvest failure with the results of a loss of confidence in an industrial system developing rapidly to meet the needs set up by the railway system under construction.

Industrial crisis would quite likely have occurred in 1846–7 even without an agricultural crisis. A financial crisis in England led to the withdrawal of large English capitals invested in French railway shares and caused a generalised loss of confidence and shortage of credit. After a period of rapid expansion to meet the demands of the railways, the metallurgical industry found the flow of orders drying up, so the crisis was extended. A lack of demand for the products of the textiles industry was observed in the Bas Rhin as early as 1844, due initially mainly to high raw cotton and wool prices. In the Lille-Roubaix-Tourcoing complex a depressed situation from summer 1845 was blamed on English competition, overproduction and insufficient credit. All these causes, however, were soon overtaken by the fall in demand consequent upon harvest failure. In 1848 revolution and the subsequent years of political unrest added political elements to the situation. Even when harvests improved, business confidence remained at low ebb until the political situation was stabilised by the *coup d'état* of December 1851. However, a new period of bad harvests, 1853—7 prolonged economic difficulty, making the long period 1846—57 one of continual crisis which had a prolonged after-effect on the economic structure. By eliminating marginal producers and stimulating technical improvement to reduce costs in a period of difficult sales, this period at mid-century accelerated the transition to a national market structure which railways would make possible.

With the railways, the development evident due to the slow improvement of communications since the 1750s was completed. Fluctuations in agricultural prices were evened out, and the consequentt fluctuations in demand for industrial products due to the inflated cost of foodstuffs all but eliminated. This was to be reinforced by improved living standards and a less inelastic demand for cereals. Also because of railway development the markets for industrial products were extended, particularly for the more efficient producers. The internal market became increasingly urban as migration transformed the population structure, a development which further reduced dependence on agricultural prosperity.

Efficient communications created new market structures, and intensifying competition required a concentration of production. Efficient communications strengthened the links of interdependence between the various sectors of the economy — industrial, commercial, financial and agricultural — even if reducing substantially the effects on the economic cycle of the latter. A growing number of factors served to increase the aspect of uncertainty and instability in the business situation; the increased scale and complexity of business operations; the growing difficulty of estimating demand once it ceased to be primarily local in character; the growing requirement for large capital investments, and dependence for these on sources external to the particular business; and dependence on international sources of raw materials.

A number of developments exemplified this. Thus in textiles the American Civil War engendered crisis by causing a shortage of raw cotton and high and continually fluctuating prices. The weakening of the competitive position of cotton textiles stimulated the expansion of woollens and linens, both of which proved to be over-extended once the supply position in cotton returned to normal. More generally the frequent tendency for over-production to occur as competitors sought to over-reach each other led as a consequence to continual anxiety amongst businessmen and to a loss of confidence in the future at the merest hint of possible difficulties. The most cautious restricted production and investment, the most adventurous found themselves starved of credit as banks anxious to preserve liquidity became extremely reluctant to lend.

Capital Investment

The behavious of entrepreneurs seems to have been determined essentially by the opportunities for profit available as both regional and national level — the *patronat* of Alsace and the north being especially favoured by circumstances, capital was transferred from land to industry, a better area of profitable investment opportunities. Although ownership of land remained the hall-mark of success, it became gradually more of a symbol of success and increasingly less attractive as a source of wealth.

Profits being the cause of investment and the source of capital it is worth briefly looking at the variations in profit levels. From 1732 there occurred a long period of slow rise in prices and revenues, interrupted by the rapid inflation of the revolutionary period but resuming from 1798 to about 1817—20. Due to imports of bullion from South America the monetary stock perhaps doubled in this period, and the effects of this on prices were increased by the growing use of bills of exchange and other commercial paper. Evidently this stimulated enterprise, but the effects were limited by an economic and social structure which restricted demand, and also by the still slow circulation of money throughout the economy.

If the effects of falling prices on profits during the period 1817 to 1851 were partly offset by more rapid mechanisation and particularly by pressure on wages, that is by efforts to reduce costs, it remained true that profitability as a lure to investment was less significant than it would be in the succeeding period of 1851 to 1873. Then again, due to the influx of bullion, but also now to structural changes in the economy permitting the more rapid circulation of money and increased demand, prices rose by some 30 per cent, and profits even more rapidly.[39] In this new situation, where railways and the reduction of tariff protection were transforming market structures, continued and increased profitability was increasingly associated with continuing and ever more frequent modernisation of the techniques of production, both to counter competition and make the most of new opportunities. This process, evident especially in the larger enterprises, was forced on the smaller ones.

Before the last two decades of the eighteenth century little technical change had occurred since the Middle Ages. In particular industry was still dependent on water- and wind-power and wood as fuel. The basic changes that now took place were two: the use of energy produced by steam, and the widespread introduction of powered machinery – with coal as fuel. Prior to this empiricism rather than science dominated, techniques being transmitted orally from father to son and master to apprentice. Government efforts to stimulate technical innovations, particularly the introduction of new English techniques, met generally with apathy and lack of capital. The value of new machines had to be proved to the mass of entrepreneurs by long experience. If during the period of 1780 to 1792 their use was spreading, the whole process of diffusion was slowed by the uncertainties of the years of revolution and Empire. The basic English inventions were known before the wars imposed isolation, but it was not just the caution of entrepreneurs that restrained changes. The fear of unemployment caused by machines and the widespread luddism of the 1780s also played their part. Inventions existed, the will to innovate to reduce costs of production did not. This will could only be created by the prospect of larger profits, or the fear of competitors, both external and internal. Both these stimuli were essentially creations of a new market structure of increased demand and increased competition; both developed with the means of communication. By the end of the Second Empire, if archaic techniques continued to coexist with modern, the predominance of the latter could not be doubted. Substantial capital investment had secured the re-equipment of the most dynamic sectors of industry. The statistics, which show a slowing of overall industrial growth in this period, tend to conceal this vital fact.

Economic activity depends not only on market structures and the situations they create, but on human enterprise and the ability to be creative in these situations. Economic development in France has often been considered in relation to the supposed virtues and vices of a real and/or potential entrepreneurial class, and judgement of economic activity has often taken on moral overtones. It has been condemned for its lack of modernity. Values and activities, to be considered in a meaningful historical manner must, however, be discussed in relation to a total social context.

Much has been made of the adverse effect on capital accumulation, the direction of investment, and economic growth, of the prevalence of aristocratic values, enshrined in the judicial concept of *dérogeance*. Prior to 1789 loss of noble status occurred when a nobleman engaged in activities whose essential purpose was the making of money. It was considered that occupation should be solely for honour and this was gained primarily through service to the king, especially in the field of arms. Although, as we shall see, significant forms of economic activity were conceived of as honourable and loss of noble status in the case of old-established families was during the lifetime of the transgressor alone it remained true that degrading activity was avoided, and not simply because of questions of honour but, before 1789, from fear of losing the very real tax privileges noble status guaranteed.

Even if, during the eighteenth century a significant change in values occurred which reflected the growing prestige of economic activity, most nobles of old family retained their contempt for business whilst the merchant or financier, ennobled by purchase of office, or who merely aspired to a style of life associated with landownership, more than any other felt bound to renounce activity incompatible with his new and hard-won position in society. This ethic of the gentleman required premature retirement from business and the movement of capital out of industry and commerce. The situation was not peculiarly French, nor did it end in 1789, but it was the inevitable product of the status system and investment opportunities offered by a fundamentally agrarian society.

The major form of wealth until the latter part of the nineteenth century was land. The possessing class, whether noble or bourgeois in status, was wealthy primarily because it owned land, and accumulated capital primarily from revenues gained from the land.

Urban bourgeois, in cities like Orléans seem to have possessed relatively little wealth. At Reims, during the first Empire, amongst a large number of small manufacturers and merchants, only three or four assumed an economically significant position, and possessed real wealth.

The dynamism of wealth varies with the structure of society and with that of capital. The scale of enterprise must depend in large part on market structure. Where markets were geographically restricted and purchasing power low, investment opportunities were correspondingly reduced. This, rather than social ethos, determined the rate of economic growth. Within the limits imposed by social structure the possibilities offered for profitable investment and awareness of their existence counted increasingly more than concepts of honour.

Most nobles and landowners undoubtedly remained strangers to industry and trade. Most lacked the capital and information which might have persuaded them that honour could be worth compromising. It has been observed that even the participation of nobles in industrial activity often proceeded from an essentially feudal spirit. In one respect it had the same causes as the more familiar seigneurial reaction, in the need to increase revenue in a period of rising prices. In another it often involved the exploitation of the resources on one's land — and especially

143

water and wood. Whatever the motives, this led to the development of a 'bourgeois' attitude towards business. That its social purpose was reactionary, in the effort to secure the economic underpinning of social status and rank is another matter.

Successive Governments, in an effort to encourage economic development, introduced edicts which exempted from *dérogeance* such activities as sea-borne commerce (1669), large-scale commerce (1701), mining, glass-making, and metallurgy (1722). Conversely, successful merchants were ennobled.

The nobles in industry enjoyed several advantages over their non-noble competitors: as proprietors of running water and forests; as frequent beneficiaries of concessions from the Government of royal rights over the subsoil.

The bourgeois owners of *seigneuries* and land enjoyed similar benefits, but in Hainault at least seem to have been more reluctant to develop the full potential of their land then nobles, probably because they were less sure of their social status. Nobles also enjoyed tax privileges and the benefit of contacts in Government, which brought exemptions from regulations, subsidies and orders for goods produced.

These advantages ensured a predominant rôle for nobles in industrial sectors such as mining, metallurgy and glass-making. In industries characterised by rapid growth their presence was important. According to the enquiry of 1771–80, of 603 forge-masters in 21 generalities 304 were nobles (50.4 per cent), whilst the Church owned a further 57 enterprises (9.4 per cent). The figures cover a variety of situations and in many cases the landowner simply owned a forge, and by renting it to a manufacturer thus enjoyed a 'rentier' revenue. Nevertheless this interest did represent a capital investment. Others were more deeply involved: the Duke de Penthièvre in Champagne; the Marshal de Lorges and Comte d'Orsay in Bourgogne; de Wendel and Dietrich families in Lorraine; in mining, the Prince de Croy at Anzin, Castries at Alès, the Solages of Carmaux; in textiles, the Duke d'Orleans at Orléans, and in Alsace the Baron de Waldner and the Duke de Deux-ponts represent the effort of the *grande aristocratie* to retain and extend its economic pre-eminence.[40]

The extension of shareholding through the multiplication of *Sociétiés de Commerce* made possible the participation of more passive elements in investment and its fruits. These possibilities seem especially to have been realised by the court nobles resident at Versailles and elsewhere by robe aristocrats — again the explanation rests on information and opportunity. This in a sense represents the embryonic development of the joint stock company more typical of late nineteenth century capitalism.

Noble participation in commerce, for example in the very profitable

144

slave trade, tended to be limited to the purchase of shares. The typical merchant was bourgeoris and in the given state of economic development, with limited industrial concentration, commercial activities still dominated productive ones. Once the profitability of industry increased, merchants transfered capital from commerce to industry and were able to increase their dominance over industrial activity. It would however be unwise to underestimate the contribution of artistocrats to economic development, both as entrepreneurs and *rentiers*. For as long as the economy remained dominated by agriculture, that is until the second half of the nineteenth century, the significance of investment by landowners remained great. As steam-engines and coal replaced water-power and wood, landowners supplied more exclusively capital rather than natural resources and enterprise. This can be seen clearly in Normandy, where the large number of water-mills, constructed on estates after the Revolution tended to go out of use from the 1850s. But in the developing sectors of industry, coal-mining, metallurgy and to a lesser extent textiles and chemicals, expansion was insured by a combination of very wealthy nobles and bourgeois, representing a social polarisation between the rich and others — the latter including poor nobles as well as poor commoners.

It was technical change which created the modern entrepreneur. Mechanisation demanded larger capitals, more technical knowledge and a closer involvement in the day-to-day organisation of production. It was the family business, growing by means of re-investment of profits, devoting all its energies to survival and growth, and in a competitive situation forced increasingly to modernise or disappear, which typified French industry in the first half of the nineteenth century.

Due to the small initial capital required this *patronat* was recruited from a wide section of society, but given that few workers could hope to accumulate even a small capital, industrial entrepreneurs were often former 'putting-out' merchants, involved in rural industry or else owners of small urban workshops.

Some of these enterprises succeeded, due to a combination of practical hard-headedness and fortunate circumstances. Some grew into large-scale producers. Thus at Reims during the First Empire one could clearly differentiate from the large number of small producers the three or four large who engaged in mechanised production. In the textile industry of the north, the character and circumstances of the entrepreneur engaged in rural industry in Picardy and Avesnois differed markedly from those of the factory-owners of Lille, Roubaix and Tourcoing.

More generally, as the century progressed — and the process was especially evident during the Second Empire as market structures rapidly changed — a concentration of ownership or of control occurred, even in

145

the textiles industry where family concerns remained of greatest significance. Particular industries were increasingly dominated by the few large enterprises, whose price competition fixed prices for the whole industry, for example by the joint stock company, often administered by directors with national influence, men like Schneider of Le Creusot or Casimir Perier, and later Thiers in the Anzin mining company. In such companies, the patron had become a financier, using his contacts and expertise to acquire interests in a variety of companies, leaving day-to-day administration to managers and engineers. This was a new type of capitalism, with a new kind of capitalist. A new aristocracy was being created, which whilst being numerically small yet dominated the far more numerous industrial bourgeoisie, still mainly involved in family businesses.

The point has often been made that company law, as defined in the code of Commerce of 1807, was not particularly favourable to the mobilisation of capital. By this code certain distinctions, essentially those between societies of persons and those of capital, already made during the eighteenth century, were clarified. The principle of limited responsibility, both in partnerships and wider associations was firmly established. However, the formalities required before authorisation was granted, including investigations by a Committee of the Conseil d'Etat — the time consuming and expensive character of this process undoubtedly increased reluctance to apply for authorisation.

Before the 1860s, joint stock companies (*Sociétés anonymes*) remained rare. Even in the period 1840–50, when 19,258 companies were founded, only 221 of these, that is 1.05 per cent, were established on this basis. The reason of this should however be looked for less in the restrictive nature of the legal framework than in the character of the economic structures.

Given the restrictions on the scale of production imposed by market structures large capitals were not always necessary, and individual enterprise remained the norm. Where large capitals were required shares were floated with high values, purchasable only by the wealthy. Companies issued in general only a small number of shares to facilitate continued control by the original directors. The floating of shares, before the railway area, did not consequently involve a mass appeal. It remained an attempt to raise money from a narrow geographical area and social group. The widening of the appeal beyond the ranks of family and friends was a gradual process, acceptable only as an unavoidable necessity, as the costs of industrial re-equipment grew.

The *Société en Nom Collectif,* with all its participants liable for the total debt, remained the most usual form. Liability in practice required that each member had confidence in his fellows, a fact which tended to restrict membership to three or four, mobilising a limited capital, and usually with an ephemeral existence. But the *Société en Commandite,* a form of a limited partnership in which the distinction was made between those responsible for the administration of the company, and a species of sleeping partner, enjoying limited liability, permitted capital accumulation and expansion within the limits set by general economic development. The practical evolution of this form made it in many instances a disguised form of joint stock company, used, in the Dauphiné for example, in the metallurgical, mining, silk and paper industries.

Compared with 157 authorisations of joint stock companies, with a capital of 392 million francs, in the period 1826–37, that of 1,839 of these limited partnerships with a capital value of 1.2 milliards was recorded.[41] The problem of legal liability was by these means solved in France long before it was in England.

Joint stock forms had been taken prior to the 1840s mainly by banks, assurance and gas companies. The large capitals required for railway construction obliged growing recourse to the mass of small investors and therefore the issue of lower value shares and also of fixed interest debentures in an effort to reduce speculation. This created the habit of investment and in proving the value of the joint stock company as a means of mobilising capital, at a time when the pressures for industrial re-equipment were growing, established the need for legislation less restrictive in character.

Thus a law of 23 May 1863 allowed the formation of joint stock companies without authorisation, providing their capital did not exceed 20 millions, and a law of July 1867 abolished this last restriction. The effects, not only of this, but the changing volume of investment in the economy and the growing modernity of financial structures can perhaps be judged from the fact that on the Paris Bourse in 1851 118 shares were quoted with a capitalisation of almost 11 milliards, whilst by 1869 this had risen to 307, capitalised at 31 milliards.[42]

Investment in industry, as opposed to land or state funds, is based on a belief that higher returns are likely. It predicates a new awareness of investment opportunities, and changing attitudes towards them, involving not only economic calculation but broader social attitudes, on the part of both entrepreneurs and outsiders to whom appeals for loans and investments are made. It requires, beyond a certain scale, a more deliberate, organised, channelling of funds to where they are required, if growth is to be sustained.

During the eighteenth century the capital requirements of most enterprises were small. At the end of the century, according to one estimate, the vast majority had capital values of less than 75,000 livres. Large capitals were, and this is symptomatic of the whole future development, most apparent in mining and metallurgy — thus the mining company of Anzin had an estimated capital of 9,270,000 livres in 1781.[43]

The initial investments required were normally small. Too large perhaps to make social promotion of the worker an easy affair, but sufficiently low for a mass of men with small capitals to enlarge these by industrial activity. As late as 1840 it was possible to set up in the weaving of cloth with about 3,000 fr., due to the lack of mechanisation. Probably the easiest place to start was as a merchant organising rural industry. Here the workers themselves usually supplied the equipment needed, which minimised the capital investment required of the entrepreneur.

The vast majority of businesses were family enterprises, using the savings of family and perhaps friends, and growing, if at all, by means of the re-investment of profits. As we shall see later, self-investment was usually a necessity, given the general unwillingness of those with capital to lend or to risk it in the insecure world of the small business-man. But the whole outlook of men who had laboriously built up an enterprise by their own endeavour was one which forbade appeals to outside investors. Debt might be regarded both as immoral and dangerous to independence and survival.

Examples of this kind of psycho-social tendency are numerous across the whole spectrum of French industrial life, from the textile *patronat* of the north to the technically more advanced Alsatian industry. Here, exceptionally, mechanisation occurred rapidly from 1804—10 by means of heavy borrowing, on the Bâle capital market. But after the economic crisis of 1826—8, which was caused in part by the excessive immobilisation of capital in stock and debt servicing, a successful effort was made to reduce indebtedness and rely on self-financing for further development. Even in coal-mining — in the development of the coal-fields of the north, and as late as that of the Pas-de-Calais during the Second Empire — influenced perhaps by the attitudes and habits of the textile entrepreneurs of the region who provided much of the capital and administrators, capital sums at foundation remained relatively small, the number of shareholders limited, in this case by a desire to see a rapid increase in the value of shares and high dividends. Growth occurred by means of re-investment of profits. Increasing demand made for large profit margins in many cases which facilitated this. The rate of profits in textiles in the first half of the nineteenth century has been estimated at 20—30 per cent, high enough to permit the self-financing of rapid expansion.

There is no doubt though, that as techniques improved, as the scale of production became larger, and as the relatively static artisanal world gave way to a more competitive and more dynamic industrial development, the level of investment required to maintain competitiveness increased and recourse to outside investment became increasingly necessary.

For the larger enterprises of earlier years a major problem, where economic exchange and cash flows were limited, was always a lack of liquidity, a shortage of the working capital necessary, for example, to pay workers. This had often made the call for external investment or loans an unavoidable necessity. But from the 1820s and especially the 1850s the process of industrial re-equipment was setting up demands for capital on scale never experienced before, even if the necessity to attract outside capital was still conceived of as a last resort.

This new and pressing level of demand was most clearly evident in the expansive years of 1852–7, and particularly 1854–7, years of railway construction and the transformation of heavy industry. At the beginning of the upturn, the demand for capital was restrained by the return into service of previously under-used productive capacity, but the keenly felt incentives and pressures of economic growth, the unification of the national market and tariff reform seemed to require further concentration and modernisation.

New techniques were expensive. Thus in 1853 at Pont l'Eveque a new water-wheel cost between 6,000 and 12,000 fr. and a hundred horse-power steam-engine necessary to supplement water-power to maintain continuity of production in time of low water cost 200,000 fr. In metallurgy, too, there are similar examples of growing costs: the primitive Catalan furnace had cost 25,000 to 30,000 fr., a blast-furnace, using charcoal fuel, 50,000 to 100,000 francs, but one using coke 200,000 fr.; and with increase in the scale of production came also larger investments in raw materials, wages, etc.[44] The new investment levels were most evident in heavy industry, but affected also large numbers of textile firms.

In this new situation, where the protective isolation of regional markets rapidly disappeared, competition and consequently modernisation were inescapable. The penetration of new techniques, whose financing was beyond the means of individuals or small groups, of new forms of company organisation, better adapted to commercial and financial management, became far more rapid. Self-investment remained generally the ideal, even in large enterprises, but investment decisions could not always be postponed to await the accumulation of profits.

Did sufficient capital exist, and was it effectively mobilised to meet these increasing needs?

A variety of factors helped to shape investment decisions: the desire for revenue, for security, for social status – and also inertia. Save for a small minority, of the very wealthiest, most possessors of capital were ill-informed and if they made investment decisions these reflected the broad consensus of opinion amongst investors. They followed like sheep. Major changes in the pattern of social investment occur only as a result of the appearance of new and, at least apparently, much more profitable investment opportunities, creating for the moment a heightened interest and more reflective attitude on the part of investors.

The supply of capital available for investment and the form investment takes must in large part reflect the existing economic structure. Prior to large-scale emigration land values and revenue generally were increasing as competition to own or lease land increased. This fact made land ownership profitable and acted as a major disincentive to investment in industry or commerce.

The importance of social structure, and patterns of land ownership have also been stressed, as factors determining the way in which the monetary surplus generated by agriculture was used. The large proportion of peasant small owners, saving to buy land, must have immobilised large quantities of money.

The period of rising prices in the eighteenth century was one of rising profits and a more rapid rate of capital accumulation, in all sectors of the economy. How much of this capital was invested in luxuries, in land, or in state loans, it is impossible to judge, but it does seem to have been easier to obtain capital for industry and commerce than ever before. The economic behaviour of this period can only be judged in relation to its opportunities, awareness of them and social aspirations. Examples of business failures were too common to make industrial investment an attractive prospect for many of those with capital to spare. Much of the capital employed in industry and commerce had simply been inherited, its initial form being thus determined by a previous generation. In addition there were investors attracted by the risks and possibly high rewards of speculation, those with so much capital that they could afford to risk a little, or else men with resources on their land waiting to be exploited, as was the soil itself. Investment patterns need to be examined at local and regional levels, for just like other markets, that for capital was fundamentally localised before the railway era. For the majority, even of wealthy men, land provided an adequate income, prestige and security for old age, and a prestigious inheritance for one's children.

This was the main factor which shaped investment, determined by the deisre to create a secure patrimony for the family, with security rather than high revenue as the basic aim. Only once this had been achieved did any surplus become available for more adventurous investment, that is speculation.

The Revolutionary and Imperial periods temporarily increased the attractiveness of land as an investment by reinforcing the desire for security, and increasing the opportunity for purchase of land. Rather

than the destruction of seigneurial privilege or any reduction in the
social prestige conveyed by land, it was the growth of investment
opportunities in subsequent years which speeded up the reorientation
of investments. This process was most evident in Paris, where greater
awareness of new opportunities existed, due to the concentration there
of financial enterprise. The social élite was able to make investments in
industry which were both secure and more profitable than land. The
mass of small investors, less well informed, were often less successful.
Other centres, the Atlantic ports for example, which had disposable
capital with the decline in colonial trade adopted a more traditional
pattern of investments in land or local commerce.

The whole process was accumulative — the economically more
advanced areas provided opportunities for investment and developed
ever more rapidly, whilst the more isolated and economically backward
areas tended to stagnate and fall further behind. Industrial investment
in Dauphiné, for example, which had depended on the revenues of
landowners, became increasingly inadequate in the last quarter of the
eighteenth century, as technical change began. The region was one
largely of mountains and of a poor agriculture, so that the revenue
drawn even from large properties was limited. Beyond a certain technical
level, and level of investment, this limit to capital accumulation served
to obstruct modernisation.

Examination of the wills of the wealthiest bourgeoisie in Paris in the
first half of the nineteenth century revealed that about 55 per cent of
their wealth was held in liquid forms of capital. Lyon and Lille soon
revealed similar patterns. Other provincial centres, such as Toulouse
(40 per cent in 1850), were more backward with additionally much of
their liquid capital held in the traditional form of state stock.

One estimate of the structure of investments, using information on
inheritance, indicates the following:[45]

	1851–5	1856–60	1861–5	1866–70	1871–5
Stocks and Shares	6.9	5.2	5.7	5.8	8.6
Other moveable property	25.9	37.9	30.5	39.1	36.2
Total moveable property	32.8	43.1	44.2	44.8	46.8
Total fixed assets	67.2	56.9	55.8	55.1	53.2

The exactness of the statistics is ppen to question, but they do reveal a
clear shift in investment preferences.

In a number of ways railway development was to be decisive in
shaping the evolution of investment. It helped create the habit of
investment in industry, especially once state guarantees secured
dividends. The broad economic effects were of course decisive — the
creation of a national market required modernisation. The process of

industrial re-equipment, which was already well under way in places like Alsace, was extended and intensified, providing for the first time a large number of investment opportunities. As the scale of industry increased, if self-financing remained the ideal, it became less and less possible.

Financial Institutions

To what extent did new financial institutions develop to meet those new needs? Before the 1860s the banking system was characterised by three essential traits: geographical fragmentation; an orientation towards commerce rather than industry; and the involvement banks with only very narrowly limited social groups. The structure of the banking system in effect, in its archaisms, merely reflected those of the general market. Industry and trade developing only slowly, because of the lack of effective demand, did not require a developed system of finance.

Capital, for long- and short-term industrial and commercial needs, was amassed through a variety of customary and interpersonal contacts at a local level, creating a network which because of its private character is difficult to clearly outline.

Professional banking functions were carried on by individuals, engaged also in a variety of other occupations, including the semi-public financial officers of the crown, money-changers, merchants and notaries. The latter were especially significant in rural areas as recipients of individual savings for investment. The individual functioning as a banker used the money entrusted to him as if it were his own. The whole system depended on the trust of depositors in the honesty of the bankers, and effectively on personal relationships.

The limitations of such a system are obvious. They included the small amount of capital which could be accumulated by the individual banker, the inadequate division of risks because of the geographical limitation of the area of operation and the nature of investment decisions taken on the basis of inadequate information, concerning economic development generally, and often influenced by ties of friendship.

The main activities of such institutions, and of banking generally, was speculation on a variety of merchandises — grain, for example, which was so subject to price fluctuation. This, however, gave way rapidly in the nineteenth century to loans and particularly the discounting of commercial bills. Given the limited amount of capital accumulated, and also the limited demands of small-scale enterprises, both supply and demand were primarily for short-term credits.

Centralisation of the financial market was far from complete, even in the 1840s, when regional centres like Bordeaux, Besancon, Dijon, Strasbourg, Le Mans, Tours and Grenoble remained important as sources of credit. In Paris in 1826 there were at least 220 private banks, a sign of their individual insignificance.

If capitals were of local origin, it is certain that even in the eighteenth century the technical means for transfer existed. They were used for commercial transactions. Yet the capital accumulated in ports like Marseille, Bordeaux, and Nantes was rarely used for industrial development, either locally or elsewhere. The main explanation of this was lack of opportunity, but also of importance was the fact that in the absence of a developed and dependable banking system the basic guarantees of security and information on which long-term investment would depend were lacking.

A certain limited coherence was given to this fragmented financial system, by the pre-eminence of Paris and certain Parisian financiers. Before and after the Revolution this Haute Banque of about a dozen houses prospered from the floating of state loans, and through the rôle of commercial paper drawn on Paris and used throughout France. To a degree Parisian operations regulated the discount rates which primarily determined the credit situation. The establishment of the Bank of France (decree of 28 *nivose en* VIII) institutionalised this pre-eminence. Its council of regents was dominated by the representatives of these great private banks. During the first half of the nineteenth century the outlook of these bankers remained nevertheless that of merchant bankers, properly speaking, interested in state loans, short-term speculations — financiers of the *Ancien Regime* rather than investment bankers. Their influence in a period of monetary shortage and of immobilisation by hoarding and in state loans was vital. The control they exercised over credit was restrictive in the extreme. As late as September 1851 the note issue of the Bank of France was 529 million francs, against a metallic banking of 620 millions.

The rôle played by the Haute Banque in the financing of railway development seemed, however, to herald a new era. The scale of investment was unprecedented, and in the early years, in particular, the rôle of the merchant banks pre-eminent. Thus when the Nord Railway Company was founded in 1845, the initial capital of 200 millions was mobilised by a group which included the merchant bankers Rothschild, Pereire, Hottinguer and Laffitte-Blount.

The creation of branches of the Bank of France had already done something to improve banking conditions. Now in periods of crisis the provinces made fewer demands on Paris; competition forced local bankers to improve their methods. But there were too few of these branches — 30 in 1852 — and the compensatory effect between sectors and between regions with capital surpluses and those needing capital remained inadequate.

The decisive changes came later, with the development of branch banking, made possible by the establishment of rail and telegraph networks, which alone made possible the central control and administration of the banking network. Changes in economic conditions associated with the establishment of a national market limited the disruptive effects of crop variations, and created the greater stability necessary for banking, whilst also stimulating industrial re-equipment and increasing the need for assured sources of capital. The new banks were established only where the railway already existed to develop exchanges and create the need for their services.

In all this the real innovation was not the actual establishment of banks, but the concept of a network, established by means of the reorganisation of existing private banks and the creation of new, making possible an appeal to the whole saving public through a multiplicity of branches. Capital could be effectively drained from areas of surplus. It was used not to meet local needs but wherever the rewards for its employment appeared to be greatest, with this use determined by decisions taken mainly in Paris.

Capitals accumulated over long periods and previously invested locally, particularly in land, were attracted by the hope of larger and more trouble-free returns. At Toulouse, a centre of a predominantly agricultural region, previously only land purchase and lending on mortgage or else state loans had provided outlets. The years following the establishment of branches of the Crédit Foncier (1853), Société Générale (1867) and a local stock exchange (1856) were followed by an extraordinary speculative fever, in direct contrast with the traditional caution. The financial education of the general public was occurring with the increased diffusion of bank-notes, state loans, and railway shares.

As the needs of industry increased, so, though with a certain time lag, new financial institutions developed to meet them. As early as 1825 Laffitte had founded an investment bank (Société Commanditaire de l'Industrie), using only his own capital. This soon failed, due to the illiquidity of his assets in a period of economic crisis. The Crédit Mobilier (1852) was to enjoy a longer success, but ultimately to fail for similar reasons.

In contrast with later years industrial investment during much of the 1850s—60s proved attractive to the new as well as the old banks. In fact the two were inseparable. The old Haute Banque had participated in the foundation of the new credit institutions. In the establishment of the Société Générale in 1863 the participation of men like Bartholomy, Blount, Talabot and Schneider, important in the railway and metallurgical worlds, and close associates of Rothschild, was evident. Through the old merchant banks, the new branch banks, and by means of the Bank of France and its monopoly of note issue, and control of discount rates, the centralisation of financial control was greatly accentuated and the economic power of a small group of men assured.

The most significant investment activity of the banks was undoubtedly railway finance and closely associated with this investment in, and continuous short-term loans to heavy industry, insured by the close personal links between individuals, and the interlocking directorates of a whole series of major banking, railway and heavy industrial companies. In effect this was the creation of the new industrial economy. Whatever their reluctance to accept external interference, metallurgical companies found it difficult to finance, solely from profits, the re-equipment essential for survival. Once engaged in industrial finance, banks found it difficult to disengage without risking the loss of capital already advanced. Thus close links were maintained from the 1840s between Le Creusot, Fourchambault, Wendel, and the banking house of Seillière. Thus the rôle of the Belgian Société Générale in collaboration with the Rothschild banks in developing the ironworks at Anzin, and the Nord Railway Company, pursuing a coherent development of these interlinked interests.

This bank involvement was always limited. In the first place little capital was provided for small, medium-sized or new enterprises. At the most these categories could hope for discount facilities. Banks were prepared to extend credit facilities, essentially to already well-established enterprises, to whom lending did not constitute a risk. This policy inevitably favoured the process of concentration of ownership and production.

The Parisian banks could choose from amongst the whole range of possibilities for profitable lending, and could afford to ignore the small enterprise. Symptomatically they extended little credit to the textile industry, where mainly family firms were even more reluctant than large enterprises to borrow, and if they had to, solicited loans from local banks with a specialised knowledge of the textile industry and with less awareness of possibilities, as well as fewer opportunities, for speculating alongside the larger banks.

Even during the adventurous period of banking involvement in industry from the 1840s to 1860s banks remained reluctant to risk immobilising capital through long-term loans. These were constantly in short supply. The bank failures in the crisis years of 1838–9 and 1846–8 served to remind bankers, if this was necessary, of the risks of illiquidity. The eventual failure of the Crédit Mobilier was merely a confirmation. Although before the banking crisis of 1866 the share-holdings of the Crédit Lyonnais had reached a value of 6.5 million, they were soon to be substantially reduced.

One of the apparent paradoxes of the development of the French financial system was that at the very moment when strong links appeared to have been created between finance houses and heavy industry, seen, for example, in the large numbers of representatives of metallurgy, mining and railways on the boards of the new joint stock banks, and vice versa, at a time also where large capitals were being accumulated, bank lending to industry sharply declined. Substantial re-equipment had been facilitated but substantial archaisms remained.

The already evident reluctance of banks to lend and industrialists to borrow was, in the closing years of the Second Empire, greatly intensified. This was a reflection of growing internal and international political uncertainties. A desire for security restrained that for profitability. The investment portfolio of the Crédit Lyonnais fell from 6.5 to 2.3 million fr. between 1866 and 1869. During the so called 'Grève du Milliard' large capitals were held unproductive, awaiting a future of greater optimism. In the years of international depression, beginning around 1873–4, loans to foreign governments increasingly attracted the banks, because of the large commissions their floating brought. The export of capital was thus encouraged and facilitated. In relation to internal demand capital was anyway over-abundant, given the restraint of industrialists and also on government borrowing after the hectic years of the Empire.

The new banks made innovations in the collection of resources rather than in their employment. But even accepting this, it remained true that without such factors as the extension and intensification of their activity in the field of short-term loans and discount; the mobilisation of capital which they encouraged and the reduction in interest rates that this made possible; the assured supply of working capital; the facilities for the marketing of shares and debentures that they provided; the increased supply and acceleration in the circulation of money in the widest sense which they made possible – without, in short, the establishment of modern banking structures – economic growth could not have been maintained. More than direct involvement, it was the importance of this creation of a banking network which should be stressed. Just to take one illustrative example; the Bank of France discounted bills for 1817 millions in 1847 – the highest total since the beginning of the century; discounted an annual average of 5,571 millions in the period 1851 to 60; and 14,615 millions in that from 1861 to 1875.

The circulation of merchandise by rail required that of money at a comparable speed, in growing volume and cheaply. The means of payment and credit had to adapt to new demands and new rhythms. The dependence of economic growth on circulation of money had long been acknowledged. The Société Industrielle du Departement de la Drôme in 1827, for example, had been established with the hope of

156

providing precisely this aid to industry. One of the characteristics of an underdeveloped economy is the slowness with which money circulates, and the sheer lack of it in other than peculiarly favoured places. Until about 1850, whilst discount had been possible at 3 per cent or even 2.5 per cent at some places at moments of abundance, for example at Paris, a centre of international accounting, where liquidities without employment were found, and at Lyon and Mulhouse, conveniently close to Geneva and Bâle, elsewhere little credit had been available. Generally even in manufacturing towns, commercial paper alone compensated for the shortage and lack of mobility of money. It was usually necessary to borrow from one of the 10,000 or so notaries and at rates of 7 to 9 per cent or higher. This was inevitable when bullion and bank-notes were in short supply and the latter not really acceptable in comparison with gold.

These were all features of the traditional economy, which had restricted economic development by limiting both the demand for goods and the ability to secure credit. The volume and mobility of bank money, increased by the 1856 law on cheques, and the fortuitous contemporaneously increasing bullion supply, made possible the increased circulation of goods and capital, the two being complementary aspects of the same process of growth.

The establishment in 1852 of an authoritarian régime after years of political uncertainty did much to increase business confidence. The world economy, stimulated by an influx of gold from California and Australia, added another encouraging factor to the situation. The basic result of these years, unique in French history, was a threefold revolution in communications, techniques and credit which, in spite of the survival of archaic sectors of the economy, nevertheless served to create a new civilisation.

In comparison with the past, a massive amount of capital was successfully mobilised. Investment in the railway network for example — 282 million fr. in 1847 — declined to near insignificance during the years of the Second Republic, but attaining 131 millions in 1852, 269 in 1853, 339 in 1854 and 496 in 1855. By the 1860s investment had reached levels, judged by the old-established merchant banks and conservative financial opinion generally to be excessive — at 700 millions to 1 milliard annually without counting state loans. In the interests of sound finance interest rates werepushed up and a speculative boom restrained. Fear of war in the 1860s, particularly after the Prussian victory over Austria at Sadowa in 1866 created a mood of great caution amongst investors, who increasingly tended to hold their money inactive in the form of bank deposits. The economic boom of the 1850s—60s was short-lived.

Statistical computations of rates of economic growth do not reveal the exceptional significance of these years. In comparison with the English the French economy remained backward. The agricultural prosperity of the imperial years had made possible the further parcelation of agricultural land. But even here there were signs of economic change, imposed by the establishment of a national market. In this more competitive situation marginal land tended to lose value, and because of new techniques agriculture became slowly more capital intensive. Both these factors tended to encourage a movement of capital out of agriculture into other investments, almost everywhere save in lower Languedoc, where the crises of traditional industry and the prosperity of wine producers encouraged, at least until the vines were ruined by phylloxera, a reverse tendency.

New market structures established by transformed communications created increased demand and growing competition, both stimulating industrial re-equipment, that is creating a growing demand for capital, which for the first time could be adequately mobilised because the new communications permitted the parallel establishment of a credit network. The two combined to accelerate the circulation of capital and cash, and to have such an evident and enormous effect on economic life and the conditions of existence that mentalities were transformed. An accumulative society was created. Growth rather than subsistence was its hall-mark.

The State and the Economy

It would be wrong to link these developments closely to a particular political régime. In Western Europe, given the lead established by Britain they were probably inevitable. Equally it would be wrong to ignore the important rôle of the Second Empire, and of the State more generally in contributing to the establishment of the overall situation in which economic development occurred.

Economic development occurred within a framework of particular but changing political and juridical institutions. The policies of pre-1815 administrations towards industry were far more obviously interventionists than those of their successors.

Direct intervention by the intendants, encouraged by successive controllers generally took the form of the distribution of loans, grants, semi-monopoly privileges, tax exemptions, the distribution of examples of the most advanced machinery, and efforts to attract foreign and especially English specialists: Holker, Milne, and Wilkinson for example. The encouragement of mechanisation was especially evident from the 1770s. In the Dauphiné aid was given to the development of the silk, cotton, hosiery and steel industries. In a period when capital resources were limited this government aid was important. The more dynamic enterprises as well as those whose directors had influence, were encouraged and their innovating example followed by others. In metallurgy in particular, the new enterprises depended heavily on a combination of state aid and orders, but suffered considerably from fluctuations in these, and often delayed payments reflecting the problems of government finance. The most significant aspect of this interventionist policy was less direct, namely the desire of the State to establish improved communications in the interests both of centralisation of authority and economic development.

These policies and the whole tangle of regulations at national and municipal levels, which governments tolerated, if they did not always encourage, have often been presented as gravely restraining the capacity of the French economy to develop.

The corporations which existed in many towns possessed legal power to regulate a trade. These powers were used to limit competition as well as protect consumers. Entry into a trade and the quantity of production were both restricted. Until the 1730s—50s, administrations continued to exert pressure on unorganised professions to form corporations. In the new economic climate developing from this period intervention and controls began to seem increasingly less than necessary. Over-production and social unrest were less likely in a period of economic expansion. Not only did opposition grow, amongst producers and merchants, symbolised by the growing attachment to liberal economic ideas, but this attitude was increasingly shared by administrators. Intendants and the inspectors of manufactured goods were influenced by these new ideas and undoubtedly also by the growing resistance to regulation. However, opposition to change also remained strong, as can be seen from Turgot's attempt to abolish corporations: successful in January 1776, but revoked in August of the same year, though not in its entirety.

In company with changing administrative practice the corporations themselves in many cases changed. Increasingly *Métiers Libres*, less restrictive, replaced the *Métiers Regles*, especially in the more dynamic economic centres, like Nantes. The growth of rural industry, particularly in textiles also evinced the will of commercial capitalism to by-pass restriction.

In many places the revolutionary legislation abolishing corporations and state regulation merely completed a process long under way, a process stimulated by the growth of opportunities for making profits. In many places, especially it seems in the Dauphiné, the majority of trades and workers had never been organised outside the larger centres of population. At Montélimar, for example, of 37 trades 32 had not had a corporate organisation.

The ineffectiveness of eighteenth century regulation made of it a not very significant cause of economic backwardness, and in consequence, one should not exaggerate the significance of the revolutionary legislation abolishing it. Nevertheless, the laws of 2 March 1791 (*Loi d'Allarde*) abolishing corporations, privileged manufactures and state regulation by means of inspection, and of 14 June 1791 (*Loi le Chapelier*) forbidding association between workers or masters as likely to interfere with the free negotiation of contracts, were to be of some economic and much greater social importance in the post-revolutionary period, particularly in their effects on attitudes and social relationships.

In the immediate future state intervention rather than disappearing was intensified. War and internal unrest demanded economic controls, and government intervention was a constant feature of the whole period of Republic, Consulate and Empire, although the intervention of prefects had, because of the approved ideology of economic freedom, to be more discreet and restrained than had been that of the intendants.

With the coming of peace from 1815 direct intervention declined, but certainly did not disappear. The mining inspectors and the engineers of the Ponts et Chaussées assumed many of the functions, previously carried out by *inspecteurs des Manufactures* — exercising controls over forests, mines, furnaces, some machines, and especially communications. Even during the Second Empire, in refusing to allow the free amalgamation of coal-mining companies — even forcing the re-division of the Companie des Mines de la Loire — state intervention, in the supposed interests of preserving competition, prevented the mining industry from enjoying the full fruits of economies of scale. Thus an interventionist tradition survived, partly from habit, partly from necessity, stimulating and organising activity where, particularly before the development of a financial network, and large-scale enterprise, there were no alternative dynamic centres.

Besides forms of direct intervention, government activity impinged on the economy in so many ways. Fiscal policy is one obvious aspect. Taxation, the flotation of loans and sales of office diverted some capital from productive investment, but redirected more into it. The question of consequences is extremely complicated. During the eighteenth century, for example, if internal customs dues and various tolls on road traffic acted to restrain trade, to what extent were these offset by the tax exemptions enjoyed by many towns, and also by the introduction of exemptions from customs dues: coal for example was exempted from 1761 in an effort to increase production. To what extent did the generally low levels of taxation on the profits of industrial and commercial activity ease the problems of capital accumulation?

During the century there was growing dissatisfaction with a taxation system which appeared arbitrary and which by means of indirect taxes on consumption threw such a great burden on the poorer classes, to the relief of the privileged. Arbitrariness was believed to restrain investment, privilege to cause suffering to the masses and excessively low tax receipts for the State. Reform introduced by men like Orry in 1733 and Laverdy in 1767, and taxes like the *dixième, cinquantième* and *vingtième* were partial attempts to reduce these failings.

These efforts were continued during the Revolution, Empire and Restoration, with more success as the capacity for resistance by the privileged classes had been somewhat reduced. The Constituent Assembly went so far in 1791 as to abolish the taxes on consumption, but they were reintroduced in 1804 to meet the growing financial needs of the Empire. Between a law codifying earlier legislation in 1816 and the reforms of July 1914 and July 1917, the basic structure remained unchanged. 46.4 per cent of the tax revenue in 1830 and 54.5 per cent in 1881 were raised by indirect taxation whilst the wealthy classes with political influence remained substantially undertaxed in relation to their income and capital.[46] Although the basic characteristics of the tax system reflected the strength of class privilege, there were also features of general economic and social development which helped determine its characteristics. Effective assessment of wealth required the creation of a large, technically skilled bureaucracy. In the absence of this, taxation was necessarily based on external, easily identified signs of wealth. Thus, prior to the Revolution and afterwards in the form of the *octroi* there were various taxes on exchange including internal customs dues and tolls, which facilitated the raising of revenue but undoubtedly reduced the volume of trade.

Similarly in the case of direct taxation: the manifestations of wealth were taxed, such as the possession of land, use of a factory, habitation of a house — in the latter case by a tax on doors and windows. Only a very vague relationship was established between these external signs and real wealth.

The land tax was based on a cadastral survey which estimated the productivity of a piece of land in terms of its area, fertility and costs of exploitation, or else indirectly in relation to rentals earned or comparison with similar properties. During the pre-Revolutionary period, such a system had existed in some areas (areas of *taille réelle*). By 1845 the necessary surveys had been completed for the whole country.

The new system reduced the arbitrariness of assessment and by its relative fixity and the absence of progressive taxation encouraged both saving and investment. Both the *patente*, the tax on business premises, and the land tax were revised perhaps only every twenty years. Investment in both agriculture and industry was encouraged by a certainty that taxation would be unchanged for long periods and would even with reassessment, be unlikely to increase very much. On the other hand the disproportionate burden placed on consumption contributed to the maintenance of low levels of demand, and in consequence limited profitability. In this respect it is probable that saving was encouraged to a greater degree than investment, and the instability of the economy signified by frequent and often violent crises, increased.

The effects of war and political unrest on economic development can be described with greater certainty. War was inevitably disastrous. Even in time of economic upturn, by the closure of external markets it tended to cause a crisis of over-production. If war coincided with the general crisis caused by a poor harvest, then the consequent deepening of the crisis had dreadful social consequences. The Seven Years War is calculated to have caused a 60 per cent decline in external trade. Recovery was rapid, but then intervention in the American War of Independence caused another crisis. Significantly for prospects of economic development in the eighteenth century, wars were less frequent and far less destructive than they had been in the previous century. Some industries, particularly cotton and iron, were even stimulated by the temporary decline in international competition.

The period of revolution and empire combined intense internal political change with the longest wars of the century. The effects were in some respects stimulating through the suppressions of customs barriers, and the enlargement, even if temporary, of markets by conquest and the stimuli afforded to some industries by military procurement. Overall, however, the consequences were disastrous. Increased taxation, inflation due to *assignats,* price and wage maxima, requisitioning, all discouraged economic activity. The most significant effect was the dislocation of international trade. The prosperity of the major ports and their hinterlands had depended on colonial trade. This had been the most dynamic sector of the eighteenth century economy. During the period 1792–1815 British mastery of the seas was more complete than ever before and the loss of the key West Indian colonies more serious. The revolt by slaves in Santo Domingo, which had been the focus of three-quarters of the colonial trade, compounded the damage. Industrial output at Marseille fell from 50 million francs to 12 million by 1813. The whole south-west, particularly its textile industries, was propelled from precocious growth into the beginning of a process of de-industrialisation. The period had the added effect of strengthening the potential for economic survival of the peasantry and stimulating investment in the land for the security it offered. These developments restrained overall structural change in economy.

Although contact with England, centre of technical innovation, was restrained, most of the basic innovations were already known. A more serious factor restraining innovation was the absence of competitive pressures. The military opening-up of markets to the East and the Mediterranean involved industrialists in competition but with generally more backward economies.

In contrast with this violent period, the nineteenth century was characterised by long periods of peace in Europe, during which government economic policy was more positive in intent, and devoted essentially to providing an environment suitable for economic activity. This was achieved by conservative budgetary policies, ensuring the balanced budgets essential to financial confidence, by preserving public order as defined by the possessing classes, and the establishment improved communications and educational systems. For contemporaries, the key aspect of the establishment of conditions encouraging investment was tariff policy.

The general acceptance of an ideology of freedom for the economic activity of both producers and merchants of agricultural and industrial products, did not mean quite what it appeared to. State intervention was welcomed or rather demanded when these groups thought they might benefit, and most noticeably in the cases of tariff protection and the preservation of order. Associations and strikes by workers to improve their conditions were forbidden. In these cases it was maintained that wages must be regulated by natural laws. These were not allowed to regulate trade however.

The fervour with which protection was upheld can be seen in the case of opposition to the proposed commercial treaty with Belgium in 1846. It is easily explained. For the inefficient producer protection seemed to promise survival, and for the efficient inflated prices and profits, due to the lack of competition. In many cases protection was a dogma, not based on a rational examination of markets. Thus, on hearing of the 1860 commercial treaty with Britain many textile manufacturers closed or laid off workers in the mistaken belief that survival was impossible without high tariff protection.

The treaty of 1786 with England, which suppressed prohibitions and reduced tariffs, had not produced very happy results. It had been replaced in 1792 by an even more intense protectionism. The initial act of the Restoration in 1814 was to reduce the tariffs, but pressure of opinion soon led to a reversal. During the July Monarchy protectionism again prevailed. Even after modifications introduced in 1836 tariffs of 70 per cent on pig-iron and 110 per cent on cast-iron typified the system.

There was, and has been much argument about the economic effects of such protection. One fact which should be born in mind in relation to this whole question is that of communications. Whatever the level of tariffs, distance, and the high costs of transport, before the application of steam-power, served as an effective enough protection for most industries. Therefore, in explaining the rate of economic development the level of tariff protection should assume a secondary place.

The purpose of high tariffs, obviously, was the protection of domestic industries. Their existence must have reduced the pressure to modernise, but paradoxically it is doubtful if the initial investments would have occurred in some industries without protection. This offered a certain security, a guaranteed domestic regional market, the supply of which would permit a certain level of development. The Director of Mines, in justifying the application of tariffs to iron imports, in 1822 observed that given a low level of demand, only high prices made possible a remunerative enough return to compensate for the high costs of borrowing money. In effect investment in modernisation required as a pre-requisite promise of high profits. That archaic industries were also thereby allowed to survive was an unavoidable consequence.

It could also be maintained that coal-mining required protection, on the basis of the stagnation of the Valenciennes coal-field during the First Empire, when the more advanced Belgian coal-fields had been incorporated into France. Subsequently not just the frontier, but the canal system, was used to give this protection. The Canal de St Quentin opening Paris to coal from the Nord was opened in 1810. Completion of the Sambre-Oise canal, linking the Charleroi field to the same market, was deliberately delayed until 1838, by which time the Valenciennes field was competitive.

The cotton industry too had needed protection. The continental system and the blockade preceding it had, by serving as an extreme form of protection, served to stimulate the demand for cotton products, and also the mechanisation of the industry. Thus in the industrial complex Lille-Roubaix-Tourcoing, the number of spindles had increased from 32,000 in 1800, 114,000 in 1808 to 177,000 in 1810, whilst the mule had at the same time tended to replace both jenny and water-frame. English competition at this time could not have been supported.

But if some industries profited from protection, others probably suffered. Engineering was adversely effected by high iron prices and significantly when railway development began in the early 1840s rails had to be bought in large quantities from England, because of the inadequacies of French supplies in both quantity and quality.

If the cotton industry needed protection, woollens and silk probably did not. All three were adversely affected by high tariffs on raw materials, as were coal users, forced because of insufficient domestic supplies to import English coal. Tariffs on English machinery, if helping the development of domestic engineering, hindered the mechanisation of other industries.

In the period of depressed prices from 1817 to 1851, tariffs did little to counter the tendency for prices to fall. This was one factor countering the deleterious effects of protection on modernisation. Innovation was encouraged by the desire to reduce costs and prevent a decline in profits. However a more obvious and more commonly applied method of reducing costs was to intensify the exploitation of labour, particularly by wage reductions.

Out of the welter of competing interests and the evident technical backwardness of France compared with England grew a movement in favour of tariff reform, involving merchants from the great ports, wine and silk producers and even some of the most strongly established entrepreneurs in other sectors, such as Alsatian cotton printers. An 'Association for free trade' was formed in 1845. More significant was the current of opinion created by theoretical economists and the influence this had on politicians, and in particular on Napoleon III, during the period of the authoritarian Empire, when he could act whatever the strength of opposition in the *corps législatif,* to negotiate a series of commercial treaties beginning with Britain in 1860.

The consequences of tariff reform are difficult to disengage from the effects of a variety of other factors operative at the same time. One can safely say that reduction in tariffs, affecting about 80 per cent of imports, including almost all manufactured goods by 1861, must have increased competition. However, in the case of metallurgy, continued tariffs of 30 per cent on pig-iron (25 per cent from 1864) still offered a real protection, especially given the additional transport costs English producers had to pay. British exports of pig-iron to France in the last five years of the 1850s averaged 74.247 tons; from 1860 to 1865 138, 116; 1865 to 1870 184, 687; and 1870 to 1875 82,400 tons. The statistics for wrought-iron and railway equipment do not even show this temporary increase. It was hardly on the scale necessary to inundate the French market. This seems to indicate that French metallurgy and engineering became rapidly competitive. Indeed significant reductions in tariff protection for coal, iron and steel, in 1853 to 1855 had previously warned them of the need to modernise. These changes stimulated modernisation and the reduction of prices, encouraging a process already under way which was of great benefit to iron-using industries. The combination of the establishment of a national market and declining prices additionally caused the most serious crises yet, indeed the rapid disappearance, of the traditional charcoal-using iron industry.

The consequences for the textile industries are even more difficult to judge, because especially of the American Civil War and the resulting cotton famine. The woollen and worsted, the Lyon silk industry (though not that of St Etienne) protested little and appear to have been generally competitive. Demand for other textiles increased as raw cotton prices rose sharply. The costs of re-equipment were reduced by the reduction of tariffs on English machinery, and a fall in domestic iron and machinery prices. In short, if it is difficult to judge the extent, tariff reform seems generally to have stimulated modernisation through accelerating processes of structural change already occurring, but mainly due to the development of internal competition through the establishment of improved communications.

The results of the commercial treaties of the 1860s were not entirely happy. They helped create a feeling of uncertainty, of insecurity amongst entrepreneurs, seen in the more rapid development of professional associations to defend interests and fix prices. Estimates of potential foreign competition were not always rational, and the treaties tended to be blamed for all manner of economic ills. This lack of confidence, the fear of war, and then the consequences of war, the slowing of the rate of growth of internal demand once the major structural changes had occurred, all contributed to effect a deceleration in the rate of overall economic growth during the period of free trade 1860–92. Without any doubt, however lower tariffs, in combination with cheaper transport, in intensifying currents of international trade, helped stimulate the modernisation of the French economy.

The economic policies of the State thus had considerable effects on economic development. Of greatest significance was the political framework they provided. The growth of economic activity required security; without security long-term investments in particular tend to be postponed. Thus periods of revolution and war are a disincentive to investment. From 1789 many potential investors sought the security of land purchase rather than industry or commerce. The economic and legal position of the peasantry was strengthened. Legislation designed to introduce freedom of internal trade could provide only a limited stimulus to development as long as poor communications did not allow for much freedom to trade, and the whole period of Revolution and Empire was one in which transport conditions deteriorated.

The effect of the Revolution on economic activity was great, as had been those of previous periods of war and internal unrest, but no change in the basic economic structure was effected. If anything the predominance of agriculture was increased. In the whole period of growth beginning around 1730, the revolutionary crisis seems to have been one of a number of intervals. One positive gain of the revolutionary period was the rationalisation of the process of government. A professionalisation of the bureaucracy occurred with the abolition of purchase of office after 1789. Service of the State became more largely the central consideration for bureaucrats rather than private gain.

The period of constitutional monarchy has been characterised as one of weak central government. The economic consequences of this can be seen at their most serious in the slowness with which crucial decisions were taken on railway development by the parliaments of the July Monarchy, divided as they were by competing local interests. Perhaps the most significant government decisions in this period were in the field of education – the primary education law of 1833 being of especial importance. Christopher Johnson has however shown how during the July Monarchy the bureaucrats of the Conseil des Ponts et Chaussées in conjunction with the industrial and commercial 'grande bourgeoisie' of Paris and other major cities, aware of the need for transport development to stimulate economic growth, sought to impose a rational public works policy. The achievement was limited by opposition from ministers, and in the Chamber of Deputies from representatives of essentially local interests. Nevertheless basic decisions were taken on routes and financing and construction of the network commenced. During the authoritarian Empire, relieved of these political restrictions, this alliance of financiers and technocrats was to enjoy far greater freedom and a transport revolution occurred.

The establishment of an authoritarian régime in December 1851 was generally welcomed by entrepreneurs after the long period of economic and political crisis from 1846. The security it seemed to offer, the decisive decions taken in respect of railway development, the favourable international scene all served to release a wave of pent-up speculation. It was during this early period of Empire that the structure of the economy changed. It was then that the *Ancien Régime Economique* came decisively to an end. The initial euphoria, the confidence in the régime, the favourable international economic situation, did not last, but by the 1860s a long period of growth had culminated in structural change, symbolised and made possible by the existence of a railway network.

Labour

The structure of employment changed slowly before the middle of the nineteenth century and even after, and although change accelerated it was, on the whole, less radical than the changes in the contribution of each sector of the economy to net domestic product, due to different trends in productivity.

Numerically, in 1866 7,535,000 individuals were active in agriculture (49.8 per cent of the active population); in 1896 the figure had risen to 8,500,900, but the proportion had fallen to 44.9 per cent.

The active agricultural population has been estimated at 80 per cent of the total active population around 1700, 75 per cent around 1790–1815, and 70 to 73 per cent around 1830.[48] Sectorial relocation

167

Employment of active Population 1851–81[47]

	1851 (86 Depts)	1856	1866 (89 Depts)	1881 (87 Depts)
Agriculture, forestry, fishing	64,4%	51,3%	49,8%	47,7%
Liberal professions and public service	4,1%	6,7%	6,7%	7,1%
Industry		31,1%	29,0%	26,8%
Transport	27,4%	4,4%	1,7%	1,7%
Commerce, banking service			6,4%	9,7%
Domestic service	4,1%	6,5%	6,4%	7,0%
Total	100,0%	100,0%	100,0%	100,0%

occurred far more rapidly subsequent to this date than before. Previously in an essentially pre-industrial situation large reserves of underemployed rural labour had proved a disincentive to technical innovation. Urban demand for labour was more than satisfied by the permanent drift of population from the countryside and whatever labour shortages occurred were for particular categories of skilled labour. labour. The creation of new conditions in the labour market by a substantial increase in urban employment opportunities was an aspect of the overall process of modernisation and industrial development. Large-scale migration from the countryside required first the provision of opportunities, but itself became subsequently an element sustaining growth through the provision of both labour and demand for industrial products. Conversely the declining supply of rural labour consequent upon migration and the intensification of agriculture in many regions reduced the labour cost advantage which had been the major attraction of the countryside to industrial entrepreneurs.

In its early stages the new industrial labour force, especially in textiles, was composed mainly of unskilled, uneducated labour, with a high proportion of women and children. The main concern of entrepreneurs in mechanised establishments, at least until the middle of the nineteenth century, was with maximising the use of machinery and improving the organisation of the productive process. As the supply of unskilled labour was plentiful and the techniques of production relatively uncomplicated, there was every facility to maintain labour costs at as low a level as possible to permit rapid capital accumulation. The main problem faced in respect of this labour was to persuade it to adopt new and more regular work habits, attuned to the needs of power machinery rather than the whim of the individual. This need for an industrial discipline explains the draconian character of factory regulations. The creation of new attitudes was a process taking generations, and the deficiencies of French labour in comparison with

English were for many entrepreneurs a justification for continued tariff protection.

The introduction of new techniques transformed many trades. Often professional training was no longer necessary. Apprenticeship, the organisation of which had clearly been declining in the eighteenth century, became for many factory workers an unnecessary and inaccessible luxury. Yet skills, old and new, continued to be needed, and wage differentials between those with skills judged to be valuable and those with redundant skills or with none at all indicated the real bargaining power of workers identifiable as a scarce resource. Most valuable of all, at least in the larger-scale establishments, were the trained specialists from the *Grandes Ecoles,* occupying managerial and engineering rôles, and at the lower levels the products of the five Ecoles d'Art et Métiers existing by 1857. The small number of specialists trained by these establishments — the Ecole Générale des Arts et Manufactures produced only 3,000 engineers between 1832 and 1870 — indicates the limited requirements due to the limits to industrial development. The training of all these specialists was technical rather than scientific, preparing them to improve machinery and factory organisation rather than make scientific discoveries.

Workers in old professions unaffected by mechanisation, such as building, various luxury trades, or sectors in expansion such as mining were often able to maintain or increase their wage levels. Elsewhere, at least until the 1850s, declining or at best stagnant nominal and real wages seem to have been more characteristic, as population and labour supply increased. Wages, which varied regionally and over time, tended to be around what was estimated to be subsistence level, fluctuating primarily with bread prices. Piece rates, and the activity of labour contractors, intensified the compeition between workers for employment. Hostility to the introduction of machinery, resulting in quasi-insurrectional situations at various times, indicates the desire of workers to resist a worsening of their situation, but without real organisation, enfeebled and brutalised by low wages and abysmal living conditions, repressed by police activity, the capacity of workers in the industrialising economy to resist exploitation was limited.

The Le Chapelier law of 1791 forbidding association by workers, completed by the 1810 penal code and a law of April 1834 evinced the Government determination to repress worker protest as a threat to social order.

Such legislation was always partly evaded especially in communities and trades which had traditions of organisation surviving in the form of mutual aid societies, for example in Paris, and other major cities. Migration and technological change causing dislocation and deprivation, restricted ability to organise defence against employer pressure, but the contagious example of artisanal groups and the experience of living and working together grew as a more sedentary working class came into existence. This, with less repressive attitudes on the part of the State evident in the 1864 law permitting strikes, led gradually to increased organisational activity.

The great diversity of styles of action, from the spontaneous short-lived protest against wage reductions typical of the textile worker, to the offensive action of the artisan, carefully organised to occur in a period of economic prosperity when the employer would be more likely to make concessions, evinced the variety of working and living conditions in the working class. The most open to exploitation remained the out-workers, those employed in rural industry. The development of the system of *marchandage,* or subcontracting for labour, particularly in the 1840s in rural industries and in building represented perhaps the extreme point in exploitation. Demands for its abolition were a major feature of workers' aspirations for social reform following the 1848 revolution.

Not only differing wage levels between various occupational groups but differences in family income, number of children and their ages determined revenue per head and living standards for families. Illness, unemployment, strikes, the first births, led almost inevitably to debt, especially to local shopkeepers and landlords. Such insecurity tended to make men cautious. Protest and strikes were the result of momentary impulse, or took place as a last resort. Dismissals in periods of crisis were always selective – the known troublemaker went first, the 'good' worker and the subservient could hope to retain his job, and ease his family's suffering. Most workers remained patient and moderate due to fear of unemployment and the survival of a vague sentiment of community of interest with the patron and of deference towards him. Workers commonly admitted their subordinate position. Rather than social revolution they dreamt of being accepted on a footing of closer equality. As real income increased in the 1840s they sought in public to appear as bourgeois by their modes of dress. The more ambitious hoped for social promotion for their sons, if not for themselves, but they were relatively few.

Worker pressure on employers to reduce exploitation had limited effect. This was a factor facilitating capital accumulation but not necessarily of encouraging investment, for it permitted the maintenance of low labour costs, and gave little incentive or opportunity to workers to improve their skills and increase productivity. It was a system of barbarous exploitation. Possibly at the time it was an inescapable system, but its barbarity remains difficult to deny.

For some groups of workers from the 1840s, and more generally in the next decade, a number of factors led to the beginning of an improvement in conditions. From 1851 a period of rising prices, growing quantity of production and increased profits made employers more willing to make concessions. More rapid mechanisation involving the establishment of factories with high overhead costs made employers more reluctant to lay off workers in periods of depression, easing the insecurity and threat of total destitution for so long part of the industrial situation, especially for domestic workers, whose employers met no overhead costs and could simply stop supplying raw materials when demand for the product fell off. In addition the supply-demand relationship for labour was transformed. The permanent migration of large numbers of people from areas of over-population to those of labour need, if it served to restrain the increase of wages in the latter, stimulated an increase in the former, leading to a growing national uniformity in wage levels.

In this period of more rapid structural change in industry, and in part explaining it, productivity could be increased, and costs reduced only by means of technical improvement. By the middle of the nineteenth century the physical limits to the exploitation of human labour seemed to have been reached. Further economic growth could only occur as part of a broad innovatory process, which included a more intelligent use of labour and of its potential. Quality, physical and intellectual, was slowly seen to matter, as well as quantity, and to provide for this higher wages, better working and living conditions, and primary education were provided, gradually but more quickly than before.

Conclusion

The gross national product of France grew at a relatively slow rate compared with other major industrial countries, but if *per capita* growth is calculated, bearing in mind the low rates of population growth in France, then the eighteenth and nineteenth century achievement is more impressive. The inadequacies of the statistics available, presenting the possibility of a large margin of error, should however make the historian hesitate before drawing too many conclusions from them.

Evolution of gross national product in France[49]

	GNP in millions of francs	Population (in millions)	per capita product in francs
1701–10	2,818	20,0	141
1781–90	4,760	26,8	178
1803–12	5,693	29,0	196
1825–34	7,458	32,6	229
1835–44	9,047	34,2	264
1845–54	10,405	35,8	291
1855–64	12,308	37,4	329
1865–74	14,052	36,1	389
1875–84	15,360	37,7	408

In reviewing the history of an economy and a society the historian is required to enlarge the simple concept of growth, attractive because it is relatively easy to measure, into a more general concept of development. Throughout the ages French society had shown a capacity for recovery from crisis, for growth over greater or lesser periods, but not for sustained growth, not for structural change.

The basic realities in history are perhaps those of social structure. Industrialisation required fundamental change in the structure of the economy, and in social behaviour and attitudes. Not only increased production, but the introduction of new methods of production in key economic sectors. Such a change was made possible and worthwhile by the creation of fluid conditions for the supply of capital, raw materials and labour, and by the establishment of new market structures.

Far more decisive than political and institutional revolution, in permitting a decisive break with established economic and social structures, were the series of developments beginning in the decade 1840−50. Substantial archaisms survived. Change manifested itself first in particular places, at various 'Poles of Growth' and then spread, slowly in many cases, throughout the economy. But without any doubt, with the development of the railway, the economy of the *Ancien Régime,* which had survived until the middle of the nineteenth century, finally succumbed. An economic and social structure, whose rhythms had been determined by its means of communication, gave way as new systems and new rhythms were established, making possible the most radical changes French society had ever known.

Notes

1. Labrousse, E., *Aspects de l'evolution économique et sociale de la France et du Royaume-Uni de 1815 à 1880,* 1949, p. 8.
2. Dupeux, G., *La Société française, 1789−1960,* 1964, p. 44.
3. Lévy-Leboyer, M., *La Croissance Economique en France au 19ᵉ siècle,* A.E.S.C., 1968, p. 790.
4. Crouzet, F., 'Essai de construction d'un indice annuel de la production industrielle française au 19ᵉ siècle', *A.E.S.C.,* 1970.
5. Dupeux, op. cit., pp. 45−6.
6. Bouvier, J., Furet, F., and Gillet, M., *Le mouvement du profit en France au 19ᵉ siècle,* 1965, p. 270.
7. Léon, P., *La naissance de la grande industrie en Dauphiné (fin du 17ᵉ siècle − 1869),* 2 vols, 1954, pp. 666−7.
8. Lévy-Leboyer, M., op. cit., p. 788.
9. Markovitch, T.J., 'Le revenue industriel et artisanal sous la monarchie de julliet et le second empire', *E.S.,* 1967, pp. 10, 91.
10. Desmerest, J., *Evolution de la France contemporaire, la France de 1870,* 1970.
11. Vial, J., *L'industrialisation de la sidérurgie française, 1814−1864,* 1967, pp. 412−13.

12. Chaunu, P., 'Le bâtiment dans l'économie traditionelle', in Bardet, J.P., et al., Le bâtiment. Enquete d'histoire economique XIVe–XIXe siècles – Maisons rurales et urbaines dans la France traditionelle, 1971, pp. 18–19.
13. A. Hunt of the University of East Anglia is preparing a doctoral dissertation on 'The Building Industry in the departments of Ardèche, Drôme, & Isère: in the second half of the 19th century.
14. Désert, G., 'Apercus sur l'industrie française du bâtiment au 19e siècle' in Bardet, J.P., et al., Le bâtiment. Enquête d'histoire économique 14e–19e siècles, Vol. 1, 1971, pp. 73–6, 78, 84–6.
15. Chatelain, A., 'La main-d'oeuvre dans l'industrie française du bâtiment aux 19e et 20e siècles', T.A.S., 1956.
16. Désert, op. cit., p. 214.
17. Bois, P., 'La crise dans un department de l'ouest. La Sarthe', in Labrousse, E., Aspects de la crise et de la dépression de l'économie française au milieu du 19e siècle, 1956, p. 295.
18. Fohlen, C., L'industrie textile française au 19e siècle, 1956, p.192.
19. Markovitch, T.J., L'industrie française de 1789 à 1964, 1964, p. 47.
20. Labrousse, op. cit., p. 85.
21. Toutain, J.C., Le produit de l'agriculture française de 1700 à 1958, 1961; and Markovitch, op. cit. A maximum of 6,500 metric tons was attained in 1905–13.
22. Courtheaux, J.-P., 'L'impératif industriel au 19e siècle', R.H.E.S., 1969.
23. Dunham, A.L., The Anglo-French Treaty of Commerce of 1860 and the Progress of the Industrial Revolution in France, Ann Arbor, 1930, p. 161–3; cf. somewhat different figures in Fohlen, C., 'Charbon et révolution industrielle en France, 1815–50', in Trénard, L. (ed.), charbon et révolution . . . , pp. 146–7.
24. Gille, B., La sidérurgie françiase au 19e siècle, Geneva, 1968, pp. 62, 234; Fohlen, op. cit.
25. Gille, op. cit., p. 47.
26. Fohlen, op. cit. p. 46.
27. Vial, op. cit., pp. 271–3.
28. Dunham, A.L., The Industrial Revolution in France, 1815–48, New York, 1955, p. 85.
29. Gille, B., 'Les plus grandes compagnies houillières françaises vers 1840: Essai sur le structure du capitalisme', in Trénard, op. cit.
30. Armengaud, A., 'A propos des origines du sous-développement industriel dans le sud-ouest', A.M., 1960, p. 76.
31. Fohlen, op. cit., p. 42.
32. Chaunu, P., 'Malthusianisme démographique et malthusianisme économique', A.E.S.C., 1972, pp. 7, 11–12.
33. Markovitch, op. cit., p. 46.
34. Jones, E.L., and Woolf, S.J., Agrarian change and Economic Development, 1969, p. 15.
35. Labrousse, E., et al., Histoire économique et sociale de la France, II, 1970, p. 503.
36. Wolkowitsch, M., L'économie régionale des transports dans le centre et le centre-ouest de la France, n.d., p. 207.
37. Désert, op. cit., p. 103.
38. Léon, P., La naissance de la grande industrie en Dauphine, (fin du 17e siecle – 1869), 2 vols, 1954, pp. 777, 783–4, 786.
39. Dupeux, op. cit., p. 136.
40. Labrousse, et al., op. cit., pp. 256–7 and especially Richard, G., Noblesse d'affaires au 18e siècle, 1974.

41. Gille, B., *Recherches sur le formation de la grande entreprise capitaliste 1815–48*, 1959, p. 37.
42. Palmade, G., *Capitalisme et capitalistes française au 19ᵉ siècle*, 1961, p. 150.
43. Labrouse, *et al.*, op. cit.
44. Vial, op. cit., pp. 346–7.
45. Michalet, C.-A., *Le placements des épargnants française de 1815 á nos jours*, 1968, p. 100.
46. Bouvier, J., 'Sur l'immobilisme du système fiscal française au 19ᵉ siècle', *R.H.E.S.*, 1972.
47. Bairoch, P., *Révolution industrielle et sous-développement*, 1969, pp. 341–3.
48. Levy-Leboyer, M., 'La décélération de l'économie française dans la seconde moitié du 19ᵉ siècle', *R.H.E.S.*, 1970, p. 484.
49. Bairoch, op. cit., p. 346.

Further Reading

Ardant, G., *Theorie sociologique de l'impôt*, I, 1965.
Ariès, P., *Histoire des populations françaises et de leurs attitudes devant la vie depuis le 18ᵉ siècle*, 1948.
Armengaud, A., *Les populations de l'est-aquitain au début de l'époque contemporaine*, 1961.
Armengaud, A., 'A propos des origines du sous-développement industriel dans le sud-ouest', *A.M.*, 1960.

Bairoch, P., 'Le rôle de l'agriculture dans le création de la sidérurgie moderne', *R.H.E.S.*, 1966.
Bairoch, P., *Révolution industrielle et sous-développement*, 1969.
Bairoch, P., 'Free trade and European Economic Development in the nineteenth century', *E.E.R.*, 1972.
Ballot, C., *L'introduction du machinisme dans l'industrie française*, 1923.
Bendix, R., *Work and Authority in Industry*, New York, 1963.
Bergeron, L., *L'épisode napoléonien, 1799–1815*, 1972.
Bergeron, L., 'Problèmes économiques de la France napoléonienne', *R.H.M.C.*, 1970.
Bergeron, L., 'Une relecture attentive et passionnée de la révolution française', *A.E.S.C.*, 1968.
de Bertier de Sauvigny, G., *La Restauration*, 1955.
Blanchard, M., *Essais historiques sur les premiers chemins de fer du midi Languedocien et de la vallée du Rhône*, Montpellier, 1935.
Blanchard, M., 'The Railway Policy of the Second Empire' in Crouzet, F., *et al.*, *Essays in European Economic History*, 1969.
Bois, P., 'La crise dans un départment de l'ouest: la Sarthe' in Labrousse, F., *Aspects de la crise et de la dépression de l'économie française au milieu du 19ᵉ siècle*, 1956.
Bouvier, J., *Histoire économique et histoire sociale*, Geneva, 1968.

Bouvier, J., *Naissance d'une banque: le Crédit Lyonnais,* 1968.

Bouvier, J., 'A propos de la crise dite de 1805. Les crises économiques sous l'empire', *R.H.M.C.,* 1970.

Bouvier, J., 'Sur l'immobilisme du système fiscal française au 19e siècle', *R.H.E.S.,* 1972.

Bouvier, J., Furet, F., Gillet, M., *Le mouvement du profit en France au 19e siècle,* 1965.

Bozon, P., *La vie rurale en Vivarais,* 1963.

Butel, P., 'Crise et mutation de l'activité économique á Bordeaux sous le consulat et l'empire', *R.H.M.C.,* 1970.

Cameron, R., 'Profit, croissance et stagnation en France au 19e siècle', *E.A.,* 1957.

Caralp-Landon, R., *Les chemins de fer dans le Massif Central,* 1957.

Caron, F., *Histoire de l'exploitation d'un grand réseau. La compagnie du chemin de fer du Nord, 1846–1937,* 1973.

Caron, F., 'Recherches sur le capital des voies de communication en France au 19e siècle (en particulier le capital ferroviaire)' in Léon, P., *et al.* (eds.), *L'industrialisation en Europe,* 1972.

Caron, F., 'Les commandes des compagnies de chemin de fer en France, 1850–1914', *R.H.S.,* 1962.

Caron, F., 'Banques et industrialisation au 19e siècle', *A.E.S.C.,* 1965.

Chanut, A., *et al.,* 'Aspects industriels de la crise: le département du Nord' in Labrousse, F. (ed.), *Aspects,* 1956.

Chatelain, A., 'La main-d'oeuvre dans l'industrie française du bâtiment aux 19e et 20e siècles', *T.A.S.,* 1956.

Chaunu, P., 'Le bâtiment dans l'économie traditionelle' in Bardet, J.P., *et al., Le bâtiment. Enquête d'histoire économique XIV–XIXe siècles – Maisons rurales et urbaines dans la France traditionelle,* 1971.

Chaunu, P., 'Malthusianisme démographique et malthusianisme économique', *A.E.S.C.,* 1972.

Chaussinand-Nogaret, G., 'Capital et structure sociale sous l'ancien régime', *A.E.S.C.,* 1970.

Chevalier, M., *La vie humaine dans les Pyrenées Ariègeoises,* 1956.

Clause, G., 'L'industrie lainière rémoise à l'époque napoléonienne', *R.H.M.C.,* 1970.

Cobban, A., *The Social Interpretation of the French Revolution,* 1968.

Coornaert, E., 'Artisanat et concentration industrielle de 1815 á 1848', *I.H.,* 1953.

Coornaert, E., 'Le protectionnisme sous le monarchie censitaire (1815–48)', *I.H.,* 1953.

Courthéoux, J.P., 'L'impératif industriel au 19e siècle', *R.H.E.S.,* 1969.

Crouzet, F., 'Essai de construction d'un indice annuel de la production industrielle française au 19e siècle', *A.E.S.C.*, 1970.

Crouzet, F., 'Encore la croissance économique française au 19e siècle', *R.N.*, 1972.

Crouzet, F., 'Le charbon anglais en France au 19e siècle' in Trénard, L. (ed.), *Charbon et sciences humaines*, 1966.

Crouzet, F., 'Les origines du sous-développement économique du sud-ouest', *A.M.*, 1959.

Crouzet, F., 'Wars, Blockade and Economic Change in Europe, 1792–1815', *J.E.H.*, 1964.

Crouzet, F., 'Agriculture et révolution industrielle', *C.H.*, 1967.

Dardel, P., *Commerce, industrie et navigation á Rouen et au Havre au 18e siècle*, Rouen, 1966.

Daumard, A., *La bourgeoisie parisienne de 1815 á 1848*, 1963.

Daumard, A., 'L'évolution des structures sociales en France á l'époque de l'industrialisation', *R.H.*, 1972.

Daumard, A., 'Le fortune mobilière en France selon les milieux sociaux (XIX–XXe siècles)', *R.H.E.S.*, 1965.

Daumard, A. (ed.), *Les fortunes françaises au 19e siècle*, 1973.

Dauzet, P., *Le siècle des chemins de fer en France*, Fontenay-au-Roses, 1948.

Desert, G., 'Aperçus sur l'industrie française du bâtiment au 19e siècle', in Bardet, J.P., *et al.*, *Le Bâtiment*, 1971.

Desert, G., 'Les paysans du calvados au 19e siècle', *A.N.*, 1971.

Desmarest, J., *Evolution de la France contemporaine, la France de 1870*, 1970.

Deyon, P., 'Aspects industriels de la crise: le cas de Rouen', in Labrousse, E., (ed.), *Aspects*, 1956.

Dolleans, E., *Histoire du travail en France*, I, 1953.

Dreyfus, F.G., 'La crise dans un département de l'est; le bas-Rhin' in Labrousse, E., (ed.), *Aspects*, 1956.

Dufraisse, R., 'Régime douanier, blocus, systéme continental', *R.H.E.S.*, 1966.

Dunham, A.L., *The Anglo-French Treaty of Commerce of 1860 and the Progress of the Industrial Revolution in France*, Ann Arbor, 1930.

Dunham, A.L., *The Industrial Revolution in France, 1815–48*, New York, 1955.

Dupeux, G., *La société française, 1789–1960*, 1964.

Duveau, G., *La vie ouvrière en France sous le second Empire*, 1946.

Fohlen, C., *L'industrie textile au temps du second empire*, 1956.

Fohlen, C., *The Industrial Revolution in France*, 1970.

176

Fohlen, C., 'L'industrie textile française au 19e siècle', *I.H.*, 1954.

Fohlen, C., 'Naissance, d'une civilisation industrielle, 1765–1875', in Fohlen and Bédarida, *Histoire générale du travail III L'ere des révolutions, 1765–1914*, 1962.

Fohlen, C., 'Charbon et révolution industrielle en France, 1815–50', in Trénard, L., *Charbon*, 1966.

Fohlen, C., 'Bourgeoisie française, liberté économique et intervention de l'état', *R.E.*, 1956.

Gille, B., *Recherches sur le formation de la grande entreprise capitaliste, 1815–48*, 1959.

Gille, B., *Les origines de la grande industrie métallurgique en France*, n.d.

Gille, B., *La siderurgie française au 19e siècle*, Geneva, 1968.

Gille, B., *La banque en France au 19e siècle*, Geneva, 1970.

Gille, B., 'Les plus grandes compagnies houillères françaises vers 1840: Essai sur le structure du capitalisme' in Trénard, L. (ed.), *Charbon*, 1966.

Gillet, M., 'Au 19e siècle – industrialisation linèare ou industrialisation par bonds?', *R.E.*, 1972.

Gillet, M., 'The Coal Age and the Rise of Coal Fields in the Nord and the Pas-de-Calais', in Crouzet, F., *et al.*, *Essay in European Economic History*.

Gillet, M., *Les Charbonnages du nord de la France au 19e siècle*, 1973.

Girard, L., *La politique des travaux publics du second Empire*, 1952.

Godechot, J., 'La crise de 1846–47 dans le sud-ouest de la France', *Etudes XVI*, 1954.

Goubert, P., *L'ancien régime*, I, 1969.

Guichard, P., 'D'une société repliée á une société ouverte: l'évolution socio-économique de la région d'Andance, de la fin du 17e siècle á la révolution', in Léon, P. (ed.), *Structures économiques et problèmes sociaux du monde rurale dans la France du sud-est*, 1966.

Habakkuk, A.J., 'The Historical Experience of the Basic Conditions of Economic Progress' in Falkus, M.R. (ed.), *Readings in the History of Economic Growth*, 1958.

Hardy-Hemery, O., 'Le Valenciennois industrial: cohérence et incoherence d'un espace géononique', *R.E.*, 1972.

Hufton, O., *Bayeux in the Late Eighteenth Century. A social study*, 1967.

Hunt, A., 'The Building Industry in the Department of the Isère in the second half of the nineteenth century' (Ph.D. thesis in preparation at the University of East Anglia).

Jardin, A., Tudesq, A.J., *La France des Notables,* 2 vols, 1973.

Johnson, C.H., 'The Revolution of 1830 in French Economic History', in Merriman, J.M. (ed.), *1830 in France,* New York, 1975.

Jones, E.L., Woolf, S.J., *Agrarian change and Economic Development,* 1969.

Jouffroy, L.M., *Une étape de la construction des grandes lignes de chemin de fer: le ligne de Paris á la frontière d'Allemagne,* n.d.

Jouffroy, L.M., *L'ére du rail,* 1953.

Kahan-Rabecq, M.M., *Alsace économique et sociale sous le régne de Louis-Philippe,* I, 1939.

Kemp, T., *Economic Forces in French History. An Essay on the Development of the French Economy, 1760–1914,* 1971.

Labasse, J., *Les capitaux et le région. Essai sur le commerce et le circulation des capitaux dans le région Lyonnaise,* 1955.

Labasse, J., 'La circulation des capitaux en France au 19e siècle',*J.H.,* 1955.

Labrousse, E., *Aspects de l'évolution économique et sociale de la France et du Royaume-uni de 1815–1880,* 1949.

Labrousse, E., *La crise de l'économie française á la fin de l'ancien régime et au début de la révolution,* 1944.

Labrousse, E., *Le mouvement ouvrier et les idées sociales en France de 1815 á la fin du 19e siècle,* 1952.

Labrousse, E., 'Preface to VIIIe colloque d'histoire sur l'artisanat et l'apprentissage', Aix-en-Provence, 1965.

Labrousse, E., *et al., Histoire économique et sociale de la France,* II, 1970.

Lambert-Dansette, J., 'Le patronat du Nord: sa période triumphante (1830–80)', *B.S.H.M.,* 1972.

Landes, D.S., 'Technological Change and Development in Western Europe, 1750–1914', *The Cambridge Economic History of Europe,* VI, 1965.

Lasserre, A., *La situation des ouvriers de l'industrie textile dans la région Lilloise sous la monarchie de juillet,* Lausanne, 1952.

Laurent, R., *L'octroi de Dijon au 19e siècle,* 1960.

Lefevre, A., *Sous le second empire: chemins de fer et politique.* 1951.

Lefranc, G., *Histoire du travail et des travailleurs,* 1957.

Lemarchand, G., 'Le 17e et le 18e siècles en France: bilan et perspectives des recherches', *A.H.R.F.,* 1969.

Léon, P., 'La naissance de la grande industrie en Dauphiné (fin du 17e siècle – 1869)', 2 vols, 1954.

Léon, P., *Economies et sociétés pre-industrielle, 1650–1780,* 1970.

Léon, P., 'Tradition et machinisme dans la France du 18e siècle, *I.H.,*

1955.

Lévy-Leboyer, M., *Les banques européennes et l'industrialisation internationale dans le première moitié du 19e siècle,* 1964.

Lévy-Leboyer, M., 'La croissance économique en France au 19e siècle', *A.E.S.C.,* 1968.

Lévy-Leboyer, M., 'La décélération de l'économie française dans la seconde moitié du 19e siècle', *R.H.E.S.,* 1970.

Lévy-Leboyer, M., 'Le patronat française a-t-il été malthusien', *M.S.,* 1974.

Lhomme, J., *La grande bourgeoisie au pouvoir, 1830–80,* 1960.

Lhomme, J., *Economie et histoire,* Geneva, 1967.

Lutfalla, M.,'Aux origines du liberalisme économique en France: Le Journal des économistes', Analyse du contenu de la première série, 1841–1853',*R.H.E.S.,* 1972.

Mandrou, R., *La France aux 17e et 18e siècles,* 1967.

Markovitch, T.J., *L'industrie francaise de 1789 a 1964,* 1964.

Markovitch, T.J., 'Le revenue industriel et artisanal sous la monarchie de juillet et le second empire', *E.S.,* 1967.

Markovitch, T.J., 'L'industrie lainière française au debut du 18e siècle', *R.H.E.S.,* 1968.

Markovitch, T.J., 'L'histoire du 18e siècle et de la revolution française: bilan et perspective de recherches',*A.H.R.F.,* 1969.

Michalet, C.-A., *Les placements des épargnants français de 1815 á nos jours,* 1968.

Mousnier, R., *La Société française de 1770 á 1789,* I, 1970.

Palmade, G., *Capitalisme et capitalistes français au 19e siècle,* 1961.

Papy, M., 'Quelques fortunes bordelaises au milieu du 19e siècle', *R.H.E.S.,* 1965.

Pautard, J., *Les disparités régionales dans la croissance de l'agriculture française,* 1955.

Perrot, M., 'Aspects industriels de la crise: les régions textiles du Calvados' in Labrousse, E. (ed.), op. cit.

Perrot, M., *Les ouvriers en grève. France 1871–90,* 2 vols, 1974.

Pierrard, P., *La vie ouvrière á Lille sous le second Empire,* 1965.

Pinard, J., 'Géographie industrielle et problèmes financiers' in *La pensée géographique française contemporaine. Mélanges offertes à André Meynier,* Saint-Brieuc, 1972.

Pinchemel, P., *France: A geographical Survey,* 1969.

Pinkney, D.H., *Napoléon III and the re-building of Paris,* Princeton, 1958.

Price, R.D., 'The Change from Labour abundance to Labour Shortage in French Agriculture in the 19th Century', *E.H.R.,* 1975.

Priouret, R., *Origines du patronat français*, 1963.

Prost, A., *L'enseignement en France, 1800–1967*, 1968.

Renouard, D., *Le transport de marchandises par fer, route et eau depuis 1850*, 1960.

Richard, G., 'Un essai d'adaptation sociale á une nouvelle structure économique. La noblesse de France et les sociétés par actions á la fin du 18ᵉ siècle', *R.H.E.S.*, 1962.

Richard, G., *Noblesse d'affaires au 18ᵉ siècle*, 1974.

Rist, C., 'Une experience française de libération des échanges au 19ᵉ siècle. Le traité de 1860, *R.F.S.P.*, 1956.

Rochefort, M., *L'organisation urbane de l'Alsace*, Gap, 1960.

Rosier, B., *Structures agraires et dévéloppements économiques*, 1968.

Rouff, M., *Les mines de Charbon en France au 18ᵉ siècle, 1744–91*, 1922.

Sée, H., *Histoire économique de la France*, 2 vols, 1942.

Sée, H., 'Remarques sur le caractère de l'industrie rurale en France et les causes de son extension au 18ᵉ siècle', *R.H.*, 1923.

Seignour, P., *La vie économique du Vaucluse de 1815 á 1848*, Aix-en-Provence, 1957.

Silly, J.B., 'La disparition de la petite métallurgie rurale', *R.H.S.*, 1961.

Silly, J.B., 'La concentration dans l'industrie sidérurgique en France sous le second empire', *R.H.S.*, 1962.

Soboul, A., *Le société française dans la seconde moitié du 18ᵉ siècle, Structures sociales, cultures et modes de vie*, 1969.

Soboul, A., *La France à la veille de la Révolution*, I, 1966.

Soboul, A., 'Problèmes de l'apprentissage (second moitiè du 18ᵉ siècle). Réalités sociales et nécessités économiques', in Labrousse, E. (ed), *ville colloque*, Aix-en-Provence, 1965.

Sorlin, P., *La société française, 1840–1914*, 1969.

Sutcliffe, A., *The Autumn of Central Paris: The Defeat of Town Planning, 1850–1970*, 1970.

Thuillier, G., *Aspects de l'économie nivernaise*, 1966.

Toutain, J.C., *Le produit de l'agriculture française de 1700 á 1958*, 1961.

Trempé, R., 'Analyse du comportement des administrateurs de la société des Mines de Carmaux, vis-à-vis mineurs, *M.S.*, 1963.

Trenard, L., 'Le charbon avant l'ère industrielle', in Trénard, L. (ed.), *Charbon*,

Tudesq, A.J., *Les grands notables en France. Etude historique d'une psychologie sociale*, 2 vols, 1964.

Vial, J., *L'industrialisation de la sidérurgie française, 1814–1864*, 1967.

Vidalenc, J., 'La situation économique et sociale des basses-Alpes en 1848', *Etudes*, XVI, 1954.

Vovelle, M., *La chuté de la monarchie, 1787–92*, 1972.

Wolff, J., 'Decazeville: expansion et déclin d'un pôle de croissance', *R.E.*, 1972.

Wolkowitsch, M., *L'économie régionale des transports dans le centre et le centre-ouest de la France*, n.d.

Woronoff, D., *La république bourgeoise de Thermidor et Brumaire (1794–99)*, 1972.

Woronoff, D., 'Tradition et innovation dans la sidérurgie: un example de gestion d'entreprise en Haute-Marne sous le consulat et l'empire', *R.H.M.C.*, 1970.

Wrigley, E.A., *Industrial Growth and Population Change*, 1962.

Zarka, A., 'Un example de pôle de croissance: L'industrie textile du nord de la France, 1830–1870', *R.E.*, 1958.

POPULATION

Recently historians have highlighted the enigma of the increase in population in France from the first third of the eighteenth century in the seeming absence of an agricultural revolution before the second half of the nineteenth century. This apparent paradox is an illusion, for once this period is looked at within a wider historical context, a continuity with the past becomes evident. Fundamentally what happened in the period 1730–1850 was that the full potential for the development of agriculture and the growth of population within the traditional society was developed. This growth might well have been followed, as it had been throughout the history of man, by a renewed crisis in which massive mortalities revealed that the resources available to feed an enlarged population were inadequate, but from the middle of the nineteenth century a relatively rapid increase in the supply of these resources occurred, and in a comparatively short period the character of human society and the quality of life were transformed. For the first time in human history the fear of famine was banished. More accurately than by any other measure the ending of endemic malnutrition provides a means of estimating the success of economic development during the transition from a pre-industrial to a modern economy.

The population of France is estimated to have grown in the following manner:[1]

1750–51	21 million	1850–51	35.8 million
1800–01	27.3	1860–61	37.4
1820–21	30.5	1872	36.1
1830–31	32.6	1880–81	37.7
1840–41	34.2	1890–91	38.3

Growth was the product of an excess of births over deaths, plus immigration – essentially the first factor.

The expansion of the population in the eighteenth century should be viewed in relation to the disastrous period of epidemic and famine of 1690–1720. The effects of this on population were evident in the 1730s due to the reduced numbers of children being born to age-groups decimated at the turn of the century. Population growth during the eighteenth century meant in large part a recuperation of densities achieved during the seventeenth century. recuperation occurred, as always because high mortality reduced, temporarily ulation pressure on resources. An additional cause was a decline in the severity

182

crises, due not only to the reduction of population pressure, but to climatic variations and changes in the pattern of epidemics. In the eighteenth century, in contrast with the seventeenth, few people actually starved to death although chronic undernourishment was commonplace. In contrast with the hecatombs caused by famine and disease in the earlier period undernourished populations were capable of procreating numerous children, who although also poorly fed were more likely than previously to survive into adulthood. The example of India today is proof of the capacity to multiply of undernourished peoples. If in general agricultural productivity just about kept pace with population growth, this meant that the economic structure of the *Ancien Régime* survived, and with it the possiblity of a renewal of the more intense crises of earlier periods. Throughout human history sheltered, prosperous periods seem to have alternated with those of crisis and demographic decay.

Mortality

From about 1750 there appears to have been a tendency — no more — for mortality to decline. This was not a continuous decline, as rates of mortality fluctuated significantly from year to year. Between 1789 and 1815 it has been estimated that mortality fell from about 32 per 1,000 to 27 per 1,000. Losses due to the wars of the Revolution and the Empire have been estimated at 1.3 million, representing little more than one year's mortality, and demographically significant less for this than because the dead were mainly young men whose deaths affected the equilibrium between the sexes and the dynamism of the population.

During the period of the constitutional monarchies the death-rate remained high. The statistical information available is more accurate and more useful from this period. Between 1816 and 1831 it hovered around 25 per 1,000, but with the cholera epidemic of 1832 rose to 28.5 per 1,000, remaining at 27.8 per 1,000 in 1834. (In Paris, where the cholera epidemic was especially severe, the death-rate for the age-group 20–39, i.e. the age group which ensures demographic growth, averaged 56 per 1,000 in the years 1831–5.) This was followed by a slow decline to a low point of 21.2 per 1,000 by 1845, followed in the crisis years of 1846–50 by an average mortality rate of 23.9 per 1,000, and then another decline to 22.3 per 1,000 in the years 1851–3, rising in 1854–5 to 27.4 per 1,000 and 26 per 1,000; and by 1859 to 26.8 per 1,000. The death-rate in 1860 was down to 21.4 per 1,000 and remained for the decade generally between 22 and 24 per 1,000, but with renewed highs due to war and its effects in 1870 and 1871: 28.4 per 1,000 and 35.1 per 1,000.

The key elements for an understanding of this are the continued prevalence of undernourishment and the slowness with which general living conditions improved. Regional variations in mortality are perhaps indicative. Prosperity was the most effective protection against death — prosperity measured in terms not only of regional levels of productivity, but also the social division of the product.

One interesting example of how mortality varied with social conditions is provided by the development of the coal-field in the Pas-de-Calais. Mortality in 1851—61 was 20 per 1,000, but with the coming of industrialisation living and working conditions deteriorated. This was reflected in a mortality rate of 38 per 1,000 in the decade 1861—71. Then due to increased wages, better conditions and improved medical care, and in spite of a certain ageing of the population, the death-rate fell to 25 per 1,000 in 1891.

Mortality in the large towns was generally above the average rate for France but varied significantly between towns; for example in Lyon around 1785 the rate was 27 per 1,000 whereas at Rouen it was regularly over 35 per 1,000. It varied also within towns between the richer and poorer quarters. The two extremes in Paris in 1850 were 18.1 per 1,000 and 33.7 per 1,000. This reveals an important inequality.

However, discussion of rates of mortality in terms of basic statistics is too limited, because in addition to changes in death-rates, the structure of mortality continually changed with important consequences.

This was evident in the second half of the nineteenth century when as the *per capita* level of production rose markedly and social organisation changed, the main impact of death gradually shifted from the first five years of life to old age. The process can be observed earlier but only to a very limited extent. More characteristic had been a high still-birth rate. Many infants had been born dead from preventable causes. Ignorance of the principles of hygiene combined with hard physical labour during pregnancy, and deficiencies of diet led to low birth weight and frequent premature births. Midwifery only slowly improved.

Infant mortality was also high, especially in the first year of life, mainly due to nutritional disorders and infections. Diet for the infants was generally inadequate, normally due to a lack of animal proteins. Mothers with insufficient milk often fed babies solids too early. Weak children were unable to resist measles and pneumonia in the colder months, or gastro-enteritis in the summer. Smallpox remained a major killer of infants until at least the end of the eighteenth century. Innoculation was an important cause of the reduction of infant mortality, but the consequences should not be exaggerated.

The practice by which urban parents sent children to a wet-nurse a few days after birth was important. Wet-nurses often transmitted diseases in their milk, and especially to the children of the poor, or the large numbers of abandoned infants passed on by the municipal authorities with little money for their care. These rural women, supplementing the inadequate income of their families, made woefully inadequate nurses. Yet where the women of the poor in the towns could not afford to cease working to look after children, there was little choice for them but to send their infants away. In Lyon throughout the second half of the eighteenth century from 1,000 to 1,500 legitimate and 500 to 700 abandoned children were sent each year to wet-nurses. The practice was slow to decline and this would depend on the spread of new attitudes towards infants, one that was less resigned to the possibility of their deaths.

If a decline in infant mortality occurred in the eighteenth century it was primarily due to the same factors affecting general mortality and above all the decline in the intensity of food crises. There was a great deal of variation between regions and rich and poor parishes in the same area. The decline of infant mortality was negligible in some regions like in Normandy, or Lyon to take an urban example, whilst in other areas the survival of more and more infants into young adulthood meant the enlargement of child-bearing age-groups.

However, infant mortality remained relatively high until almost the end of the nineteenth century, at above 180 per thousand live births until 1831–5, then falling to 166 and 156 per 1,000 in the next two quinquennia but with high annual variations, e.g. 215 per 1,000 in 1859 and 150 per 1,000 in 1860 (compared with 17 per 1,000 in 1950).[2] There were also high variations between social groups, as seen in the fact that half the children of manufacturers, merchants and managers in the industrial centre of Mulhouse reached 29 years in the 1830s, whilst half those of weavers and spinners were dead by the age of two. Not only social differences, but also differences between the sexes can be observed. Male mortality was generally greater than female, except in the age-groups 20–29 and especially 30–39 due to deaths in child-birth. Seasonal variation in death-rate was also common: in Anjou it was high in winter, but the maximum came in spring and autumn, with a minimum in summer, reflecting vulnerability to cold in winter and to digestive complaints and fevers in spring and autumn.

Thus death-rate, even as late as the Second Empire remained high, although usually below eighteenth-century rates, and declined only very slowly. It remained susceptible to marked aggravation. A final break with the *Ancien Régime* pattern was clear only in the closing years of the nineteenth century when the decline in mortality rates became more rapid, due especially to the fall in infant mortality, and to improvements in the standards of every-day living.

The first major change in the character of death, occurred with the oft-mentioned decline in the intensity of crises early in the eighteenth century. No longer was the surplus accumulated during a few decades free of crises likely to be destroyed in a few years or even months, although in some ill-favoured regions the toll exacted by disease maintained extremely high levels of mortality. In this respect it is worth quoting the example of the Sénéchaussee of Angers, where in the two periods 1775–8 and 1786–8 there occurred 71,786 births, and 61,999 deaths, an excess in seven years of 9.769 births, but between those two periods, in the years 1779–85 there were epidemics, particularly dysentery causing 80,385 deaths compared with 70,626 births, i.e. in seven years an excess of 9,759 deaths. Thus in a period of fourteen years, the net increase of population was 10.[3]

If the balance between population and resources remained precarious everywhere rates of population growth indicated variety in local situations. Thus in the eighteenth century increase was most rapid in the east and north. The possibility of growth depended on pre-existing population densities and their relation to food resources. In much of the west, south-west and centre of France as early as 1750 densities were already too high to sustain further growth and stagnation occurred.

The effects on demographic statistics of traditional crises due to poor harvests, remained evident until the 1850s, though with declining frequency and lesser intensity. The years from 1846 to 1850 were notably difficult, and represented an increased mortality due to a crisis of subsistence, which, if less marked than earlier crises, in its severity, in its widespread effects, and in the disturbances it provoked, remained a typical crisis of the *Ancien Régime,* indicative of a society characterised by massive inequalities and widespread insecurity and undernourishment.

Birth-Rate

The other side of the population growth question is that of birth-rate. The overall birth-rate depends on the age composition of the population and on the rate of child bearing at each age. In the years following the catastrophic crises of the 1693–1720 period a number of age-groups reduced in size came to maturity. This and the retarding effects of the crisis of 1739–43, meant that relatively few children were born each year and population growth was unlikely to have occurred in most areas before the 1750s.

For most of the eighteenth century the birth-rate was around 40 per 1,000 inhabitants, with a tendency to decline towards the end of the century at least in Normandy, Brittany and Languedoc. Although breast-feeding causes temporary sterility in most women, it is probable that high infant mortality, in interrupting breast-feeding, reduced its importance in limiting births, so that given the limits imposed by physiological capacity and the length of marriages the number of births came close to the natural potential.

What is especially significant about France, however, is that long before other countries, in fact from towards the end of the eighteenth century a decline in birth-rate occurred which is explicable only by deliberate limitation of the number of births, and which meant that in spite of a slowly declining death-rate, the excess of births over deaths remained lower than elsewhere, and so consequently did the rate of population growth.

If we accept an average figure of about 37 per 1,000 for the period 1779—89, by 1792 the birth rate had fallen to 34.6 per 1,000 and to 31.8 per 1,000 by 1800—10. Thus there was a fall of something like 15 per cent in twenty years, which is especially significant because from 1790 the marriage-rate rose as changes in social structures and mentality produced by the Revolution led to earlier marriage. But there was no corresponding increase in the number of births.

From this level the birth-rate fell below 31 per 1,000 by 1827, 30 per 1,000 by 1832, 29 per 1,000 by 1837 and 28 per 1,000 by 1844. Between 1851 and 1868 the tendency to decline was less evident, with a certain oscillation around 27 per 1,000, possibly induced by the greater political and social stability.[4]

Declining birth-rate resulted in a tendency towards a higher average age of the population, reinforcing that towards a declining birth-rate. In the countryside, especially from the 1850s, high migration more rapidly contributed to the same effect, which was not compensated for by the preponderance of young in the developing urban areas because immigrants soon accepted the lower birth-rates of the towns.

To explain social history it is always necessary to review regional as well as national developments. This is particularly true of demographic history. Great stress has been laid upon the variations between micro-regions, and within them of the fundamental influence upon sexual behaviour of influential social groups.

Contrasts between rural areas are at least as significant as their similarities. Thus in East Aquitain in the 1840s the backward Ariège retained a high, unrestricted birth-rate much later than the more prosperous Garonne. In the lower Auvergne the birth-rate , even in the eighteenth century was lower in the plain than in the mountains. It has been suggested that rather than deliberate restriction of conception the explanation of the lower rate there was undernourishment, declining sexual appetites and the increased incidence of sterility.[5]

There is a tendency, too, to easily contrast town and country. Variations between towns was also clear. In Lyon the birth-rate dropped significantly from 1760—70 probably because of an increase in the number of immigrant girls working in the silk industry. These tended to marry late after amassing some savings, so that their period of fertility was relatively short, although the interval between births was shorter than in the countryside due to the recourse, even by artisan families, to wet-nurses rather than the mothers breast-feeding. At Foix, in the under-developed Ariège, even in the quinquennia 1841—5 the birth-rate was as high as 45.5 per 1,000 falling steeply to 20.1 per 1,000 by 1871—5. Over the same period by contrast the birth-rate at economically more advanced Toulouse fell from an already low 24.4 to 22.9 per 1,000. Conversely in the more dynamic urban centres attracting large-scale immigration, and consequently having a young age structure birth-rate was late to decline. At Lille in 1876 it was 41.6 per 1,000 in the Pas-de-Calais from 1861—71 it averaged an incredible 60 per 1,000, declining to 40 per 1,000 in 1891 as the population became more stable and its structure less young.

From what we have already said it begins to look as though birth-rate can be related to economic development, but not in a simple manner. Economically backward areas, in town and country were likely to have high birth-rates, but so were the most dynamic urban areas.

It seems that an intergenisic interval of more than twenty-eight months is an indication of limitation of births. In a variety of areas, from the second half of the eighteenth century such intervals are evident. In Crulai in Normandy for example a decline is evident from 36 per 1,000 around 1760 to 20 per 1,000 by 1810, whereas, given the age and matrimonial structure, without birth-control the birth-rate should have been about 31 per 1,000. Traditionally, amongst workers and peasants, procreation had been something natural, the result of processes which were not to be ruled. If a family's resources had seemed inadequate to provide for the needs of new babies then the response had often been infanticide and abandonment. (The huge number of foundlings regularly taken into institutions in Paris is indicative of this.) These were important factors in restraining population growth. The other alternative to these means and the poverty implied by large numbers of children was postponement of marriage which was also common.

In the upper classes first, especially in the second half of the eighteenth century, there developed a growing disgust at the female condition of repeated pregnancy. A new reasoned attitude to marriage developed, a new optimism about the possibility of social ascension for a limited number of children to whom one's resources should be devoted. The means adopted for the limitation of family size were abstinence from sexual relations, coitus interruptus or withdrawal and, if necessary, abortion.

This spread slowly to the masses. The social changes, the reduction in the influence of the Church, the contacts made by conscripts during the period of the Revolution and Empire speeded the diffusion of new attitudes. Most evidently effected were the four regions of Normandy, Gascony, the south of the Massif Central and the Ile de France.

Thus a complex of factors, moral as well as economic induced a fundamental change in human attitudes, a radical modification in the sexual behaviour of a large number of married couples. The change was increasingly evident even in the areas in which the Catholic Church retained its moral authority, though contraception did tend to spread somewhat less rapidly in these. The initial diffusion of the notion of limitation did not occur through the means of written propaganda and did not provoke a reaction from the religious authorities susceptible of modifying the situation until it was too late. Couples rejecting the Church's teaching on contraception must often have done so from ignorance of these teachings. Indeed the traditional condemnation by the Church of sex as a pleasurable act, especially by priests influenced by Jansenism, combined with the fact that pregnancy must have seemed to be a confirmation of this sexuality might well have, initially, before the Church's position had been clarified encouraged efforts to reduce the number of pregnancies. The growing secularisation of human existence tended to result in an increasing reluctance to talk to confessors about sexual relations and a general unwillingness to accept interference with the intimacies of married life.

Whilst stressing the importance of a changing moral outlook, the significance of economic changes in intensifying the desire to limit family size should also be stressed. A less intense fear of famine, greater security and a more optimistic attitude to life stimulated ambition, in particular after the 1830—40s. It was from that point especially, that the high frequency of conception typical of the earlier periods was modified and one of the main features of life transformed.

This transformation was found in prosperous areas rather than poor, amongst property owners or those who aspired to own property, amongst the ambitious rather than those without hope.

Birth-control was not a reflex of distress but of the desire for a better life. In areas in which economic and social structures and attitudes were slow to change, the act of procreation as an aspect of these was also slowly transformed.

Illegitimacy in the countryside, especially in the eighteenth century was very low. Various figures have been presented, e.g. 0.5 per cent of births in the Beauvaisis, 0.3—0.4 per cent in Languedoc, or an unusually high 3 per cent at Troarn in present-day Calvados. From the middle of the century in some areas it tended to increase. National figures of 4.9 per cent for 1800—5, 7 per cent for 1816—20 have been presented, with subsequent stagnation at 7.2—7.6 per cent in spite of urbanisation. Illegitimacy was more common in the towns, not only due to the urban context but because pregnant girls from the countryside often sought shelter there. In the period 1851—6 rural illegitimacy was 4 per cent and urban 12.1 per cent.

The great majority of births however occurred within marriages, and high rates of pre-nuptial conception, if indicating differences in moral outlook and social customs, e.g. 3 per cent of the first-born at Crulai, 30 per cent at Sotteville-le-Rouen, 15 per cent at Ingouville, 23 per cent at Troarn (all in Normandy) do not detract from this.

Marriage

The rate of marriage consequently acted as an important determining element of birth-rate. This is a factor especially true of rural societies where frequently 'the household is the principal unit of economic production as well as consumption, which means that the marriage pattern is tied in very intimately with the performance of the economy as a whole'.[6] In such a situation marriage was a matter of concern for families rather than individuals. In a particular area the age of marriage was determined by the resources available. In many areas population growth was restrained and a precarious balance between population and resources maintained by the practice of postponing marriage. Thus birth-rates could vary considerably between areas, and in the same areas over time, even without the practice of contraception. In large towns marriage was often postponed because of the economic difficulties in the way of establishing a household.

It becomes evident from looking at the statistics on age of marriage that until about 1860 the rate of marriage varied inversely with the price of cereals. High prices were reflected in lower rates of marriages, and vice versa.

In crises marriages were postponed. Following the crisis, in compensation marriages increased, but this did not alter the fact that the number of children likely to be born in marriage was reduced, by perhaps one child for every two years of postponement.

Birth-rate was reduced not merely by such postponement but by a complex of emotional and physical factors. Undernourishment and poor diet, general debilitation might cause temporary sterility of women, though this was less marked as the intensity of crises diminished. The physiological response to psychological uncertainty must have had some effect, and more obviously, due to physical weakness, abstinence from sexual relations was likely. The traditions of continence during religious festivals made this easier.

The declining severity of crises of subsistence in the second half of the eighteenth century meant a reduced effect on birth-rate, and in most years an excess of births over deaths, especially in the 1760—70 period. Marked exceptions were the crisis years of 1772—7, 1779 and 1783. Epidemics if increasing mortality had a far less marked effect on the marriage rate and on conceptions.

The tendency of mortality to decline also had significant effects on marriage. Fewer marriages were ended prematurely by the death of one of the partners. Thus longer-lasting marriages would, at least until the diffusion of the notion of limitation of family size, have more children. The Revolution and Empire, in increasing economic opportunity for some, and as a means of avoiding conscription for others, promoted an increase in the marriage-rate, but by this time contraception was sufficiently common to limit the effects of this on birth-rate.

As the idea of family limitation spread and reduced the fear of one of the consequences of early marriage, impoverishment due to too many children, so also from the 1860s due to the assured provision of food supplies, the link between food prices and marriage-rates disappeared, following a last confirmation of this association during the crisis years 1846—52. In general the economic constraints on emotional relationships were being reduced or transformed. The entire psychological climate of existence was changing.

Food Supply

A variety of factors made sustained population growth possible: the decline in the intensity of crises, the gains of the Revolutionary period in terms of a fairer distribution of produce, agricultural improvements, and the expansion of rural industry. By the middle of the nineteenth century, however, the dominant characteristic of the French countryside was the presence of the poor. In most rural areas it was in this period that maximum population densities were achieved. This was seen in the subdivision of land-holdings, in the competition for farms and for the right to sharecrop, in the growing number of agricultural labourers available and in their underemployment. Significant improvements in agricultural methods had occurred, but these had been insufficient to halt this process of pauperisation. In many areas the adoption of the potato around the turn of the century had permitted a continuation of population growth, but the addition to food supplies and to security this offered as an additional crop were not sufficient to alter the basic situation of misery and degradation in which people lived. Paradoxically more substantial innovation was restrained by the pressing need of the growing population for food, and the general unwillingness or inability to take risks.

The gains of the Revolution had not permitted the breaking out from the constraints of the existing economic system. The abolition of feudal dues and the reduction of taxes obviously increased peasant resources — e.g. in the province of La Marche the land tax had previously amounted to about 30 per cent of revenue, and subsequent to only one-sixth. But the gains were soon countered by population growth. In the Haut Vivarais these changes, combined with the appearance of the potato seem to have stimulated a more rapid growth of population. Conversely the loss of colonial trade caused by the Revolutionary wars led particularly in the south-west and Normandy to the decline of rural industry, an important source of income to supplement that from the land. Increased competition from more technically advanced, urban-based industry was to constitute another threat of growing importance. Other forms of supplementary support were also under attack, including customary rights to pasture, following the law of 1827 designed to safeguard forests from too rapid depredation.

Geographical variations in human conditions were of course evident but not in strict relation to the agricultural potential of particular regions. Much depended on the social structure, on the extent to which a wealthy landowning class was able to exact a surplus at the expense of the mass of consumers, or else on the degree to which widespread subdivision of the land encouraged more rapid population growth, and a more evident over-population. A contrast has been made between the area of plain and that of hillside in the Cevennes. In the first area large estates were owned by a small number of people who themselves absorbed, for consumption and sale, much of the produce. On the slopes the land was subdivided and supported a much larger population, dependent in addition on rural industry and seasonal migration.

More generalised contrasts can be drawn, and have been, between the potentially rich cereal plains of the north and the east, with their monoculture of cereals and chronically undernourished populations; the *bocage* of the west with a more variegated agricultural production but again a social structure and also a more pronounced technical conservatism which engendered misery; the Mediterranean region with a climate favouring an intensive agriculture and the possibility of importing food by sea, but with poverty everywhere although a smaller proportion of dependent labourers; and the mountains where cultivation was always difficult because of relief and soils, and where rights in the forests and seasonal migration were especially important.

At the end of the July Monarchy the countryside generally, with a few exceptions, was on the verge of over-population. The development of rural industry and seasonal migration revealed the severity of the situation, especially in the north-west, east, the Limagne, Lyon region, and in Aquitaine. The enquiry of 1852 estimated the number of seasonal migrants at 878,000. In the mountains — the Alps, Pyrenees and Massif Central — the desperate cultivation of cereals occurred at high altitudes, in clearly unsuitable conditions. Everywhere the cultivation of inferior marginal land, was indicative of the situation. In many areas, particularly where the growing demands of a more intensive agriculture and new industries were as yet unfelt, population was growing more rapidly than employment opportunities.

The crisis of 1848—51 revealed that almost the whole of France was in a state approaching that of relative over-population in which the growth of resources and the distribution of employment opportunities were not adequate to meet the needs of a growing population. Even though the rate of growth was far below that of contemporary underdeveloped countries, the fact remained that France in the middle years of the nineteenth century was extremely susceptible to a crisis of the traditional type associating harvest failure with generalised economic difficulties. The survival of these crises well into the nineteenth century reveals more than anything else the slowness with which the social structure was changing. Only due to massive structural changes in the national and international economies would famine be avoided.

In spite of a significant increase in agricultural productivity before the middle years of the nineteenth century, as productivity increased and more land was brought into cultivation, the food resources available remained subject to the climatically induced fluctuations of harvests, and commonly yielded 50 per cent below or above average, with even greater variations in marketable produce after the necessary deduction of seeds. It has been estimated that, even in a good year, following provision for the consumption of the producers themselves only about 30 per cent of the cereals harvest was marketed. These short-term variations in the product of agriculture were the major events of human existence. These rather than long-term price movements movements were felt by contemporaries.

There was without doubt a reduction in the severity of crises in the eighteenth century. The amplitude of cyclical price movements, experienced in the south-east in 1688—1704 and 1705—20 was not repeated, nor was the quadrupling of grain prices which occurred in Anjou in 1661—2. The crises of the eighteenth and nineteenth centuries rarely occurred on a national scale, for example 1778—82 were crisis years in the south alone, 1782 in the north-north-east and 1786 in the west, although significantly the crisis of 1788—9 affected 27 of the 32 generalities into which France was divided.

For a variety of reasons — the more favourable climate, limited agricultural improvements, gradual development of communications and more effective action by the authorities to ensure food supplies —

crises were attenuated, but none the less frequent. Periods of relative calm might still be followed by periods of more intense crisis. Progress was not constant.

In the south-east the period 1729—60, when the amplitude of crises was reduced, was succeeded by major crises. In Anjou, the relatively good period of 1726—67 was followed by a long period of difficulty due to wet springs and summers in 1768, 1769, 1770, 1782, 1787, and 1788, to exceptional dryness in 1781, 1784, and especially 1785, and exceptionally cold winters in 1784, 1785 and 1789. The effects of these were various. The humid springs and summers were most directly disastrous to the crops but dry summers, in reducing the amount of fodder available, forced the sale of many animals, a decline in the application of manure to the land, a decline in the cereals harvests due to the inadequate number of draught animals, insufficient seeding and lower yields. Cold winters, by freezing the rivers, prevented movement of provisions and the working of water-powered mills.

The age of crises did not end with the eighteenth century. In the Ariège marked crises due to harvest failures were experienced in 1812, 1817, 1829—31, 1837, 1853 and especially 1845—6. For France generally the period 1845—7 was very difficult. For example between July 1845, a moment of roughly normal prices, and April 1847, the point of cyclical high, the price of a hectolitre of wheat on the market at Evreux (Eure) rose from 17.50 fr. to 39 fr. At Draguignon (Var) the increase was from 24.50 fr. to 32 fr. This illustrates the importance of regional differences, but also the general increase experienced at this time: 100 per cent in the first case, and 50 per cent in the second.

A poor harvest inevitably means reduced supply, and in a situation of under-developed communications, regional shortages could not be adequately compensated for by areas with surplus. Even in normal years large numbers of peasants and labourers needed to purchase foodstuffs on the market, and this number greatly increased in years of poor crops. In other words at the very moment when supply was reduced, demand tended to increase. This imbalance was more evident in the centre, east and north, that is the most continental, most populated areas, which were also most dependent on cereals. It was least severe in the Mediterranean areas because of access to international trade and the prevalence of a more varied polyculture, and less severe along the Atlantic coast in the south-west and west. It ought also to be remembered that to a degree plants adapt to local climates and identical conclusions concerning the effects of climate on crops tend to be over-simple.

The question of price fluctuation is a complicated one. In the first place, seasonal fluctuations need to be taken into account along with cyclical. In spring and summer, that is immediately before the harvest,

194

when stocks were running low prices tended to rise, and then in autumn, following the harvest, to fall. The amplitude of such movements, even their direction would vary with the scale of reserves and the quality, or even expectations concerning the crop. Generally seasonal movements tended to reinforce cyclical tendencies, and as late as the first decade of the Second Empire when communications remained poor in many areas, and the isolation of local markets had not everywhere been reduced, price increases of 50—100 per cent were not uncommon. The increased demand for transport facilities during a period of regional shortage served to inflate transport costs, and was a further important factor in price rises.

The influence of stocks must also be taken into account: large stocks might partly offset a poor harvest, whilst the exhaustion of stocks, following a series of poor harvests might result in high prices for several years after the bad harvests whilst stocks were reconstituted. Generally, however, facilities for stocking were very limited. It has been suggested that the traditional notion of the harvest year is too simple, and that in explaining price fluctuations it is necessary to take into account the varying calendar for the maturing of different grains and that for post-harvest tasks like threshing and milling.

Additionally it is maintained, with some justice, that insufficient attention has been paid to possible substitutes for cereals. In a region like Languedoc the consequences of a poor cereal harvest could vary significantly between lower Languedoc, heavily dependent on cereals, and the Cevennes where chestnuts were an important element of the diet, or upper Languedoc where maize often figured as a substitute. It should not be forgotten however the cereals were the major source of foodstuffs and that all food prices tended to reflect those of cereals. Moreover lack of money restricted the extent to which the poor could have recourse to substitutes. The importance has been stressed for lower Auvergne of the availability by 1770 of spring cereals which could be sown to replace a failed autumn-sown crop provided the latter had obviously spoiled early enough. The same possibility existed in the Paris region and provided a limited safeguard against famine.

On the importance of speculation in pushing up prices there is general agreement. The very hint of shortage, and the fear it aroused would serve to unleash actions designed to withhold foodstuffs from markets until prices reached their maximum, thus artificially increasing shortages. Not only the relatively wealthy, but a mass of small men — everyone with a surplus above personal needs — tended to become involved. In the Doubs in June 1817 it was reported that grain was being offered in return for a verbal promise of the repayment of twice or three times as much after the harvest. Those who could afford to laid in stocks for their personal use which also contributed to forcing up prices.

The market situation was often due as much to the lack of money in an economy where exchange was still limited as to actual physical shortage of grains. The supply of coins was limited. Peasants who sold part of their crop, or who engaged in rural industry to obtain money to pay taxes rarely retained reserves of money themselves. The great majority was moreover unable to benefit from the rise in prices. They produced, especially following a poor harvest, insufficient to generate a surplus for sale above their own needs. Those who were in the worst situation were most dependent on the market, especially day labourers without land of their own. But in a bad year most of the population would gradually enter the market to buy grain at inflated prices, which, particularly before the abolition of feudal dues and the tithe, they might have themselves produced, or sold at low price immediately after the harvest to meet their immediate needs, and which they were now forced to repurchase. The wealthy alone possessed buildings with significant storage facilities, accumulating grain by means of feudal dues, sharecropping, rents in kind and purchases, and could make substantial benefits from a situation of shortage, or in every year from seasonal fluctuations. In the nineteenth century this possibility remained an important source of revenue for large landowners, and served to generate hostility against them.

The question of food shortage is related not solely to production but to the distribution of the product in society. Generally the lives of the poor in town and country were fraught with insecurity. Seasonal unemployment affected most trades. Fluctuations in the demands for the products of industry were frequent. Wages and to a degree living standards varied between regions according to the relationship between the supply of and the demand for labour, and local price levels. By and large over-population permitted the reduction of wages to a subsistence minimum. If only part of the population was wage-earning, wage-levels tended to reflect the living standards of all. In an economy dominated by agriculture, where industry, depended above all on demand from the rural population, or from those whose revenues were derived from the land, a crisis in agriculture invariably caused a crisis in industry, and unemployment and reduced wages, especially in the textile industry and the hypersensitive building industry, by far the major employers of urban labour. On the land, too, a poor harvest meant that less labour was required.

The condition of the majority of the poor in town and country, their physiological misery and psychological insecurity, was in glaring contrast with that of the better off, who enjoyed greater security and the ability to profit from the misfortunes of their fellows during a food shortage.

The situation was not stagnant; the conditions and problems of the poor varied over time. The production and distribution of food just about kept pace with an increase in population of perhaps 30—40 per cent in the period 1700—89. Better weather meant fewer harvest failures; improved communications and better-organised commerce improved the distribution from areas of surplus to those of deficit. Thus in the Toulouse region where population increased by 45—50 per cent in the eighteenth century, far outstripping the rate of growth of productivity (which increased by 15—20 per cent from 1730—9 and 1770—89), better communications facilitated provisioning.

The long rise in cereal prices contributed to the increase in road and water traffic by reducing the proportional cost of transport.

The growth of industry and the cultivation of industrial crops permitted the accumulation of money with which to purchase foodstuffs and alleviated conditions in many areas, but this only marginally reduced feelings of insecurity because of dependence on the fluctuating demands of rural and, especially before the Revolution, on colonial markets.

The active intervention of the municipal authorities and of the intendants has been stressed as a vital element in the explanation of better-provisioned markets. The growing effectiveness of the Administration characterised the eighteenth century, although the limits to this remained narrow. Massive intervention on the scale of that of the Revolutionary years with governments preoccupied with the need to feed the armies and Paris, and secondly to provision towns on the main routes to the capital to secure the movement of supplies, led to the dislocation of traditional patterns of supply, and with the imposition of a price maximum on grains in May 1793 to refusals by grain producers to sell in the open market. Official intervention was generally limited to normal purchase operations and distribution at non-profit-making prices. This was a form of charitable activity which appealed to many private citizens also, sharing official fear of the disorder which might otherwise ensue. The urban poor, because of the greater threat they posed to order, were especially likely to invite intervention.

The introduction of new crops, and in particular of the potato and maize were also means, as we have seen, of adapting to increasing population densities, but represented nevertheless a qualitative impoverishment of diet, whilst often providing only a breathing space eventually wiped out by continued population growth. Together with other changes in crop patterns they did provide a growing multiplicity of alternatives to cereals in diet. If everyday lives and the quality and quantity of food consumed changed little between the years of dearth of the eighteenth century and the middle of the nineteenth particularly

197

in those areas isolated from the major zones of communication and trade, this multiplicity, better weather, and improved distribution all but eliminated the killing character of food shortage, but chronic undernourishment survived.

The closing years of the reign of Louis XV and the whole reign of Louis XVI were marked by climatically induced crises, especially severe in the Toulouse region, Languedoc, Provence, and to a lesser extent throughout Northern France. These illustrate the degree to which the *Ancien Régime économique* survived in its fundamental features — high transport charges, and the fragmentation of markets. Only the rich were free of chronic insecurity, and the threat to order which the deprivation of the poor caused, threatened even them.

The decline in the tax burden brought about by the Revolution, in modifying the distribution of resources again temporarily relaxed the pressure of population, postponing the major crisis for another half a century. The intervening period saw recurrent crises and a gradual process of pauperisation in many areas accompanying the growth of population, and in the absence of a radical improvement in agricultural methods and yields. Possibly by the period 1840—50 the upper limit of population, giving the existing resources, had been reached. Severe harvest failure was increasingly likely as densities increased and the cultivation of marginal land, less reliable in its yields, increased, as did the overuse of land more generally.

Examples as diverse as the Paris region and the Ariège can be advanced to indicate this degradation. The population of the capital seems in the 1780s to have had a diet adequate to increase its resistence to epidemics, but the impoverishment of diet in the nineteenth century, until around 1850—60, can be seen in the prevalence of tuberculosis and of epidemics of cholera. In the Ariège population expansion had continued because of the adoption of the potato. From 1845 to 1851 potato crops were more or less bad, causing intense suffering. In the departments of lower Normandy meat consumption per head declined noticeably during the July Monarchy.

Major structural change in the French economy occurred from the middle years of the nineteenth century. Compared with the immediately preceding period there was now to be relative stability of both seasonal and cyclical food prices. Shortages like those of 1817, 1829, 1847 or even 1854—6 disappeared. The combination of railway and telegraph made rapid cheap transport possible. The whole economic mechanism was no longer dominated by movements in the price of cereals. To illustrate the point it is worst observing the change in differences between price minima and maxima. In 1847 the maximum gap had been 20 fr. between the 20 fr. recorded in the Aude and Ariège and the 49 fr. of the Bas-Rhin. After 1859 2—3 fr. became normal. In 1855 when it had been necessary to import 10 million hectolitres of cereals, the still inadequate railway network took eight months to move this stock. In 1861 only three months were required. The ending of this age-old fear had tremendous effects on popular psychology.

The psychology of dearth survived as long as did massive price fluctuations. Although the intensity of crises declined, they remained severe enough to maintain the collective fear of famine. Years of malnutrition, a lifetime dominated by the struggle for food dominated mens behaviour and attitudes. Poverty might be accepted with resignation for as long as it appeared to be inevitable and death often with apathy, but the fear of famine provoked panic. The hungry abandoned the fields, and went around the countryside begging. The increased traffic in grains as supplies were moved into areas of deficit gave credence to all manner of fantastic rumours, often involving a plot by the rich to starve the poor. In the market-places sellers were often forced to part with their grains at what was regarded by mobs as a fair and just price. This was the pattern in those areas most severely affected by shortage, until the 1850s.

These disturbances were one result of unreliable agricultural supplies and population pressure on resources. More invidious was the almost permanent state of undernourishment in which most of the population existed. The rich always escaped, and those of the poor living in the regions of most active and varied economic life, particularly in the north, seemed to have enjoyed normally superior physiological conditions to the populations of most of France, but conditions generally were not good. Only a minority of prosperous peasants artisans and highly skilled workers escaped misery.

Diet

Probably nothing reveals more clearly the standard of living of populations whilst also providing a key to the understanding of mortality and birth-rates than an analysis of diet.

Before the coming of the railways, people ate what they grew or at least what was grown locally. Diet reflected local natural conditions and traditions and was affected only to a very limited extent by commerce. There was thus considerable regional variation, but generally the basis of diet was cereals, used to make bread or porrage. The most significant variations were due to the existence of a genuine polyculture where population densities were low enough to permit the use of land for the cultivation of crops other than cereals. This was more evident in the south, and in the mountains, than in the north and east.

Diet did not, however, exactly reflect production. Often the richer cereals were produced for sale to pay taxes and feudal dues, whilst the

the poorer cereals were retained for popular consumption. Nowhere was this phenomenon as pronounced as in Brittany, where similarly, if there were a relatively large number of cows these were bred to supply the demand for meat from Normandy and Paris, and meat consumption in Brittany remained very low. However, in compensation relatively large supplies of milk and butter were available for local consumption, as well as export, and this was a significant element of quality in the diet of the poor, made possible by the survival of large areas of wasteland.

In the mountains of the Auvergne large areas of wasteland allowed for the breeding of cows, of pigs, reared on the residue of cheese production and also of sheep and goats. Thus diet was more varied than in the cereal producing plains, although more lacking in fruit and vegetables.

In many areas consumption of meat, and dairy products, was restricted by the lack of pasture and by the low milk yields of diseased and badly cared-for animals. Meat and wines were consumed primarily on occasions of festivity and during periods of especially hard work. Such luxuries would be sold rather than consumed. A common tradition was the slaughter of one pig in the year, the meat being salted to provide the year's meat supply.

The provision of vegetables and fruits from gardens, and of additional meat through poaching were important supplements to diet, but again primarily where space allowed for forests and gardens.

The diet of the mass of town-dwellers was scarcely any better, although it is significant that in Brittany in the eighteenth century the poorest cereals disappeared from common consumption the major towns long before they did in the countryside. However in the 1840s the Lille worker still subsisted on a monotonous fare of bread and potatoes.

It is difficult to determine the exact significance of bread in the popular diet, but even given the existence of alternatives like potatoes or chestnuts, it remained true that the price of bread was the major determining factor in total living standards. Throughout the first half of the nineteenth century increases in its price, in requiring that a higher proportion of probably reduced income be devoted to the purchase of bread, resulted in a marked decline in the quantity and quality of an already impoverished diet. In the Auvergne, for example, oatmeal of lower nutritional value tended to replace rye. More generally populations faced with the possibility of starvation because they had insufficient money ate the cheapest food available including green fruits, unripe grain and meat from diseased carcasses. In the towns where adulteration of foodstuffs was normally common, further decline in quality occurred. The Revolution, although reducing tax burdens and permitting temporary improvements, produced no significant change in the character of diet. Prior to the railway era the changes which did occur paradoxically owed much to severe shortages.

In general eating habits were only slowly modified, but some changes occurred rapidly and then usually out of desperation. The introduction of the potato is a good example. This possessed certain advantages as a substitute for or a supplement to cereals, particularly in upland areas where unsuitable growing conditions caused especially marked irregularities in cereal crops. It could be successfully cultivated in most soils up to 1,400–1,500 metres, and even in shade its yields were high. Most significantly perhaps in respect of this supplementary rôle it did well after humid springs, precisely the conditions under which cereals suffered. The potato entered the popular diet in Alsace during the period 1740–70; in Auvergne with the crisis of the 1770s; in the Nivernais especially after the crisis of 1812–13. In the Pyrenees its cultivation reached a maximum extension by the 1840s; the failure of the potato currently with that of cereals in 1845, due to disease, was there to be especially disastrous.

This, together with the gradual extension and intensification of agriculture, was the major change occurring in food supply in the eighteenth and first half of the nineteenth century. Any attempt to relate the statistics available on population density and population growth to those available on food production and supply is fraught with danger. Much of the product of agriculture in a self-subsistence economy does not enter commerce and cannot be measured. The statistical sources are simply inadequate. After reading the reports, of the enquiry of 1848 and other descriptive sources, one is inevitably left with the overwhelming impression that until the middle of the nineteenth century undernourishment was chronic and normal for the majority of the population throughout France, that for the masses the basic problem of life was how and what to eat, that if few people actually died of starvation the levels of energy and of health in such a civilisation could not be high. In short France was characterised by the survival of the *Ancien Régime alimentaire*, and the various problems arising from this.

Recent research into diet supports the conclusion that before the middle years of the nineteenth century change was slow. In terms of calorific value and nutritional content diet was similar to that in modern under-developed countries. Toutain calculates an average daily consumption rising from 1,700 to 2,000 calories from the end of the eighteenth century to around 1830, followed by a more rapid increase to 2,800 and 3,000 calories by 1880. He further estimates that 80 per cent of these calories were supplied by cereals in 1789 and 72 per cent in 1850 (30 per cent in 1960–4), whilst the contribution of meats was only 7 per cent in 1789 (15 per cent in 1960–4), and of dairy products under 5 per cent from 1789 to 1880 (10 per cent 1960—4). Protein supply was similarly dominated by cereals to the extent of 70 per cent as late as 1880 with meat and milk products contributing around 10 per cent each.[7] Diet was everywhere unbalanced, even if the nature of this lack of balance varied between areas: in the Limagne, for example, the population of the plains suffered from a lack of animal protein; in the mountains, by contrast, there was a lack of fruit and vegetables. Whatever the nature of the disequilibrium its presence was constant, as can be seen from the physiological misery of the masses, and their susceptibility to disease.

The historian suffers from a lack of precise scientific analysis of human nutritional needs and of the effects of deficiencies. However, in 1840, when Charles Dupin reported on the physical condition of military conscripts he was convinced that a degeneration of the race was occurring. Even in 1860 26.8 per cent of the young men examined were rejected as medically unfit, and the figure rose to 32.7 per cent, when those rejected for inadequate stature were included. The condition of older age-groups and certain social groups, including the growing factory proletariat was even worse.

The basic problem was undernourishment, due to insufficiency of food in both quantity and quality, deficiencies in vitamins, proteins and certain oligo-elements, causing malformation of the skeletal structure and general physiological deficiencies, including lack of intellectual and physical energy and constant bad health. The physical development of young men was often retarded, affected even before birth by the undernourishment of their mothers, and if surviving birth often congenitally inadequate, liable to typical nutritional maladies like rickets and scurvy, to skin diseases due to malnutrition and dirtiness, to goitre and cretinism and to general mental underdevelopment caused by protein malnutrition. There were evidently regional variations. The nature of the staple food usually determined the type and severity of malnutrition. To take simply the example of the Auvergne towards the end of the eighteenth century. Here there was a clear contrast between the population of the mountains, superior in physical vigour and spirit, and longer living than the population of the plains, because their agricultural conditions provided a more varied and richer diet. Due to lack of animal protein and especially milk the lowland population seemed to have suffered from something akin to Kwashiorkor common in contemporary Asia. In the 1840s probably the most extreme cases of misery were to be found in the Pyreneean areas of the department of Ariège where the causes were over-population, food shortage, and also consanguine marriages, all typical of the closed, underdeveloped economy. Here more than anywhere else the social system, by means of limited access to foodstuffs, limited social mobility and restricted mental horizons created generation after generation of suffering individuals, both effect and cause of its survival, because in such a situation 'the whole manner of life is adapted to an insufficient supply of calories with results that are socially undesirable: lack of drive and initiative, avoidance of physical and mental effort; excessive rest'.[8]

The picture was not uniformly as grim, as we have already observed, but it is difficult to escape concluding of the populations we are observing that at no time before the second half of the nineteenth century had they escaped from the threat of starvation or the very real effects of undernourishment. Diet in normal times might just have been adequate to maintain reasonable standards of health, but for beings subjected to the effects of intermittent harvest failures and disease it did not provide an adequate means of recovery. If hunger did not kill directly, in the digestive illnesses to which it led, and in low resistence to sickness, it maintained high levels of mortality. The history of disease can only be understood in relation to the prevalence of this physiological misery.

Disease

The last great plague epidemic occurred in Marseille in 1720, although the fear it created meant that most epidemics continued for a considerable time to be labelled 'peste' by the poor. The disappearance of plague illustrates the point that epidemic cycles have in part a coherence of their own, and can not be linked exclusively to the economy. Man, as a zoological species must be related to historically evolving virus and bacilli as well as to the social context in the usual sense.

The disappearance of the plague cannot be seen as a sign of improved standards of life. Disease remained endemic amongst the most miserable, even in the best years and then spread more widely in years when human organisms were particularly weak and susceptible to attack.

For most of the population diet was normally unbalanced. Shortage increased its inadequacy. Epidemic inevitably followed dearth, indicating a close, if not causal relationship between disease and economic conditions in which diet largely determined capacity of resistance to disease. Epidemics often followed the harvest. The supply and quality of food was normally at its lowest point immediately prior to the harvest, which required exhausting work during a period of deterioration of diet.

The way in which mortality rates reflected social inequality was further evidence of this link with undernourishment. Perhaps the fundamental difference between rich and poor was that the former at all times ate more and better. The poor, whether in town or country were decimated by disease. The rich, although likely to be infected, according to the normal rules of contagion, were far less likely to die. Their organisms were stronger and more resistant.

This differential mortality can be illustrated using a calculation based on the mortality figures for Paris in 1817, dividing the *arrondisements* into three groups, according to levels of wealth. The calculation is crude but revealing:[9]

Mortality corrected to minimise the effect of location of hospitals

	arrondissements	
Group I (the wealthiest)	1, 2, 3, 4	23.2 per thousand
Group II	5, 6, 7, 10, 11	26.5 per thousand
Group III	8, 9, 12	37.5 per thousand

If death from starvation was rare, food shortage forced the poor to eat food of a quality even inferior to their normal provisions. Frequently the result was intestinal disorders. In areas where fruit trees were common, severe dysentery epidemics were likely when the major crops failed — caused by a combination of eating unripe fruits and undernourishment. In the late eighteenth century these epidemics were characteristic of the poorest regions. One in Anjou for example, where bacilleary dysentery of a very contagious character spread directly by contact with the sick, or indirectly through clothes, food and water, had disastrous consequences.

Another scourge was smallpox. In the Alençon plain, it and Scarlatina appeared in cycles of 6—7 years. In other areas, including parts of Brittany it was almost endemic. Innoculation spread from the 1780s, but slowly and·intermittently. The disease remained common in the nineteenth century, with as late as 1869—72 occurrence on an epidemic scale, with 50,000 cases, 17,680 of which were mortal.

Along the Mediterranean and Atlantic coasts, and in marshy regions of the interior, malaria was a common and debilitating disease, which rapidly disappeared, but only after 1850, when large-scale drainage programmes were completed.

Also related to water, in fact to deficiencies in water supply, were the common epidemics of the typhus-typhoid kind and also gastroenteritis and colitus, which would only disappear with the improvement of supplies mainly from the second half of the nineteenth century. As late as 1848, in Prades (Ariège) typhoid killed 110, one-seventh of the population, and this was not exceptional. In Paris too, typhoid remained common. Where drinking-water fountains and rivers were used for a variety of purposes, including washing the clothes of the sick, contagian was inevitable. The demographic effects of typhoid-type epidemics have been carefully examined for Normandy in the late eighteenth century and it has been concluded that if they were less dramatic than the great mortalities of the seventeenth century they were longer lasting, and due to this only a little less murderous.

The list of diseases is long. Tuberculosis was an especial sign of malnutrition and its ravages certainly did not decline in the nineteenth century. Venereal diseases became more widespread, propagated in many areas by wet-nurses, themselves infected by the children they suckled, or brought home by seasonal migrant workers. Hydrophobia continued to terrify. The wolves which transmitted it were gradually eliminated, but domestic animals still proved a threat, which if less frequent still meant horrible and inevitable death. Revealing of the standards of life was the lethal character of measles, whooping-cough, pneumonia and pleurisy, all indicative of low powers of resistance.

Cholera, appearing in 1832, signified a renewal of the ancient mortalities and revealed again the weak potential for resistance of much of the population. Cholera and tuberculosis are perhaps the symbols of misery in this first half of the nineteenth century. This first epidemic claimed 103,000 victims. Its recurrence in 1849 killed 19,184 in Paris alone. In 1854 in the region of east Aquitaine cholera followed a rise in food prices. In the period August-October, 11,266 deaths were recorded in the Ariège, 2,226 in Haute-Garonne and only 17 in the Tarn-et-Garonne. 100,000 died in France. Significantly epidemics of typhoid and smallpox were present at the same time. If in the Ariège 4 per cent of the population died, the figure rose to 20 per cent in five cantons of the Foix area, the poorest part of the department. A similar kind of differentiation between the very poor and the rest was observed in Bordeaux, where in the richest *arrondissement,* the 3rd only three deaths were recorded, whilst in the poor 8th and 10th the figures were 125 and 201 respectively.

The pattern of disease varied over time as an aspect of the history of disease, and also of changes in the socio-economic structure.

Amongst the workers in new factories scurvy, rickets, tuberculosis and alcoholism were common along with the accidents due to unguarded machinery and chemicals indicating a serious malaise due to a combination of poor wages, poor working conditions, long hours, poor food and lodgings. The situation of agricultural labour was sometimes superior, sometimes no better, depending on the region, but everywhere physical debility was common, and in poor areas like Finistère the recourse to alcohol as a means of escape was very marked, even as the nineteenth century progressed.

Morineau has recently argued that it is not necessary to link population increase to developments in agriculture or medicine, rather that the explanation is likely to rest primarily on a recession in the virulence of disease.[10] It is tempting to agree, particularly following an analysis which seeks to indicate the unrevolutionised character of French society before the middle years of the nineteenth century. Only after this did living standards substantially improve. Previously there had existed large variations in prosperity and living conditions between areas. Some had been more nearly liberated from epidemics than others, but for an undernourished population crowded together in insanitary towns and villages escape was never entirely possible. To many sickness must still have appeared as an inescapable punishment by God for the sins of man.

The limited ability of medicine to check disease has been mentioned, and the point must be enlarged upon, not only in respect of the development of medical science, but in relation to popular attitudes to medicine and hygiene.

The lack of personal hygiene and of sanitation combined with inadequate diet to explain the continuation of high death-rates. Bodily hygiene is in effect pre-determined by the water resources available, by clothing, by standards of public hygiene and by general attitudes to cleanliness, these being influenced by medical knowledge to a greater or lesser extent.

In a traditional civilisation the sources of water were diverse, but generally external to the house — in streams, wells and cisterns. Problems of collection and storage were factors limiting the quantity used. Running water was rare, even in major cities, before the second half of the nineteenth century, and spread only slowly until the early twentieth century. People were usually dirty. This was especially true of the poor, who were unable to afford soap. Villermé observed of Alsatian workers in 1840 that the poor have neither the desire nor the time, nor the means to be other than filthy. By modern standards even the well-off were none too clean, and their standards of dental health in particular were deplorable. Clothing too was dirty. The poor wore clothes until they became rags, or little better; linen was rarely changed.

This general lack of hygiene effected housing too. Accommodation was inadequately cleaned because of the lack of water and generally overcrowded. This was especially evident as urban growth occurred, and new building simply failed to provide for the influx of population. For the poor, finding a decent place to live was for long to remain a problem, especially as growing demand led to increases in rents. The possibilities of contagion in crowded accommodation, with inadequate ventilation and insufficient sanitary installations is obvious. Medical reports on Paris following the cholera epidemic of 1832 stressed the relationship between high mortality and high population densities. Conditions in most provincial centres seem to have been equally insalubrious, whilst those for peasants and rural labourers were generally rudimentary and dirty to an extent that was not sufficiently compensated by the clean country air. The streets too were unhealthy: in Paris before the reforms introduced by Haussman they were filthy, whilst in smaller centres the situation was even worse due to the practice in the countryside of keeping manure piles outside houses.

For those who could afford the cost, and indeed for large numbers of people in both town and country, the prosperous years of the Second Empire encouraged the construction of better houses. Improved communications meant the spread of new standards. In many rural areas overcrowding declined with population densities as migration developed. Improvement was slowed by the survival of traditional attitudes and often by the fact that housing came low on a list of priorities which placed acquiring new land or even constructing new farm buildings before human comfort.

If water supply was usually inadequate, the effects of this were heightened by the poor quality of the water obtained. Infiltration corrupted supplies, as did the multiplicity of uses to which sources were put. In Paris the Second Empire brought about a radical improvement in supplies, but at Nevers, for example, where at least part of the town had enjoyed the facilities of piped water from 1830, filtration was only introduced in the 1920s.

These were conditions which changed only very slowly, and before the 1850s, change was hardly perceptible. This was another respect in which the human condition remained essentially unchanged, until the second half of the nineteenth century. This was an element within a complex of ecological factors determining the spread and lethal effect of disease.

Improvements in medicine have been suggested as part of the explanation of population increase, and it is likely that a series of changes did have important results.

Midwifery certainly improved. Intendants under central government impulsion were requiring the provision of courses for midwives as early as the 1770s, which served to reduce both the number of deaths in child-birth and the deformation of children caused by maladroit delivery. Even as late as 1853 in the Nievre however, whole cantons were without midwives and babies continued to be delivered by village women. In the struggle against epidemics too, more systematic action was encouraged by governments including the dispatch of doctors, food and medicines to areas of infection. The result was that even if practical standards of medical science advanced little, the sick were isolated, made cleaner, and given a better diet, so reducing contagion and increasing possibilities of recovery. Stress should be placed on this increase in the intervention of the authorities in matters of public health, which had its limits, rather than on improvement in medical practice. Of the latter, there were some, most notable the introduction in the eighteenth century of the South American plants quinquina and ipecacuana, effective against malaria and dysentery, and the diffusion of innoculation against smallpox, which became generalised early in the nineteenth century. Otherwise medical care remained primitive. The successes of surgery were limited by the effects of shock, haemorrhage and infection. Bleeding and purges tended to be used as universal cures — and if the latter were indeed often beneficial, in the case of typhoid for example they were likely to cause a fatal intestinal perforation. In the preparation of medicines, chemistry was little employed, and normally to no good effect. Medicines were prepared from plants and animal products, and often there seems to have been little difference between the remedies offered by the recognised doctors and those of the village quacks. Medical ideas were confused. Only in 1887, to take one example, was typhoid blamed on water supply, and widespread acceptance of the idea took time.

The number of doctors was inadequate especially in the countryside and poorer areas of towns. Their competence was mediocre and their aid regarded as too expensive by most of the population. Recourse was had to their care generally only when the patient was on the verge of death.

Hospitals too were few in number, small in size, and almost non-existent in the countryside. The *cahiers* of 1789 included numerous request for hospitals. The Revolution served to reduce the hospital facilities provided by the Church, and by 1849 there had been little increase. In the 1860s the lack of hospitals in the countryside was being offered as an explanation of migration to the towns. Normally the rural sick were only accepted in town hospitals when there was room and when their communes offered payment, both of which were rare.

Although hospital conditions slowly improved Cuvier's comment that patients experienced 'the sufferings of hell' in them remained apt. Lack of hygiene and overcrowding, the mixing of patients with a variety of illnesses, multiplied the possibility of contagion. Descriptions of provincial hospitals in the 1850s echoed these complaints. Hospitals remained places to be afraid of, and the extension and the improvement of medical and hospital networks occurred mainly after the Second Empire.

Illness and old age should be stressed as constant elements in the situation of the poor, inescapable causes of poverty and degredation for much of the population, to be added to the consequences of economic crises. Hard work, especially in the countryside, made for rapid ageing. The old were often regarded as parasites, and worked until they dropped to avoid this. The social situation of the aged and infirm was perhaps symbolised most clearly by the widespread prevalence of begging. This declined rapidly after the middle years of the nineteenth century, indicative of changing conditions, but until then, for many, charity was an essential supplement to inadequate resources. 'The beggars were the product of poverty and of a recognition that however hard one worked one could do nothing other than drag out a wretched existence.'[11] Only a small élite — the wealthy, or to a lesser extent the better-paid workers who could afford to subscribe to mutual aid societies — could be reasonably confident of escaping utterr degradation. Public assistance took the form of work relief or simple charity, and the provision of free medical care for paupers. It was not adequate to meet the needs of a population, much of which normally lived around subsistence level.

From the 1850s a rapid decline in the prevalence of chronic undernourishment occurred. Whereas formerly transport costs and lack of money had combined to limit diet to locally produced food — insufficiently abundant, and in quality insufficiently differentiated — now the combination of better communications, more rapid agricultural improvement and general progress in living standards caused accelerated, extensive and sustained improvements in diet.

Until the 1880s the improvement, for most of the population was essentially quantitative due to the increased production and more efficient supply of elements of the traditional diet. Once, however, caloric saturation had been achieved — by 1880 — then further increase in living standards involved improvements in the quality of diet. Meat, vegetables and fruit were increasingly added to the popular diet. The railway network, with the extension of the range of markets it introduced, was decisive in bringing about increased security of supply and variation in production. Diet was often still slow to change. Old established habits needed to be broken. Meat for much of the population remained a luxury throughout the nineteenth century, but the decline of fluctuations in demand for meat evinced its growing acceptance as a necessity by all classes.

Improvement in diet was reflected in improvements in health. Poverty and undernourishment did not disappear. Marked differences in diet between social groups remained but the degree of differentiation declined significantly.

Initially rather than in terms of quality the change was most appreciated by the poor in terms of quantity. For the first time in human history, massive fluctuations in the supply and particularly the price of basic foodstuffs disappeared. This was the most significant result of the transport revolution in relation to human existence and behaviour. This more than anything else marked the disappearance of the *Ancien Régime économique and sociale*.

Migration

Population growth cannot be discussed without consideration of population structure. A different kind of society, based on a different kind of economy exists once inflows into the towns occur on a scale sufficient to alter the traditional balance between town and country.

Before the middle of the nineteenth century, economic development being relatively slow, the employment opportunities offered by the towns were relatively restrained. Even so substantial numbers of migrants reached the towns in search of work or of food which urban merchants and administrations made great efforts to secure for the towns, from both economic interest and in order to minimise disorder. The ambitious arrived in search of opportunity, often bringing some capital with them; the desperate sought a means of subsistence which the countryside no longer offered. More significantly, throughout the countryside there were considerable flows of seasonal migrant labour. Under growing population pressure, resources in many regions became inadequate, particularly where isolation inhibited the development of rural industry. This was the case most clearly in large parts of the Massif Central, and the Alpine and Pyreneean areas.

Harvest work in richer agricultural regions provided one alternative. Such movements were a symptom of misery, of the difficulty of earning enough to live. As population pressure increased in the first decades of the nineteenth century so seasonal migration increased. It was especially important in upland areas like the Cevennes which had, because of the altitudes, a later harvest time than in the plains.

Seasonal migrations such as that of masons from the Marche and Limousin were not always entirely due to over-population. In Cantal for example they caused a labour shortage during the period of harvest, which required the immigration of labour from poorer areas. It was simply that the wages earned in the building industry made the harvest something of secondary importance. This movement too increased in the early nineteenth century, stimulated by more rapid urban development. By mid-century from the Creuse alone 25–30,000 migrants went to Paris or Lyon each year.

From the 1840s and especially 1850–60s temporary migration rapidly began to give way to permanent. Often new crops, a changing agricultural timetable made it more difficult to conveniently harvest successively in a number of places. Industry increasingly required a more permanent labour force. The contrast between town and country, in terms of conditions of existence grew wider and if formerly temporary migration had provided a means of supplementing the income from the land in one's home area, increasingly, in permitting a growing awareness of superior opportunities and living standards elsewhere, it stimulated

210

permanent migration.

A number of changes such as improved communications, more rapid industrialisation, urbanisation, and in agriculture commercialisation, served to upset the precarious equilibrium of rural life for many, whilst providing growing employment opportunities in the towns. During the July Monarchy the rate of migration increased, but the fundamental period in which the shape of inter-sectoral transfers of labour for the future was traced was the decade 1852–62. The trend was general but especially pronounced in the south-west, southern Alps, Normandy, Picardy and much of the north-east. In these areas maximum rural population was achieved by 1860. This occurred much later in the Centre, Brittany, Vendeé, and some isolated departments like Gironde and Seine-et-Oise, but became everywhere rapid from 1890–1900.

Significantly, migration did not transform the more over-populated areas first. It seems to have developed earlier and to a greater degree from the more prosperous agricultural areas which were closer to major urban centres and to have occurred mainly over short distances and in a number of stages, spread over several generations.

Labour shortage stimulated the mechanisation of agriculture in what were for the most part already the more technologically advanced agricultural areas, whilst continued high population densities in more isolated and technically backward regions would for long hinder structural modernisation and allow for the survival not only of technical, but major social disparities between regions.

Who migrated? First the artisans and agricultural labourers, those with little or no land of their own, with less of a stake in rural society. Where the population included a large proportion of peasant proprietors migration was slower to develop and subsequently structural modification of agriculture limited. The years of the Second Empire were relatively prosperous in many areas. Only slowly did commercial pressures build up, forcing many small proprietors in the last third of century into an awareness of the fact that their farms were uneconomic. Prior to this the emigrants were young people, not heads of households: women who found employment as domestics, washerwomen and *concierges,* men who went into building and mining. Railway development did however make it increasingly easier for whole families to move.

The reasons they moved were various. Whilst recognising the artificiality of the division it is useful to divide them into factors repelling people from the countryside and factors attracting them to the towns. In real life, of course, both motives are inseparable and ought to be considered within the context of the whole complex of relations between rural and urban societies.

Migration had always occurred, but had not previously continued so as to cause a seemingly permanent depopulation of the countryside. The beginning of this more permanent movement can be seen in the growing competition of the products of mechanised industry with those of rural industry, particularly in textiles, even before the development of railways. To provide employment throughout the year and to supplement the income derived from agriculture a whole range of extra activities had been carried on. Only such a variety permitted a large population to subsist.

By the 1840s population pressure on resources was growing intense and these resources were anyway beginning to decline particularly in areas like that around Amiens due to the new factories. The agricultural crisis beginning in 1845–6 and the general economic crisis it engendered substantially reduced living standards for a period of four or five years, forcing migration of some of the more desperate, but more fundamentally creating an attitude amongst those who remained which would turn into a desire to escape once new opportunities for employment had been created.

With the development of improved communications rural industry went into rapid decline. The closure of the Catalan forges in the Ariège was typical of this. Agriculture was faced with a need to adapt to new conditions. Often adaptation meant an increased need for labour, but also longer days and harder work just when industrial expansion provided the opportunity for escape. In other areas pasture replaced arable farming and a final, successful assault on traditional common rights and rights of usage in forests removed vital supplementary resources.

This was the likely pattern in areas with poor soils where the process of adaptation of traditional subsistence agriculture to new market conditions was most difficult. Without a rapid increase in production, or a radical transformation of the social structure, living standards could only be improved by a reduction of population.

New crises such as disease affecting the vine and silk cultivation, overseas competition affecting the markets for flax and hemp, the introduction of chemical dyes to replace roots, the growing depression of world cereal prices, reaching a low in the period 1880–5, further weakened the position of much of the agricultural population.

A change in psychology occurred along with these economic changes. As awareness of the outside world increased, the rewards gained from agriculture were seen to be disproportionate to the effort required. Not only were conditions for work and living inferior to those in the towns, but the peasant's assessment of self in relation to the urban-dweller was more and more that of an inferior. Urban values and norms became universally accepted. The young especially, in part due to primary education, felt isolated from the modern world.

Their migration served to reduce the potential for dynamic action within rural society.

The combination of the destruction of the equilibrium of the closed economy and of the demographic equilibrium based upon it coupled with the broad feeling of inferiority, generated a movement away from the countryside which led to an improvement of living standards as population pressure was reduced, but not to a reversal of the psychological need to escape.

The goal of the migrant was not always the town. Much movement, and this often not revealed clearly by statistics, was within rural areas. In the Alps a slow movement down the mountains occurred. The poor from above were generally willing to work for lower rewards than those below, so that the latter too were pushed into movement. Marginal land was increasingly abandoned. The terraces laboriously constructed in the Cevennes were left to erosion. Even within communities there was a clear tendency towards concentration of population, a movement from the more isolated hamlets to a central village. The concentration of artisanal and commercial activity, and of administration meant that many small communities lost coherence and balance.

Longer distance movements occurred, from agricultural regions of low income to those which were more dynamic and offered a higher income. The goal of the migrant depended above all on the situation of his area of origin and also upon the traditions created by temporary migration. Thus although most migration tended to be step by step, over short distances, from the Creuse with its migratory building workers, direct movement to Paris was frequent.

Currents of migration were created. Even when the economic necessity for emigration ended, it continued, as relatives and friends followed each other. Migration was now for more positive reasons, in hope of a better life, than for negative, from desperation in the face of apparently inescapable poverty. It was not forced by the mechanisation of agriculture, which in general was a response to the growing problem of labour shortage, but by the attraction of the towns. Town life promised greater security, a more regular wage, better housing, medical facilities, education, leisure activities, a social promotion for oneself and the hope of even greater things for one's children. It was significant that for the remainder of the nineteenth century migration was most intense from the more prosperous agricultural areas, those with the highest wages, but which were also close to major towns and most aware of the life in them.

It is paradoxical that at the very moment when the fear of famine disappeared mass migration occurred. The paradox reveals perhaps the scale and complexity of the changes affecting the rural world in this transition from semi-closed to more open societies.

The urban population, considered by the census as including all those living in communities with a population of 2,000 or more, grew as follows:[12]

	France	rural	urban	%
1846	35,400,486	26,753,743	8,646,743	24.4
1851	35,783,170	26,647,711	9,135,459	25.5
1861	37,386,313	26,596,547	10,789,766	28.9
1866	38,067,064	26,471,716	11,595,348	30.5
1872	36,102,921	24,868,022	11,234,899	31.1
1891	38,343,192	24,031,900	14,311,292	37.4

This urban growth was large and medium city growth rather than small town. The larger the city, the more rapid the growth.

Urban growth in the period 1789–1846 was in fact less rapid than it had been for much of the eighteenth century. The Revolution, by creating problems for the urban economy and increasing the resources of the rural population, stemmed the movements to the towns. Not until the mid nineteenth century did major changes occur.

Traditionally towns were a part of the surrounding rural world. Because of poor transport conditions towns as manufacturing, commercial and administrative centres could serve only a limited geographical area. This then was a phase of dispersal of functions. Even in 1851 there were only 58 towns with more than 20,000 inhabitants, and only 6 with over 100,000, and these all very far from each other. The more urbanised regions were north of the Somme, Languedoc with Montauban, Toulouse, Castres and Carcasonne; the lower Rhône valley with Avignon, Montpellier and Toulon; the Loire valley from Orléans to Nantes and the Lyon-St Etienne region. By contrast whole regions were almost deprived of towns, including Normandy, Brittany, the south-east, and centre-east of the Paris basin, the south-west and the Alps.

If the potential for development was limited by the extent of the geographical area served, it was too by the food producing capacity of the accessible hinterland. It is perhaps significant that the growth of manufacture in the lower Languedoc in the eighteenth century around Lodève and Alais followed the improvements in conditions for food supply consequent upon the construction of the Canal du Midi.

The growth of non-agricultural employment can be related to two factors: the increased productivity of agricultural labour, and the growing efficiency of the facilities for the distribution of the product.

Before the middle of the nineteenth century, rather than a genuine process of urbanisation there had occurred a slow concentration of population in market towns. Subsequently urbanisation replaced agglomeration. Urban growth was mainly due to migration and occurred essentially where modern industrialisation was under way, this was true even in the case of cities like Bordeaux and Toulouse, which were in rich agricultural areas, and were important commercial centres, but now were additionally distinguished by industrial growth. The process is even more obvious in the growth of the complex Lille-Roubaix-Tourcoing Paris, due to the variety and importance of its functions, grew more rapidly than any other centre.

The changes in the communications structure made possible a concentration of economic activities and this created the modern urban network. Not all towns gained from this process. Many smaller towns lost traditional functions in small-scale industry and commerce, and became simply relays in a new system of distribution as their former functions were concentrated on the larger centres. In Languedoc the textile industry faced growing competition from the north, and in the second half of the century the population of Lodève declined from 11,000 to 8,000; that of Bédarieux from 10,000 to 6,000.

Paris replaced former regional capitals like Orléans as commercial centres and it became evident that the growth of towns in Champagne, Picardy and Normandy, of places like Châlons-sur-Marne, Beauvais, Arras, Abbeville, was restricted due to the regional predominance of Paris. Some centres, important in the old communications structure lost part or all of these functions. At Poitiers, for example, the railway employed fewer people than had formerly carting and the various hostelries. Beaugency, a river port on the Loire, experienced a far more marked decline. During the Second Empire most urban centres continued with their traditional functions as market places, hardly affected by economic change. It was the large, and the medium centres which were affected first, but as the communications networks became more dense in the last quarter of the century so the concentration of functions became more marked.

As urban centres grew larger they were transformed structurally. Systems of public hygiene were more obviously necessary as populations grew; better internal communications were required as commerce increased. The developments associated with Haussman in Paris were repeated in many provincial centres. The process of solving certain problems intensified others. Thus in the old Paris of narrow streets and high houses there had been less social segregation than there would be in the reconstructed areas, where higher rents intensified the drift of the poor to the eastern quarters of the city. Cheap public transport allowed the process of suburbanisation and the creation of the modern city.

Demographic evolution since the Middle Ages had taken the form of successive phases of growth and decline. The Revolution, beginning in 1789 did very little to change the fundamental bases of existence. Subsistence was and remained the great problem of traditional society, dominating all aspects of life. Once the problem of food supply was solved a different kind of economy and a different kind of society could exist.

In the first half of the nineteenth century, at least until the crisis of 1846—51 nothing had occurred to change the essential structure of and conditions of existence within French society. Descriptions of the food crises and disease common in so much of France in 1847 sound like a description of the eighteenth century food shortage and its effects. But, beginning during the Second Empire, accelerated transformation occurred due to the transport revolution, which made possible assured food supplies, industrialisation on a national scale, urbanisation, mass migration, improved living standards, and, to reflect the growing awareness of better conditions, a further decline in the birth-rate.

There are few sharp breaks in history; social development seems to occur by means of almost imperceptible transitions. The transport revolution permitted one such sharp break in destroying the most serious obstacles restraining economic growth and social change, and in ending the fear of famine.

Notes

1. Bergeron, L., *L'episode Napoléonien*, 1972, p. 122.
2. Dupeux, G., *La société française, 1789—1960*, 1964, p. 12.
3. Delumeau, 'Démographie et mentalités: la mort en Anjou (17e—18e siècles)', *A.E.S.C.*, 1972, p. 139.
4. Armengaud, A., *La population française au 19e siècle*, 1971, pp. 19, 39.
5. Poitrineau, A., *La vie rurale en basse-Auvergne au 18e siècle*, 1965, p. 108.
6. Hainal, J., 'European Marriage Patterns in perspective' in Glass, D.V., and Eversley, D.E.C., *Population in History*, 1965.
7. Toutain, J.C., 'La consommation alimentaire en France de 1789 à 1966', *E.S.*, 1971, p. 1979.
8. F.A.O. Report quoted by Clark, C., and Haswell, M. in *The Economics of Subsistence Agriculture*, 1970, p. 23.
9. Chevalier, L., 'Towards a history of Population', in Glass and Eversley, op. cit., p. 672.

10. Morineau, M., *Les faux-semblants d'un démarrage économique: agriculture et démographie en France au 18e siècle*, 1971, p. 672.
11. Hufton, O., *Bayeux in the late Eighteenth Century*, 1967, p. 86.
12. Weber, A.F., *The Growth of cities in the Nineteenth Century*, Ithaca, 1963, pp. 67–71.

Further Reading

Agulhon, M., 'La crise dans un département Mediterraneen: La Cas du Var' in Labrousse, E. (ed.), *Aspects de la crise et de la dépression de l'économie Française au milieu du 19e siècle, 1846–51*, 1956;

Ariès, P., *Histoire des populations françaises et de leur attitudes devant la vie depuis le 18e siècle*, 1945.

Ariès, P., 'Interprétation pour une histoire des mentalitiés' in Bergues, H., *et al.*, *La prévention des naissances dans la famille*, 1960.

Armengaud, A., *Les populations de l'est acquitain au début de l'époque contemporaine*, 1961.

Armengaud, A., *La population française au 19e siècle*, 1971.

Armengaud, A., 'Agriculture et démographie au 18e siècle', *R.H.E.S.*, 1971.

Baehrel, R., *Une croissance: la basse-provence rurale (fin du 16e siècle– 1789)*, 1961.

Bardet, J-P., *et al.*, *Sur la population française au 18e et au 19e siècles*, 1973.

Bauthier, R.H., *The economic development of Medieval Europe*, 1971.

Beltramore, A., *Le mobilité géographique d'une population*, 1966.

Berg, B., 'Nutrition and National development' in Berg, B., *et al.* (eds.), *Nutrition National Development and Planning*, Camb. Mass., 1973.

Bengin, J.M., 'Significance of Malnutrition and Priorities for its Prevention', ibid.

Bergeron, L., *L'épisode Napoléonien*, 1972.

de Bertier de Sauvigny, G., *La Restauration*, 1955.

Biraben, J.N., 'L'évolution de la fécondité en Europe occidentale', *A.E.S.C.* 1968.

Bloch, C., *L'assistance et l'état en France á la veille de la Révolution*, 1908.

Bougeatre, E., *La vie rurale dans le mantois et le vexin au 19e siècle*, Meulan, 1971.

Bouloiseau, M., *La République Jacobine, 1792–94*, 1972.

Bourdin, P.M., 'La Plaine d'alençon et ses bordures frontières. Essai d'histoire démographique et médicale (17e et 18e siècles)' in Bouvet, M., Bourdin, P.M., *A Travers la Normandie des 17e et 18e siècles*, Caen, 1968.

217

Bourgeois-Pichat, J., 'The General Development of the Population of France since the Eighteenth Century', Glass D.V., and Eversley, D.E.C., *Population in History,* 1965.

Bouvet, M., 'Troarn Etude de Démographie historique (17—18e Siècles)', Bouvet and Bordon, op. cit.

Bozon, P., *La vie rurale en Vivarais,* 1963.

Braibant, J., 'Etude des conditions de vie, de travail et de leur consequences pathologiques dans les milieux ouvrier anglais et français au 19e siècle', thèse pour le doctorat en médecine, Faculté de médecine de Paris, 1963.

de Cambiaire, A., *L'autoconsommation agricole en France,* 1962.

Carrière, F., and Pinchemel, P., *Le Fait urbaine en France,* 1963.

Carron, M.A., 'Prélude á l'exode rural en France: les migrations ancienne des travailleurs creusois', *R.H.E.S.,* 1965..

Chanut, A., *et al.,* 'Aspects industriel de la crise; le département du Nord' in Labrousse, E. (ed.), *Aspects de la crise et de la dépression du milieu du 19e siècle,* 1956.

Chatelain, A., 'Les migrants temporaires et la propagation des idées révolutionnaires en France au 19e siècle', *'1848',* 1951.

Chatelain, A., 'Les Migrations temporaires françaises au 19e siècle: Problèmes, méthodes, documentation.' *A.D.H.,* 1967.

Chatelain, A., 'Migrations et domesticité feminine urbaine en France, 18—20e siècles', *R.H.E.S.,* 1969.

Chatelain, A., *Valeur des recensements de la population française au 19e siècle, R.G.L.,* 1954.

Chaunu, P., 'Le bâtiment dans l'économie traditionelle' in Bardet J.P., *et al., Le Bâtiment-Enquête d'histoire économique,* I, 1971.

Chaunu, P., 'Malthusianisme dèmographique et malthusianisme Economique', *A.E.S.C.,* 1972.

Chevalier, L., 'Towards a history of population' in Glass, Eversley, *Population,* 1965.

Chevalier, L., *Le Choléra — La première épidemie du 19e siècle,* 1958.

Chevalier, M., *La vie humaine dans les Pyrenees ariègeoises,* 1956.

Clark, C., and Haswell, M., *The economics of subsistence Agriculture,* 1970.

Cobb, R., *The Police and the People,* 1973.

Corbin, A., 'Migrations temporaires et société rurale en 19e siècle: le cas du Limousin', *R.H.E.S.,* 1971.

Cravioto, J., and de Licardie, E.R., 'The effect of Malnutrition on the Individual' in Berg, *et al.*

Delumeau, J., 'Demographie et mentalités: la mort en Anjou (17—18e siècles)', *A.E.S.C.,* 1972.

Demangeau, S., 'L'approvisionnement de Paris en Fruits et légumes', *A.G.*, 1928.

Desaive, J.P., *L'alimentation populaire d'apres les archives de l'académie de médecine (1774–94); Actes–93e–Tours 1968*, 1971.

Desert, G., 'Aspects agricoles de la crise: le région de Caen' in Labrousse, E. (ed.), *Aspects*, 1956.

Desert, G., *La viande dans l'alimentation des bas-normands au 19e siècle, Actes–93e–Tours, 1968*, 1971.

Desert, G., 'Apercus sur l'industrie française du bâtiment au 19e siècle', in Bardet, J.P., *et al., Le Bâtiment*, I, 1971.

Dineur, M., and Engrand, Ch., 'Le choléra á Lille', in Chevalier, L. (ed.), *Le choléra*, 1958.

Dupâquier, J., 'La non-revolution agricole du 18e siècle', *A.E.S.C.*, 1972.

Dupâquier, J., 'Problèmes démographiques de la France Napoleonienne', *R.H.M.C.*, 1970.

Dupâquier, J., and Lachiver, M., 'Sur les débuts de la contraception en France', *A.E.S.C.*, 1969.

Dupeux, G., *Aspects de l'histoire sociale et politique de Loire et Cher*, 1961.

Dupeux, G., *La société française, 1789–1960*, 1964.

Estienne, P., 'L'étude de la dépopulation en montagne', *R.G.A.*, 1947.

Faucher, D., *Le Paysan et le machine*, 1954.

Faucher, D., *La vie rurale vue par un géographe*, Toulouse, 1952.

Fel, A., *Les hautes terres du Massif Central. Tradition paysanne et économie agricole*, 1962.

Flandrin, J.L., 'Contraception, mariage et relations amoureuses dans l'occident chretien', *A.E.S.C.*, 1969.

Flandrin, J.L., 'Marriage tardif et vie sexuelle', *A.E.S.C.*, 1972.

Fourastie, J., *Machinisme et bien-être*, 1951.

de Foville, A., *La transformation des moyens de transport et ses conséquences économiques et sociales*, 1880.

Frêche, G., 'Etudes statistiques sur le commerce céréaliere de la France méridionale en 18e siècle', *R.H.E.S.*, 1970.

Garden, M., *Lyon et les Lyonnais au 18e siècle*, 1971.

Gautier, E., *Siècle d'indigence*, 1950.

Godechot, J., and Moncassin, S., 'Démographie et subsistences en Languedoc du 18e siècle au début du 19e siècle', *B.H.E.S.R.F.*, 1964.

Goreux, L.M., 'Les migrations agricoles en France depuis un siècle et leurs relations avec certain facteurs économique', *E.C.*, 1956.

Goubert, J.-P., 'Le phenomène Epidēmique en Bretagne à la Fin du 18e siècle (1770–87)', *A.E.S.C.*, 1969.

Goubert, P., *L'ancien régime*, I, 1969.

Goubert, P., *Beauvais et le Beauvaisin de 1600–1730*, 1960.

Goubert, P., 'Recherches d'histoire rurale dans la France de l'ouest (17–18e siècles)', *B.S.H.M.*, 1965.

Guerrand, R., *Les origines du logement social en France*, 1967.

Habakkuk, A.J., *Population Growth and Economic Development since 1750*, Leicester, 1971.

Henry, L., 'The population of France in the 18th Century' in Glass, Eversley, *Population*, 1965.

Henry, L., 'L'apport des démographes et de la statistique' in Bergues, *et al.*, *La prevention*, 1960.

Hufton, O., *Bayeux in the late Eighteenth Century*, 1967.

Hufton, O., *The Poor of Eighteenth Century France*, 1974.

Juillard, E., 'L'urbanisation des campagnes en Europe occidentale', *E.R.*, 1961.

Kahan-Rabecq, M.M., *L'alsace économique et sociale dans le règne de Louis-Phillippe*, I, 1939.

Labrousse, E., *Histoire économique et sociale de la France*, II, 1970.

Labrousse, E., *La crise de l'économie française á la fin de l'Ancien Régime et au début de la révolution*, 1944.

Langer, W.L., 'Europe's Initial Population Explosion', *A.H.R.*, 1964.

Lasserre, A., *La situation des ouvriers de l'industrie textile dans le région lilloise sous la monarchie de Juillet*, Lausanne, 1952.

Lathan, M.C., 'A Historical Perspective' in Berg, *et al.*, *Nutrition*, Camb., Mass., 1973.

Laurent, R., *L'octroi de Dijon au 19e siècle*, 1960.

Lebrun, F., *Les hommes et le mort en Anjou aux 17e et 18e siècle*, 1971.

Lefevre, A., *Dans le Second Empire: Chemins de fer et politique*, 1951.

LeRhun, M. and R., 'Evolution du régime alimentaire á Plozévet, de 1800 a 1860', *R.G.L.*, 1961.

le Roy Ladurie, E., 'Avant-Propos' in Desaive, J.P., *et al.*, *Médecins, climat et épidemies á la Fin du 18e siècle*, 1972.

le Roy Ladurie, E., 'Voies nouvelles pour l'histoire rurale (16–18e siècles)', *E.R.*, 1964.

le Roy Ladurie, E., and Goy, J., 'Premiere esquisse d'une conjuncture du produit décimal et domanial. Fin du moyen age – 18e Siècle' in Goy, Le Roy Ladurie (eds.), op. cit.

le Roy Ladurie, E., and Goy, J., *Les fluctuations du produit de la dîme,*

1972.

Levillior, P., *L'Alsace au début du 19e siècle, 1815–30*, II.

Levillior, P., *Les transformations Economiques*, 1959.

Livet, R., *Habitat rural et structures agraires en basse-provence*, Aix-en-Provence, 1962.

Lottin, A., 'Naissances illégitimes et filles-Mères á Lille au 18e siècle', *R.H.M.C.*, 1970.

Mandrou, R., *La France aux 17e et 18e siècles*, 1967.

Marcilhacy, C., *Le diocèse d'Orléans au milieu du 19e siècle. Les hommes et leurs mentalités*, 1964.

Marlin, R., *La crise des subsistances de 1816–17 dans le Doubs*, Besançon 1960.

Marres, P., 'La modernisation de l'économie du bas-Languedoc et des Cevennes Méridionales', *S.L.G.*, 1954.

Mendras, A., and Jollivet, M., *Les collectivités rurales françaises: étude du changement social*, 1971.

Merlin, P., *L'exode rural*, 1971.

Meuvret, J.,'Demographic crisis in France from the late 16th to the 18th century`in Glass, Eversley, op. cit.

Meyer, J., *La noblesse bretonne au 18e siècle*, 1966.

Meyer, J., 'Le personnel médical en Betagne á la fin du 18e siècle' in Desaive, J.P., *et al.*, *Médecin, climat*, 1972.

Moreau, J.P., 'La vie rurale dans le sud-est du bassin parisien entre les vallées de l'Armançon et de la Loire', *I.H.*, 1955.

Morineau, M., *Les faux-semblants d'un démarrage économique: agriculture et démographie en France au 18e siècle*, 1971.

Morineau, M., 'Budgets populaires en France au 18e siècle', *R.H.E.S.*, 1972.

Morineau, M., 'Reflections tardives et conclusions prospectives', Le Roy Ladurie, E., Goy, J. (eds.), Premier esquisse.

Pautard, J., *Les disparites régionales dans la croissance de l'agriculture française*, 1965.

Peter, J.P., 'Les mots et les objects de la maladie', *R.H.*, 1971.

Phillipe, R., 'Une óperation pilote: L'étude du ravitaillement de Paris au temps de Lavoisier' in Hémardinquer, J.J., *Pour une histoire de l'alimentation*, 1970.

Pinchemel, P., *France – A Geographical Survey*, 1969.

Pinchemel, P., *Structures Sociales et dépopulation rural dans les campagnes picardes de 1836 á 1936*, 1957.

Pinkney, D., *Napoleon III and the re-building of Paris*, 1959.

Pitie, J., *Exode rural et migrations intérieures en France. L'example de la Vienne et du Poitou-Charentes*, Poitiers, 1971.

Poitrineau, A., *La vie rurale en basse-Auvergne au 18e siècle,* 1965.

Poitrineau, A., 'L'alimentation populaire en Auvergne au 18e siècle' in Hémardinquer, J.J. (ed.), op. cit.

Ponteil, F., *La crise alimentaire de 1847 dans le Bas-Rhin '1848',* 1925–6.

Poussou, 'Les mouvements migratoires en France et á partir de la France de la fin du 15e au début du 19e siècle: approches pour une synthèse', *A.D.H.,* 1970.

Pouthas, C.H., *La population française pendant la première moitié du 19e siècle,* 1956.

Ramalingaswami, V., 'The effect of malnutrition on the individual. cellular growth and development' in Berg, *et al.* (eds.), op. cit.

Rambaud, P., and Vincienne, M., *Les transformations d'une société rurale: La Maurienne (1561–1962),* 1964.

Reinhard, M., 'Le bilan du monde en 1815'; I Bilan démographique de l'Europe: 1789–1815'. Proceeding of the 12th International Congress of the Historical Sciences, Vienna, n.d.

Richet, C., *Pathologie de la misère,* 1957.

Rochefort, M., *L'organisation urbaine de l'Alsace,* Gap, 1960.

Rollet, C., 'L'effet des crises économiques au début du 19e siècle sur la population', *R.H.M.C.* 1969.

Sabatier, G., 'Une économie et une société en crise: L'Emblaves au début du 18e siècle, 1695–1753' in Leon, *Structures.*

de Saint-Jacob, P., *Les paysans de la Bourgogne du Nord au dernier siècle de l'Ancien Régime,* 1960.

Sauvy, A., 'Essai d'une vue d'ensemble' in Berguës, H., *et al., La prévention,* 1960.

Sée, H., 'Quelques aperçus sur le condition de la classe ouvrière et sur le mouvement ouvrier en France de 1815–1848', *R.H.E.S.,* 1924.

Seignour, P., *La vie économique du Vaucluse de 1815–1848,* Aix-en-Provence, 1957.

Soboul, A., *Les troubles agraires de 1848, '1848',* 1948.

Soboul, A., *La France á la vielle de la révolution,* I.

Soboul, A., *Economie et société,* 1966.

Sorlin, P., *La société française, 1840–1914,* 1969.

Susser, M.W., and Watson, W., *Sociology in Medicine,* 1971.

Tardieu, S., *La vie domestique dans le mâconnais rural pre-industriel,* 1964.

Thuillier, G., *Aspects de l'économie nivernaise au 19e siècle,* 1966.

Thuillier, G., 'Note sur les sources de l'histoire régionale de l'alimentation au 19e siècle', *A.E.S.C.,* 1968.

Thuillier, G., 'Note sur les sources de l'histoire régionale de l'hygiene corporelle au 19ᵉ siècle', *R.H.E.S.*, 1970.

Thullier, G., 'Pour une histoire régionale de l'eau: en Nivernais au 19ᵉ siècle', *A.E.S.C.*, 1968.

Toutain, J.C., 'La consommation alimentaire en France de 1789 á 1966', *E.S.*, 1971.

Toutain, J.C., 'Les transports en France de 1830 á 1968', *E.S.*, 1967.

Trenard, L., *L'alimentation en Flandre française au 18ᵉ siècle: Actes—93ᵉ—Tour, 1961*, 1971.

Vedrenne-Villeneuve, E., 'L'inégalité sociale devant le mort dans la première moitié du 19ᵉ siècle', *P.*, 1961.

Vidalenc, J., *Le peuple des campagnes*, 1969.

Weber, A.F., *The growth of cities in the nineteenth century*, Ithaca, 1963.

Woronoff, D., *Le république bourgeoise de Thermidor á Brumaire (1791—99)*, 1972.

Wrigley, E.A., *Industrial Growth and Population Change*, 1962.

CONCLUSION

The *Ancien Régime économique* was characterised: (1) by the predominance of the agricultural sector, which itself was primarily orientated towards the production of basic foodstuffs, the dominance of this sector being exemplified by the general economic crisis which followed a poor harvest; (2) the absence of cheap and reliable transport facilities which resulted in a compartmentalised market structure inducing substantial price fluctuations and increasing general economic instability; and (3) by the prominence within the industrial sector of consumer goods industries and in particular textiles. Richard Cobb has pointed out that the persistence of the problem of food supply — of dearth — is testimony to the survival of the traditional economy well into the nineteenth century.

More than by any other factor the pre-industrial character of the French economy before the 1840s was maintained by the restraints on demand and on innovation imposed by inadequate communications. In the absence of sufficiently large markets and of competitive pressures archaic techniques were able to survive. Isolated examples of innovation occurred but the fundamental character of the economy remained unchanged.

Social structures and mentalities in very large part determined the shape of economic development. They set limits to the possibility of change, exemplifying the human desire for stability. Local particularism reinforced this where poor communications isolated and created links of dependent solidarity within village communities. The *Ancien Régime économique* was characterised by the existence of countless local societies whose economic life rested on an awareness of their own needs and potential, largely uninfluenced by those of the wider world.

With the railway revolution this compartmentalisation, the fundamental characteristic of the *Ancien Régime,* rapidly disappeared. The isolation, the physical and also the psychological isolation of the rural community came to an end. The very roots of rural civilisation, the cultural autonomy which each village had to an important extent enjoyed, were increasingly destroyed as the forces of a developing industrial economy, an urban world and a national society penetrated within. By means of a variety of experiences, in the café and in the school, urban norms transformed the outlook of populations — not immediately or totally but insidiously and to a degree which destroyed the self-respect of the rural population. A crisis of adaptation to external pressures was experienced which has continued to the present day.

Within two decades the world of Zola replaced that of Balzac. In many respects it remained backward and life for too many was harsh and bitter. However, a modern economy had been created in which the predominance of industry and within the industrial sector of heavy industry, and especially metallurgy, was assured. This occurred because of the general availability of cheap and rapid means of transport, transforming and enlarging markets, eliminating crises caused by poor harvests and setting up competitive pressures which ensured the spread of innovation in both agriculture and industry.

The most significant contribution of railway development was to transform market structures and by so doing the conditions under which production was carried out. This was how and when the *Ancien Régime économique* came to an end; when the capitalist system assumed an overwhelming predominance over the remains of older economic structures.

Substantial archaisms survived and continue to survive. There never was and never will be a condition of perfect competition. In particular the relative slowness with which peasant agriculture continued to change and the consequent limitation of rural purchasing power reduced the stimuli to industrial modernisation. This was particularly the case during the depressed years of the late 1870s, the 1880s and earlier 1890s. But even then, if with the benefit of hindsight we can pinpoint relatively low rates of economic growth, contemporaries seem to have been aware above all of continued development.

It has, in recent times, been fashionable amongst economic historians to throw doubt upon the contribution of railway development to economic growth. Certainly old assumptions need to be questioned, but from the detail of economic development in France, the inescapable conclusion is that the element of the social mechanism which contributed most to economic development and social modernisation was the railway. Prior to the development of the internal-combustion engine, there was no alternative means of cheap and rapid transport.

With the transformation of economic structures a new balance was established between population and resources, partly due to demographic evolution, but primarily due to that of economic life. If, in spite of the improvement of living conditions, men remained discontented, this was due to the continued inequality of opportunity and reward in a class society, to the hopes and desires stimulated by improvement, and above all to the new awareness of inequality, and to the new facilities for organising resistance and for institutionalising protest provided by the transformation of the means of communication.

Not only economic life and material conditions but social and political relationships had been more fundamentally modified in a shorter time than ever before. The human condition had been transformed.

INDEX

Abbeville (Somme), 21, 93, 108, 215
Adour, river, 121
Agde (Hérault), 14
Agen (Lot-et-Garonne), 125
Agriculture, 2, 11, 65, 83, 167, 168
    and industry, 93, 97,
        99–101, 143–145,
        150, 151, 158
    labour, 29, 45–47, 50, 62,
        63, 71, 82, 84, 191,
        211, 215–219
    markets, 43–47, 53, 59,
        59, 61, 71, 72, 75, 76
    mechanization, 50, 71, 82,
        211, 213
    in mountains, 46, 52, 54,
        65, 193, 210
    specialization, 44, 46–47,
        51, 53, 54, 66, 76–78,
        80, 81, 83
    technical innovation, 43–48,
        50, 52–55, 59–66,
        68–72, 74, 76, 81–84,
        158, 168, 182, 191,
        198, 211, 212.
Agronomists, 45, 46, 63, 68
Aisne, river, 13, 60
Aix-en-Provence (Bouches-du-Rhône),
    64
Albi (Tarn), 117
Alès (Alais) (Gard), 112, 115, 121,
    123, 144, 215
Allevard (Isère), 5
Allier, river, 13–14, 121
Alps, 9, 25, 54, 65, 78, 210, 213
Alpes-M. (dept.), 72
Alsace, 15, 46–48, 63, 64, 81,
    100–102, 104, 106, 125, 128,
    129, 137, 144, 148, 152
America, 73, 139
American Civil War, 97, 104, 108,
    136, 140, 141, 165
Amiens (Somme), 2, 93, 105, 212
Ancien Régime économique et
    sociale, 1–2, 69, 70, 73, 75, 84,
    92, 97, 130, 135, 139, 167, 172,

183, 185, 186, 193, 209, 216,
    224, 225
Ancien Régime politique: government
    economic policies, 31–2, 33, 53,
    62, 67
Andrézieux, 16, 20
Angers (Maine-et-Loire), 101, 186
Anjou, 67, 108, 185, 193, 194, 204
Anzin (Nord), 93, 112, 113, 118,
    122, 123, 144, 146, 148, 155
Ardèche (dept.), 53, 64, 107
Ardennes, 82, 125, 129
Argentina, 79, 129
Argonne, 129
Ariège (dept.), 5, 57, 72, 111, 123,
    187, 194, 198, 202, 205
    river, 13
Arles (Bouches-du-Rhône), 16, 17
Armentières (Nord), 108
Arras (Pas-de-Calais), 215
Artisans, 29, 81, 92, 97–99, 125,
    126, 128, 169, 170, 211, 213
Assailly, 116
Assignats, 34
Association for Free Trade, 165
Aubusson (Creuse), 128
Aude (Dept.), 72
Australia, 79, 129, 157
Auvergne, 5, 13, 30, 32, 48, 58, 67,
    187, 195, 200, 201
Avernois, 145
Aveyron (dept.), 123
Avignon (Vaucluse), 69, 81, 107,
    108

Balance of payments, 35, 137, 138
Banking, 35, 82, 95, 137, 139, 141,
    147, 152–158
Bank of France, 34, 35, 153–156
Banks: Crédit Foncier, 154;
        Crédit Lyonnais 35, 155,
        156; Crédit mobilier, 154,
        155; Seillière, 155; Société
        Générale, 35, 154; Société
        Générale (Belgium), 155;
        Société industrielle du